THE JEWS OF OREGON

THE JEWS OF OREGON

1850-1950

STEVEN LOWENSTEIN

JEWISH HISTORICAL SOCIETY OF OREGON
PORTLAND, OREGON
1987

Jewish Historical Society of Oregon
6651 Southwest Capitol Highway
Portland, Oregon 97219

Copyright © 1987 by Steven Lowenstein.
All rights reserved.

Designed by John Laursen at Press-22.
Set in ITC Garamond type by Irish Setter.
Printed by Adprint Company.
Bound by Lincoln & Allen Company.
Manufactured in the United States of America.
First edition.

Library of Congress
Cataloging in Publication Data

Lowenstein, Steven, 1938-
    The Jews of Oregon, 1850-1950
    Bibliography: p. 222
    Includes Index
    1. Jews—Oregon—History.
2. Oregon—Ethnic relations.   I. Title
ISBN 0-9619786-0-0   Hard Cover
ISBN 0-9619786-1-9   Soft Cover
ISBN 0-9619786-2-7   Limited Edition
F885.J4L68 1987   979.5'004924—dc19   87-36660

To my parents
and to their parents
and to all the generations that have come before

To my son
and to his children
and to all the generations that are yet to come

Contents

PART III   BUILDING A UNIFIED JEWISH COMMUNITY   1920-1950

Preface

Remember the days of old,
Consider the years of many generations;
Ask thy father, and he will declare unto thee,
Thine elders, and they will tell thee.

  —Deuteronomy 32:7

I felt as if my father and mother were looking over my shoulder and behind them were Jews, millions of other departed Jews of yesterday and thousands of years ago.

  —Marc Chagall, on creating the stained glass windows
   for the Synagogue of Hadassah Clinic in Jerusalem

History is central to Jews. We remember the Exodus from Egypt; we remember the giving of the Torah, and so much else through the ages. In our own time, how could we forget the Holocaust or the transcendence of our return to Zion? We remember, and our memory is our survival. It has allowed us to persist for thousands of years as a unique and vital people despite being scattered among nations, and often confronting the most virulent hostility.

Today, those of us who live in America, in Oregon, experience as full an acceptance and participation in the broader society as has ever been available in the Diaspora. It might be easy to forget. But if we did, we would lose that kernel of ourselves which has made us who we are. I believe that we must remember not only the generations long gone, but those of our recent past, here where we have chosen to live.

I was born in January, 1938. My mother died in the fall of that same year, shortly before *Kristallnacht.* I know in the deepest places within me that I share an ineradicable bond with my brothers and sisters who suffered and died in the Holocaust. I am haunted by photographs of old bearded men and children, gone; an entire culture, a Jewish world, gone. Like so many Jews, I live my life in part as a voice for those who perished. For me, this book is in part an act of defiance, of fury at the Nazis; in part an act of remembrance of our dead kin; and perhaps, most of all, an act of celebration of our continuity despite all. I believe it is our duty to record the life of our communities so that we may honor those whose communities and lives have been destroyed. They are with us; they are surely a part of us. We shall not forget.

Where fascists and others have tried and failed, is it conceivable that America, with its enticement of assimilation, could lead to the eventual disappearance of Jewish religion and culture? I do not believe so. However, it is crucial that Judaism retain its vitality and Jews their self-awareness. While America is the wonderful land of the First Amendment, of democracy, pluralism and mobility, we as Jews continue to deeply value our roots and an intimate connection with our history. American Jews have had a singular ability to participate fully in the broader society and yet retain a vital ethnic and religious self-consciousness. This is true in part because there are so many ways to express one's Jewishness. This book is my way, my offering to my family, generations past and generations to come, and to the continuity of our Jewish family and community. Let us be part of the broad and common good in this pluralistic society, but let us always remember from whence we came.

The Jewish community in Oregon is largely unaware of its rich history stretching back to the origins of the state. Jews sometimes feel that others were central to building Oregon and that we were not significant participants. I hope this book will help our community to understand the importance of its long, illustrious role in Oregon's history.

Many non-Jews are unaware that there is a vital Jewish community in Oregon. And even those who are aware often think that Jews have only recently arrived from elsewhere. It is important that others recognize the valuable role that Jews have played in making Oregon the fine place it is today. Jews are not often thought of as pioneers, farmers, adventurers or small-town dwellers, either by themselves or by others, but we have been all of these while helping to settle and build Oregon. My perception is that anti-Semitism in Oregon—to the extent that it exists today—is generally born of ignorance, not malice. If Oregonians knew more about Jewish life, they might be more sensitive to the existence and needs of Jews. Perhaps this book can help Jewish history take its place beside the histories of the state's other religious and ethnic groups.

Today, members of Oregon's Jewish community are the beneficiaries of a proud tradition of Jews who have cared deeply for this state and have made exceptional contributions. It is important that we seek our roots and our destiny not only in Israel, in Europe, in the East or Midwest, but in Oregon—this beautiful outpost of the Diaspora—where we have chosen to live our lives.

A Note to the Reader

In writing this book my objective has been to portray accurately Jewish life in Oregon from 1850 to 1950, while also giving the reader a sense and feel for the adventurous and exciting lives that Jews have led. It is meant for general readership, although I believe there will be much new material helpful to scholars. I have generally not included footnotes so that the text will flow more smoothly; the original manuscript with source notations is housed at the Jewish Historical Society of Oregon for those who wish to consult it.

A selected bibliography encompassing the range of sources for this book is included in the appendices. A glossary is also provided for those readers who may be unfamiliar with Hebrew and Yiddish expressions that are included in the text.

It has been necessary to select and focus on certain communities, families and individuals. They have been chosen because I believe them to be representative or particularly interesting, and because there is sufficient material available. This is not a comprehensive work—and some may be disappointed to find something of interest to them omitted. However, the objective of conveying the breadth of Jewish history in Oregon during its first century in as readable and absorbing a manner as possible permits the inclusion of limited detail. There are a number of Jews who grew up in Oregon but left and later became famous; I generally do not include them as this book is about Oregon's Jewish community.

The role of women has often been ignored historically. I have tried, wherever information could be traced, to describe the lives of women and their outstanding accomplishments in the history of the Jews of Oregon. The use of names for women derived from the names of their husbands was widespread until recent decades and unfortunately could not be avoided in many instances.

In 1931, numbered streets throughout Portland were changed to avenues. I have consistently adopted the modern usage which is more familiar to readers.

In writing about history it is often difficult to determine which among conflicting accounts is most accurate. I have tried to corroborate all facts through two sources wherever possible. This policy often required original research to find a second source. Frequently the pursuit was intriguing and productive, as when I contacted John Selling to seek photographs and review certain material about his grandfather, Ben Selling. Two days later I found on my office desk a large box containing "Muzzie's" (Mrs. Ben Selling's) wedding dress, handmade in 1886, rare and valuable. So often I experienced the warmth and generosity of Jewish families who shared the excitement of rediscovering our past.

These experiences have made writing *The Jews of Oregon* particularly rewarding for me. I hope that this book will be as enjoyable for you to read, and will, as it has for me, foster pride in the history of our forebears.

Acknowledgments

The Jews of Oregon could not have been written without the work of many dedicated researchers and writers who came before. Although I have conducted numerous interviews and explored a great deal of primary data, this book is based for the most part on secondary sources and the invaluable oral histories recorded in the mid-1970s by a group of devoted interviewers under the leadership of Shirley Tanzer. William Toll's *The Making of an Ethnic Middle Class: Portland Jewry over Four Generations* (1982) and his many articles, and Scott Cline's Masters Thesis, *Community Structure on the Urban Frontier: The Jews of Portland, Oregon, 1849-1887* (1982) were particularly significant source books. Three unpublished manuscripts were also very valuable: Marianne Feldman's editing of thirty *Portland Jewish Oral Histories*, Michele Glazer's *Focus of a Community, Neighborhood House 1897-1929* and Rabbi Joshua Stampfer's *The Life and Works of Julius Eckman*. The work of Michele Glazer and Jennifer Lenway in examining and cataloguing Jewish newspaper stories on over one thousand Jewish organizations between 1893 and 1940 was also helpful.

There are so many people who have helped to bring this book to life. None have been more important than Lora Meyer and Ruth Semler, current and past presidents of the Jewish Historical Society of Oregon. Lora and the board of the Society were involved from the beginning and essential in making this book a reality. Not enough can be said about Ruth Semler, who undertook to find the elusive photographs and helped with virtually every aspect of the book's creation. Two former board members—Caroline Winfield and Arthur Markewitz—have inspired my work and that of many others at the Society. I owe the Jewish Historical Society a deep debt of gratitude.

I would like to express my appreciation to the Endowment Fund of the Jewish Federation of Portland which provided a grant to assist the project. I would also like to thank Portland City Commissioner Mike Lindberg, David Judd and the entire commissioner's staff for their generosity in providing me the leave needed away from my duties as executive assistant to write this book.

A number of individuals read my manuscript and otherwise helped a great deal throughout the process of writing. I am particularly grateful to Rabbi Joshua Stampfer, Rabbi Emanuel Rose, Rabbi Yonah Geller, Carl Abbott, Scott Cline, Toinette Menashe, Lora and Jim Meyer, Ruth Semler, Arden Shenker, Shirley and Hershal Tanzer, Chris Lowenstein and Sandra Haefker Lowenstein. Joe Hertzberg not only made innumerable substantive and editing corrections to the manuscript, but was always available with help whenever it was needed.

There were also many people who went out of their way to provide me with source materials and other assistance. While it is impossible to list everyone, the following people were particularly helpful: Edward Aiken, Joy Alkalay, Lee Arnstein, Joan Bayliss, Pam Bernstein, Harriet and George Bodner, Frances Bricker, Eva Carr, Sylvia Davidson, Frank Director, Felice

Lauterstein Driesen, Dorothy, Stuart and James Durkheimer, Fanny Eisenberg, Gerry Frank, Fannie Kenin Friedman, Leon Gabinet, Diana Golden, Nancy Golden, Tom and Alan Goldsmith, Ora Goodman, Alan and Nancy Green, the Heilner family, Harold Hirsch, Lena Holzman, Rabbi Myron Kinberg, Margaret and Daniel Labby, Evelyn and Gerald Leshgold, Marie Leton, Moe Levin, Dina and Ted Linn, David Lipman, Kimbark MacColl, Sr., Kimbark MacColl Jr., Harriet Maizels, Chella Meekcoms, Sarah Menashe, Jim Meyer, Roscoe Nelson, Sr., Sharon Nesbitt, Irving Neusihin, Eugene Nudelman, Sr., Chet Orloff, Nancy and Henry Oseran, Gussie Reinhardt, Keith Richard, Jane Rosenbaum, A. E. "English" Rosenberg, Bernice Rosencrantz, Eve Rosenfeld, Victor Rosenfeld, Sura Rubenstein, Ted Rubenstein, Kathleen Ryan, Mildred Saks, Hy Samuels, John Selling, Bruce Senders, Ardyth Shapiro, Blanche Sharff, Judge Gus Solomon, Libby Solomon, Irene Solomon, Harry Stein, Janet Stevens, Alfred Sugarman, Laddie Trachtenberg and Howard Waskow.

In addition to the Jewish Historical Society of Oregon, a number of libraries and collections were extremely helpful. First among them was the Oregon Historical Society and its staff, especially Jack Cleaver, Rick Harmon and Susan Seyl. Other generous providers of material included the American Jewish Historical Society (Waltham, Massachusetts), the Western Jewish History Center of the Judah Magnes Memorial Museum (Berkeley, California), the Bancroft Library (Berkeley, California), YIVO Institute for Jewish Research (New York City), The Library of Congress (Washington, D.C.), the Southern Oregon Historical Society (Jacksonville, Oregon) and the *Oregonian* (Portland, Oregon).

The Jews of Oregon would not have come together without the valuable assistance of editor and indexer Lynn Darroch and copy editor Catherine Gleason, mapmaker Ted Olson, the typing and endless corrections graciously undertaken by Judith Clay with the support of Sextant Consultants, Inc., and John Laursen of Press-22, who designed this book with great aesthetic sensitivity and managed the entire production process.

Finally I would like to express my appreciation to my family who helped in so many ways as I labored to write this book. Sandy, Chris, Hanns and Kris gave me the love, warmth and support that I needed. Thanks.

Steven Lowenstein
Portland, Oregon
December, 1987

PART I

THE GERMAN JEWISH PIONEERS

1850-1890

Beginnings of Jewish Life in America

The first Jews to come to the New World were Sephardim. They had lived in Spain and Portugal for many centuries, participating fully in a culture that flowered during the golden era of Moorish rule between the eighth and thirteenth centuries, until the Spanish Inquisition sought to purify Spain of all non-Catholic influences.

The first Jews to settle in America. They escaped Brazil, were captured by pirates, retaken by the French frigate *St. Charles* and are seen here landing in New Amsterdam. Painter unknown. Courtesy, American Jewish Historical Society (AJHS).

Ironically, on August 3, 1492, the day following the expulsion of Jews from Spain, Columbus began his voyage of discovery. But Columbus might not have set sail at all if Luis de Santangel, a prominent *Marrano*, or converted Jew, and Chancellor of the royal household of Aragon, had not persuaded King Ferdinand that the depleted Spanish treasury might be replenished if Columbus were to discover a more direct route to China. Several Jews accompanied Columbus, and one, Luis de Torres, an interpreter, was reputed to be the first member of the expedition to stand on American soil.

After their expulsion from Spain, the Sephardim found refuge in the Eastern Mediterranean, North Africa, Western Europe (particularly Holland) and Portugal, although they were soon expelled from that country when the Inquisition spread. *Marranos* were among the earliest arrivals in Spanish and Portuguese settlements in the New World, but here too they were pursued by the Inquisition. One of their only sanctuaries was the coastal city of Recife in Brazil, which was brought under Dutch rule in 1630. But its thriving Jewish community, boasting a synagogue, a rabbi and over a thousand persons, was again forced to flee when the Portuguese recaptured the area in 1654.

That same year, an impoverished group of twenty-three Jews fled Recife in a boat bound for the Caribbean and Holland. They were captured by pirates on the high seas, but were retaken by a French frigate, the *St. Charles*. After much negotiating, the French agreed to take them as far as New Amsterdam, the rough Dutch

The first synagogue erected in America, Congregation Shearith Israel, was built in 1730 on Mill Street, New York City. Courtesy, AJHS.

West India Company settlement that would become New York City.

These Jews are generally recognized to be the first to settle in America. Unfortunately, they met a hostile welcome. They were sued for payment by the ship's captain, and several of their number were imprisoned while the Calvinist governor, Peter Stuyvesant, tried to have them expelled from the colony. The Jews addressed urgent appeals to their brethren in Amsterdam, a number of whom were major shareholders in the Dutch West India Company. Pressure from Amsterdam prevailed, and the small band was allowed to remain. They founded Shearith Israel, the first and oldest continuous congregation in America.

Other small groups of Jews, their names lost to history, may have fled the terror of the Inquisition to enter what is now Texas and New Mexico at even earlier dates than those who first came to New Amsterdam. In 1579, the New Kingdom of León, a vast land grant stretching over much of what is today Northern Mexico and Southern Texas, was given to Don Luis de Carvajal, a *Marrano*, by King Philip II of Spain. Carvajal, more enlightened than typical conquistadors, settled Spanish families on his land

and pursued its development until the Mexican Inquisition discovered that some of his settlers were secretly practicing Judaism. The governor died in prison, members of his family were tortured, and a number of them were burned at an auto-da-fé in the great central square of Mexico City in 1596 because they would not renounce their religion. Untold others probably fled for their lives into the wilderness north of Mexico to settle new regions that would later become the Southwestern United States.

The Sephardic Period

The years from 1654 to 1820 are generally regarded as the Sephardic period in American Jewish history. Jews, primarily of Spanish and Portuguese background, settled in six cities along the Eastern seaboard: New York, Newport,

Oil painting of David and Phila Franks, two of Jacob and Abigail Levy Franks' nine children. Jacob Franks, one of New York's wealthiest merchants in the mid-eighteenth century, served as *parnas* (president) of Shearith Israel. Courtesy, AJHS.

The interior of Beth Elohim was typical of Sephardic synagogues. Built in Charleston, South Carolina, it was dedicated in 1794, a time when there were more Jews in Charleston than in any other city in America. Print after drawing by Solomon Carvalho. Courtesy, AJHS.

Jewish life for another century.

Jews strongly supported the Revolution, since they understood the immense significance of establishing religious tolerance and individual liberty as the policy of a new nation. Feelings were so strong that the Jewish communities of New York and Newport resettled in Connecticut and Philadelphia rather than live under British rule. When President Washington visited Newport in 1790, after independence had been won, the local Jewish community sent him a letter of congratulation. The president replied that all in the new republic "possess alike liberty of conscience. The Government gives to bigotry no sanction, to persecution no assistance." The father of the country gave his personal word to the Jewish community, just as the Declaration of Independence and the new Constitution had given formal recognition to them previously. All men were equal before the law; never before in Western history had age-old religious barriers been so fully renounced.

The German Period

The years from 1820 to approximately 1880 are generally considered the German period in American Jewish history. During this time, the Jewish population increased sharply, from approximately five thousand in 1820 to more than a quarter of a million by 1880, primarily as a result of immigration from Central Europe. The Sephardim with their proud traditions looked down upon the German "peddlers," and it was not until waves of German immigrants had arrived that they began to reshape the American Jewish community. For the Sephardim, all aspects of Jewish life—religious, social and philanthropic—emanated from the synagogue. But the Germans began a process of secularization that continues today. The Sephardim were located in urban Eastern enclaves; it was the German Jews who led the way across the continent, from the Deep South to innumerable small outposts throughout the Midwest and along the Pacific Coast.

Philadelphia, Richmond, Charleston and Savannah. The Sephardim tended to be proud and aristocratic people, carrying the memory of the Golden Age in Iberia to the more primitive American colonies. They were merchants, shippers, purveyors and artisans, ideally suited to help build the economy of agrarian America.

The Jewish community remained quite small through the Sephardic period, numbering approximately twenty-five hundred by the time of the American Revolution and double that number in 1820. By 1720, there were more Ashkenazim (Central and Eastern European Jews) in America than Sephardim, but Sephardic culture continued to dominate American

What prompted so many German Jews to leave their homeland in search of new lives? They were principally traders and artisans in Germany, and the primary reasons for leaving were economic. The Industrial Revolution was increasingly dislocating Central European peasants from their customary lands, peasants who had been the customers and the source of livelihood for many Jewish traders and small merchants. Cheaper, machine-made goods were beginning to undermine those made by Jewish artisans, and overpopulation in Central Europe exacerbated the economic problems.

The situation was worst in economically depressed Bavaria, where in 1813 an edict on the "Status of Jews" was promulgated. It curtailed the size of Jewish families, allowing only the oldest son to marry; limited the number of Jewish families in Bavarian towns and the occupations they could pursue; and even prescribed

Jewish family names, which were often derived from occupation (hence Goldschmidt and Silverman). Political reaction against the Jews and partial withdrawal of their newly won freedom occurred after the defeat of Napoleon and intensified after the failed Revolution of 1848. German nationalism grew, and anti-Jewish riots took place in several cities. Discriminatory taxes were levied in Bavaria and other German states, causing greater hardship in an already deteriorating economic climate.

While the taste for emancipation in the short-lived period of Napoleonic rule had stirred many Jews, retrenchment dashed their rising expectations. Economic forces and the spirit of the Enlightenment also loosened traditional bonds of Jewish communal authority, making it easier for individuals to break away in search of new possibilities. And so they did, at first in small numbers, but in a torrent by the

A peddler demonstrates his goods to a farm family about 1850. In contrast to established and proud Sephardic Jews, many German Jewish immigrants began life in America as peddlers. Wood engraving after C. G. Bush. Courtesy, Library of Congress (LC).

Downieville, California, in 1856, one of the many gold mining towns that mushroomed during the Gold Rush. Jews often worked in such towns on their way to Oregon. Aaron Meier, founder of Meier & Frank, arrived in Downieville in 1855 to help his brothers in their general merchandise store (shown fourth down on left). Courtesy, the Bancroft Library.

1840s. America was their principal destination.

They arrived in New York and other large East Coast cities after crowded, often treacherous transatlantic journeys. Most were single men in their late teens or twenties who either had relatives with whom to apprentice or who struck out on their own. They lacked capital and readily marketable skills, so they did what they knew best: they peddled.

Packs, trunks and baskets were filled with whatever salable items could be scraped together, and they took to the roadways, replacing the "Yankee" peddlers who had found employment in booming New England industries. Following the routes of continental expansion by foot, water and rail, they made their way to trading centers and then to the hinterlands, where new markets might be found. With hard work and luck they hoped to save enough to buy a

horse and wagon and one day to settle down and open a store, a dream that had been denied them in most places in Central Europe, where it was impossible for Jews to obtain a license to open a sedentary business.

The First Jews Come to Oregon

And so they made their way to Oregon. It is not certain who the first Jew in Oregon was. He may have been an unknown itinerant peddler, or he may have been a German engineer and soldier named Herman Ehrenberg who, after having fought for Texan independence, came across the plains to Astoria in 1844, where he spent two years surveying towns in Western Oregon. But it is generally accepted that the earliest known Jewish settlers were Jacob Goldsmith and Lewis May, who arrived in Portland in 1849 and operated a general merchandise store on Front Avenue.*

May was born in the German city of Worms and emigrated to America in 1840. He settled first in Shreveport, Louisiana, before coming to Portland. Goldsmith, also German-born, came to Portland from San Francisco. Although few records of these early merchants exist, it is known that they helped form the city's first Masonic Lodge in 1850. They remained in the city for only two years, Goldsmith returning to San Francisco, and May to New York, where he pursued interests in railroads and banking.

In 1851, Simon and Jacob Blumauer arrived in Portland. The Blumauers, born in Bavaria, opened their retail store on Front Avenue, and Simon went on to become a prominent figure in Portland's Jewish community, where he held the position of president of Temple Beth Israel for twenty-six years. The Blumauers were followed the next year by other young Germans. Five members of the Haas family—brothers Samuel, Kalman and Charles, and cousins Abe and Jacob—began a grocery store in Portland. The first Jewish woman in Oregon was a Mrs. Weinshank, who in 1853 opened a boarding house in Portland for Jewish bachelors.

Oregon was usually the second or third stop in America for these young Germans, and during the 1850s they seldom remained long in Portland. Instead, they spread out to smaller settlements throughout Oregon and the Northwest, where there was less competition in supplying needed goods to the early farm communities. J. B. and Maier Hirsch, brothers from the state of Württemberg in Germany, came to Portland in 1852, but by the beginning of 1854 they had moved to Salem where they began a general merchandise store. Brothers Solomon, Edward and Leopold Hirsch arrived

during the 1850s to assist them. After years of retailing in Salem, The Dalles and Silverton, Solomon became a partner in Fleischner, Mayer & Co. in Portland, a wholesale house and the largest Jewish business in the Northwest.

The primary impetus for much of Oregon's early settlement was the discovery of gold in California. Within a year of the first cry of "gold" from Sutter's Mill near Sacramento, over eighty thousand people had poured into California—traveling around the Cape, across the Isthmus of Panama, or by covered wagon across the plains—most to be disappointed by worked-out mines or false hopes. There were probably Jews among the miners, but they rapidly discovered, as did many Oregonians who tried their luck in California, that there was

One of three Oppenheimer brothers shortly after he arrived in Southern Oregon in 1857. One brother, Marcus Oppenheimer, traveled north to the Washington Territory where he founded the town of Marcus. Courtesy, Jewish Historical Society of Oregon (JHSO).

---

*The primary source for information on the Jews of Portland in the nineteenth century is the excellent Masters thesis by Scott Cline, *Community Structure on the Urban Frontier: The Jews of Portland, Oregon, 1849-1887*, Portland State University, 1982.

One of the first photographs of Portland, taken in July, 1852, looking south on Front Avenue from Ash Street toward Salmon. The first Jews to settle in Portland had arrived three years earlier. Courtesy, Oregon Historical Society (OHS).

more to be made "mining the miners" than digging for gold. More familiar and comfortable with trading and peddling, Jews sold provisions to the mining camps and opened small retail establishments wherever communities settled. Caroline and Philip Selling, parents of Ben Selling, Portland's famous Jewish philanthropist, were the first Jews married in San Francisco. For five years they sold goods to miners from a tent in Sonora, California. Caroline captured the rough spirit of the gold camps when she recalled that:

The nearby tent of a young couple caught fire and destroyed everything they had. Next morning the miners held a meeting. A giant with a red beard ended the discussion by pulling off his hat and emptying some gold in it. "Kick in you fellows," he directed. And as the hat circled, every miner poured in a little dust.

The Sellings came to Portland in 1862 and opened a small store on Morrison Street.

When one gold camp or town dried up, Jews moved on to the next, and so made their way to Oregon. Virtually overnight, Jacksonville in Southern Oregon became the most important town between San Francisco and Portland when gold was discovered nearby in 1851. By 1852, the census listed seven Jewish residents, all young men between eighteen and thirty-two and all involved in storekeeping to supply the miners. But by 1860, gold was played out and most of the Jewish merchants returned to San Francisco.

When Jews arrived in Oregon in the 1850s, they encountered small, struggling, isolated settlements of farmers in the Willamette Valley eking out their first crops after the long overland trek. These settlers were for the most part Christian families seeking a better life after years of economic depression in the Midwest. They were largely uneducated and poor and found their first years in Oregon frustrating because the only market for their produce was the erratic Hudson's Bay Company.

In the late 1840s, Jews found Portland a village of a few hundred persons nestled along the west bank of the Willamette. There were twenty-five or so houses, a few stores and tree stumps visible everywhere. But even in its infancy, Portland had a large number of settlers from New England who brought a heritage of thrift and prudence. Further, the city's location at the confluence of the Columbia and Willamette rivers made Portland the best site for the shipment of wheat and other produce from the Tualatin Plains and the Willamette Valley.

With the discovery of gold in California, economic opportunity and growth came swiftly to Oregon. The desperate need for wheat and lumber in the Sierra mining camps in turn brought gold dust to Oregon. That gold provided capital for transportation and development and freed farmers from their dependence on the Hudson's Bay Company. Portland and other Oregon towns grew rapidly in the 1850s, and while there was a brief recession in 1851 and 1852 due to an oversupply of goods in California, the discovery of gold in Southern Oregon filled the gap. By the time this new economic infusion had run its course, Oregon had become well-established.

2

Personal Histories on the Frontier

The Story of Sigmund Heilner

First-person accounts of Oregon's Jewish pioneers and the families they left behind are rare. But Sigmund Aron Heilner left a handmade trunk full of letters he received from his family as well as a diary that he kept between 1859 and 1861. His grandson, Sanford J. Heilner, recognizing the importance of these documents, edited and translated them from the original German and made them available through the Jewish Historical Society of Oregon. Sigmund's adventurous life, often full of peril and hardship, was typical of Oregon's Jewish pioneers.

Sigmund Heilner was born in Urspringen, Bavaria, in 1834. His father, Aron Heilner, was constrained to earn a modest living as an elementary schoolteacher, part-time farmer and moneylender by the restrictive edicts governing Jewish life in Bavaria, including the notorious "Jewish tax." Sigmund's older brother, Seligmann, emigrated to America in 1845 at the age of twenty-two, staying in the East until 1849 when he left to seek gold in California. After a few unsuccessful years, Seligmann began a dry goods business with Julius Simonsfeld in Crescent City on the north coast of California under the name Simonsfeld and Cohen. (Seligmann had changed his name to E. D. Cohen some time after his arrival in America to avoid being pursued by former creditors.)

In 1853, Sigmund followed Seligmann to America, landing in New York, where he stayed for a period with his cousin, Lemann Heilner.

Shortly after his arrival, Sigmund wrote to his family. That letter, like most of his others, is lost, but the return letter from his father was among those in the trunkful of papers. It captures the sentiment of families remaining in the Old World as the young men sought better fortune in a distant land. As it turned out, Aron Heilner was never again to see his son, Sigmund.

Aron Heilner, Sigmund's father, remained in Germany with his family. Two of his six children, sons Seligmann and Sigmund, emigrated to America. Courtesy, the Heilner Collection (HC).

Urspringen, Bavaria, where the Heilner family lived. This picture was painted by Sigmund, a talented amateur artist, before he left for America. Courtesy, HC.

Urspringen, July 15, 1853

Beloved Son Sigmund!

Your lovely letter arrived last Monday. I thank God for his goodness to all of us for letting you have such a fast and pleasant journey. May the Lord always be so kind and gracious to you. Your letter brought us great joy in many ways.... From our Seligmann, I have still not received a letter. You tell me he has also not written Lemann yet. God grant us that he is still well. His silence, this time, bothers me very much. I am accustomed to waiting for his letters and must keep hoping that everything is all right.

Everything with us is fine. I want to be cheerful like your dear Mother and the children and wait each day the mail arrives for a letter from our two boys in America. The one letter that we have waited for has arrived. Now we hope the other will soon come.

What you should now do, I cannot say since I do not know the circumstances there. You must trust our dear Lemann and your own intuition. Just do not delay your inten-

tions too long and do not do anything that is dangerous. At any rate, do not impose too much on Lemann and do not take advantage of his kindness, however, listen to him and be open with him. Most important is to do this: Work hard and do not do anything that will not bring honor to our name!

You know my principles: Endure, be patient, and do without if you must, but never despair! Never take refuge in that which does not agree with your conscience. God will not forsake those who remain faithful and do not despair. I, myself, have many times been in distress and knew no way out. It did not take long, however, before God showed me the way out.... Remain in New York, or, at least, in the area, and seek to build a future. Just do not try to get rich overnight. Seligmann is a good example of this. He has expected too much too fast. As soon as he writes to you, let us know.

I have nothing more at present to write to you. Joel Rotfeld died and Michael Schloss is here to visit. Whether he will remain or not, I do not think he even knows. Heinemann

Klein has been thrown out of Seminary because of a social disease and now wanders around with nothing constructive to do. If he comes to America, you stay completely away from him and have nothing whatsoever to do with him. Our business is quite slow right now. Wheat has demanded a higher price for the last while. Live well and be brave, alert, and careful. You are the apple of my eye.

I am your loving Father,

Aron Heilner

The following month, Sigmund received a letter from his brother in Crescent City, imploring Sigmund to join him.

Crescent City, August 25, 1853

My dear brother!

I received a letter today from our dear parents and brothers and sisters. I am overwhelmed with joy that you will soon be with me! I am upset, however, that you have not been a little more helpful in this situation. I do not know if you ever received the one hundred dollars I sent to Germany for you. You did not even let me know when you arrived in New York. I expect Lemann had something to do with that.

Now, pay attention to what I tell you. Ask Lemann to get you a through ticket on the Vanderbilt Line, Nicaragua. They sail the best route. Let Lemann read this letter, since he will understand it better. Do not take much baggage, because it costs too much. Try to meet a decent person on the trip who can help you with the language.

When you arrive in San Francisco, go to a man named David Bauernfreund. He lives on Montgomery Street, No. 94. He will greet you with open arms when you mention my name. He is a good friend of mine and will be helpful to you. I presently live in a town about four hundred miles from San Francisco.

I have established a rather nice business and hope, with God's help, to become very successful. I will probably be in San Francis-

co to meet you myself. Write me immediately after you receive this letter. Send your letter through the Adams & Company Express or Wells Fargo. Tell me when you are leaving and which route you are taking. . . . Take care of yourself, dear brother and stay away from danger.

Your brother,

Seligmann Heilner

Sigmund traveled to Baltimore and Washington, D.C., staying with family friends, and then returned to New York. His father was displeased and frustrated with Seligmann, who

Seligmann Heilner, also known as E. D. Cohen, (left) with unidentified friend in Crescent City, California. Sigmund's older brother, who had discovered the Enterprise Mine in Southern Oregon, met his end when he was murdered on a street in Baker in 1886. Courtesy, HC.

Sigmund Aron Heilner, born in 1834 in Urspringen, Bavaria, emigrated to America at the age of nineteen. Courtesy, HC.

was less than candid in his letters home concerning his new life. Aron therefore refused to give Sigmund permission to join his brother in California.

Urspringen, August 15, 1854

Beloved Son, Seligmann!

A few days ago, we received your letter of the 24th of June and were very happy to learn of your good health. . . .

In spite of your noble and good desire, I still have not made up my mind as to whether I should give my permission to Sigmund to come to you. There is so much danger associated with going to such a strange land and I am not sure it would be an improvement in Sigmund's chances to do well. I do not want to make any final conclusions, and, in fact, I am partially convinced because of your zeal,

however, even you tell us in your letters how difficult it is to live in California and your circumstances certainly are not the most enviable. The one thing that bothers me the most is that you never tell me completely what your circumstances are. Being the loyal son that you are, you should have no reason to keep anything secret from your parents. How often I have written to you and asked you to give me a full account of what you are doing, what is your business, what you earn, etc.? What do I read in your letters? Nothing more than general impressions of meaningless information. . . . I wish I had wings so that I could fly to you in that far, distant land. I am truly frustrated by your letters. Dear son, could you not simply write me the plain and simple truth about your circumstances? Tell me the good and the bad experiences. Everything is of interest to your parents when it concerns their distant son.

We live, as you know, very simply. We save what we can and especially our dear Mother is so efficient in this. I can assure you, I would like very much to financially help you and Sigmund, but at present, I must be concerned about our Regina. Her situation rests very heavily on my heart. All of her friends are either married or engaged. Ricka Frankel has been married two years and is living in Laudenbach. Caroline Schloss is engaged to Lob Frankel. Marle Kola has been married quite some time. Regina must get married soon, but for this, much money is needed. Dear Sigmund knows how much I worry about this. He wrote me in his last letter that although his entire savings consist of only 100f, he wants to give it all to me for Regina. I hope you will also help me if you are in a position that you can.

You know how I feel about Sigmund coming to you. I will certainly insist that if he does come, it will not be before a considerable length of time. His circumstances must be adequate and you must improve yours. You tell me that you could pay your brother $60 a month. Anyone that can pay someone else that much money in one month must be wealthy. *In two months, that is more than I make in one year. I would feel much better if you would leave California and go to the States on this side of Panama and, united with your brother, establish a business. We would also feel that the possibility of seeing you once again was more a reality. I am constantly thinking about you and your future. Your well-being lies close to my heart....*

Your dear, concerned Father

Aron Heilner

Regina finally married a Mr. Feiffer Gutmann after they were forced to wait several years for permission from the German authorities. In his next letter Aron, finally relenting, gave his permission. On December 12, 1854, Sigmund sailed steerage from New York to Panama on the *Star of the West*, and then on the steamer *Sierra Nevada* to San Francisco, where he arrived on January 6. Shortly after, Seligmann and Sigmund received this touching letter from their father.

Urspringen, March 11, 1855

My beloved Sons!

It was on Friday night, the 9th of this month between 4 and 5 o'clock, that your letter arrived. I was just going to dress for the Shabbes. Your dear mother joyfully called out, "It is from our children in California!" She was in the process of bathing Sophie. Regina, Caroline, and David came running to hear and see the letter. With joy, I held it in my hand and just looked at it for a minute before I opened it. Then, with great anticipation, I opened the little yellow envelope and could immediately see my fondest hope was confirmed. You were safely together. "They are together, my good sons," I called out as I took the two letters from the envelope. "One is from Seligmann and one is from Sigmund!"

Before I started to read the letter, I raised my tearful eyes to thank our dear God from the bottom of my heart for his great blessings, that he has once again given me. One of my

SIGMUND HEILNER'S DIARY

January, Sunday the 1st, 1860: *Rain almost all day. Spent the day as usual. Stayed at home and read. I am not included to pay visit to the . . . miners. I am longing to go home. I wish the magnet were broken that keeps me here. God show me the hour of fulfillment very soon. Oh, wishful thinking! My head is full of thoughts. Could I only be with you, my dear ones, even for a short time. But wait—I have to wait, imprisoned in this place which I hate so much. Distance, passing years, length of time.*

No, you do not steal the love, the affection which has lasted for years. No, on the contrary, New Year—new months—coming days—hours—you are leading me like a burning fire to my destination. God keep alive my dear ones. Good night, sweet thoughts.

Althouse Creek, June 27th, 1861: *Nine o'clock in the morning. Since I have been left alone, I want to convey my thoughts to this diary. After having had many disagreeable and unhappy hours . . . disagreeable . . . on account of my great disappointment, my trip home, the embracing of my dear ones, the leaving of California, collecting my money . . . and unhappy . . . after feeling compelled to return to this lonesome, monotonous, deserted, secluded from the world place. As my dear father said in his last letter, have patience. The few years of my exile will be ended soon and I hope with God to enjoy my life, which should be near to my dear ones. But I do not want to make plans now and I will leave it to God, who has fulfilled many of my wishes. Let us look toward the future with good courage. Let us not worry so much. Patience, energy and perseverance will accomplish everything, even some things of which we do not think. The sun is shining so brightly. I take that as a good omen. Even butterflies are coming to my window, flying back and forth as if they wanted to participate in my thoughts and I am enjoying taking a breath of the good mountain air. Every breath inspires me with more courage and perseverance. Should I not think that I am the happiest one to be in good health, to enjoy breathing the fresh and healthful mountain air. Therefore, why worry so much?*

From Sigmund Heilner's diary, kept between the years of 1859 and 1861 at Browntown. Sigmund was twenty-five when he began the diary and was often despondent and lonely. Courtesy, HC.

long anticipated wishes is now fulfilled. You are happily and safely together. God will now watch over you together. Such two fine and outstanding sons must receive great blessings together. Last Friday night was truly a most happy one.... I should say, a most joyful one.

First I read your letters aloud. Then, your dear mother read them aloud. Then Regina and Caroline read them aloud. The two young ones just listened. As we came to the place where you describe how you both first met in San Francisco, how we all wished we could have been there. How does one describe such feelings? With all my writing, I cannot express the feelings of my heart. If I could not so vividly picture you in my mind, I would not feel that moment as deeply as I do. I constantly think of it. We all want to thank the Lord for the joy we receive from knowing we

are all well. We live in the hope that one day God will again grant us the great joy of all embracing each other here....

Your Faithful Father,

Aron Heilner

Soon after his arrival in Crescent City, Sigmund left for Browntown, a tiny gold and copper mining settlement on Althouse Creek in Oregon, just north of the California border. For four years he ran a small dry goods store supplying miners, until he sold it to Charles Ebert and went briefly into the moneylending business. Lending money was widely practiced by those who had it, since miners were always in need, and banks not only charged exorbitant interest but were located far away—the one closest to Althouse was in the booming gold

Browntown, a gold and copper mining town, on Althouse Creek in Oregon, just above the California border. This is the only known rendering of the town and was painted by Sigmund Heilner in 1865 as a Christmas present for Mrs. L. E. Hall, who owned and operated the hotel shown in the painting. Courtesy, HC.

center of Jacksonville, fifty miles to the north. But, like most activities in Althouse, lending was risky, and Sigmund at times was despondent, feeling isolated and without enough to occupy him. He was not without friends, though. While at Althouse, two of his closest associates were the brothers Bernard and Isaac Goldsmith, who owned jewelry/assay stores in Crescent City and Browntown. Later, Bernard would go north to Portland and become that city's first Jewish mayor.

In 1861, Sigmund returned to Crescent City to go into the freight-forwarding business. He had planned to accompany Seligmann back to Germany to visit the family, but the purchaser of his Althouse store reneged on payment and Sigmund unhappily had to return to Browntown while his brother made the trip alone. When Seligmann (known as E. D. Cohen) returned from Germany two years later, he discovered the Enterprise Mine, or Cohen Quartz Ledge as it was first known, where a rich pay chute of gold was uncovered on Sucker Creek, not far from Althouse. Sigmund became president of the mine.

While he was at Althouse, a major Indian uprising occurred in Southern Oregon. Sigmund commanded an expedition carrying arms and ammunition to the volunteer militia fighting in the Rogue River Indian War. Later he was actively engaged in combat under Captain Driscoll. The conflict was significant enough to warrant articles in the *Frankfurter Zeitung*, a German paper read by Sigmund's father, bringing this plea in a letter dated October 25, 1856:

My beloved and precious Sons

Seligmann and Sigmund!

I have been deeply concerned about both of you. Reports in the newspapers concerning the unrest in California and Oregon have

From "A Personal Account of Life in Browntown, Oregon" by William Mackey, recorded in 1934. Mackey was born and raised in the Althouse area during the time that Sigmund Heilner lived there.

BROWNTOWN, OREGON

Few mining towns in Oregon have a more eventful history than old Browntown which stood on the banks of Althouse Creek.

Browntown in its early history was visited by several desperate characters and was the scene of more than one tragedy or deadly duel in which men lost their lives.

Browntown was the concentrating point for the miners of Sucker Creek, Bolan Creek and Democrat Gulch. These camps yielded millions of dollars in the precious metal. The miners from these camps spent their money with a lavish hand in the dance halls and at the gambling tables in the drinking resorts of Browntown.

Farmers in the fifties with their teams hauled farm products such as fruit, butter, bacon and vegetables from the Willamette and Umpqua valleys, distances of 150 to 200 miles, to Browntown and sold them to the miners. Many of those farmers were somewhat simple-minded and green and were called "tartars" by the miners and gamblers of Browntown. Those farmers seemed to have a mania for gambling and playing cards and were often enticed to stake their teams and products on card games, almost invariably losing all.

One time a farmer appeared in Browntown with a wagonload of good things to eat raised on a Willamette farm. He was arrested by a gambler on a charge of cheating at the gaming table. A jury was empaneled and everything bore the solemnity and dignity of a real court, over which an educated gambler, Dan Lanigan, presided as judge. He sat at a desk with a history of the United States as a pretended law book laid open before him. Witnesses were called and examined before Judge Lanigan. While the trial proceeded the miners who stood around would say in a low voice to each other, but within hearing distance of the doomed "tartar," "Oh it's a hard case, he'll get not less than 10 years." While the "tartar's" brother would go around among the bystanders crazed with grief and say "I'm afraid that it will go hard with my poor brother."

At last the "tartar" was found guilty and sentenced by Judge Lanigan to pay a $20 fine and forfeit his wagon load of produce and treat the crowd at the bar, which the luckless "tartar" gladly did, thinking that he had made a narrow escape from going to the state prison.

caused me many hours of consternation. It is good that I did not know that the danger was as great as it was. I would have been beside myself. Again, I thank our Eternal Father for his grace, but also I am more convinced than ever that you both must not remain in such a dangerous place. How I wish you would return and establish yourselves in Germany where people live like human beings....

Your Father,

Aron Heilner

By the mid-1860s, precious metals were largely depleted in the Althouse area and most of the people Sigmund had known had already left. After a brief, unsuccessful attempt at quartz mining, he, too, departed for Portland, where he lived for some time with his friend, Bernard Goldsmith. He tried his hand at packing goods to the inland wilderness, penetrating as far as Bear Gulch, Montana. Then he took up portrait and landscape painting, in which he had received training in Germany, and later, in Port-

The Heilner Block in Baker housed the Heilner Commercial and Commission Company. Here an extensive wholesale and retail trade was conducted. Courtesy, HC.

land, was employed by the Alaska Fur Company.

In 1872, Sigmund Heilner moved to Sparta in Union County, Oregon, a mining camp with several hundred Chinese residents where he established a general merchandise store. Although Sparta is a ghost town today, the store built by Heilner still stands. He returned to Portland in 1874 to marry Clara Neuberger, a young German immigrant whom he had met while living in Portland. The Neuberger family later provided Oregon with its second Jewish United States senator, Richard Neuberger. Clara and Sigmund Heilner settled permanently that year in Baker City, Oregon.

At this time, Baker City, later just called Baker, had over one thousand inhabitants and was the major town in Eastern Oregon. Sigmund became a prominent figure there, establishing the Heilner Commercial and Commission Company, which eventually became the Neuberger-Heilner Banking Company, the first bank in Baker and a forerunner of the First National Bank of Baker. He also ran a successful hide and wool business, operated a freight-forwarding firm, and owned an insurance agency and the Mammoth Mine in Sumpter.

The Heilners had four children: Jesse, Joseph, Millie and Sanford, the youngest, who was the only child to go into business with his father. The family was raised in a large house built by Sigmund that was frequently used for High Holiday services by the small Jewish community of Baker. In 1882, the *West Shore* magazine called the Heilner home "not only one of the handsomest, but probably the most elegantly furnished private residence in Eastern Oregon." Sigmund retired before World War I, and Sanford continued to operate the Heilner store and other enterprises until he too retired in 1977 at the age of ninety-four, a year before his death. Clara died in 1915, Sigmund in 1917; they are both buried in the Beth Israel cemetery in Portland. Sigmund Heilner's children and their offspring are the only remaining descendants of Aron Heilner's family. Seligmann, who never married, was murdered during a dispute in Baker in 1888, and all the family who stayed in the old country perished in the Holocaust.

The Story of Bernard Goldsmith

Bernard Goldschmidt (later changed to Gold-smith) was born in Bavaria on November 20, 1832, in the small town of Weddenburg, which lies between Munich and Nuremberg.* He would one day become the first Jewish mayor of Portland, slightly more than a century before Neil Goldschmidt, unrelated but sharing the same name, would become Portland's fourth Jewish mayor in 1972. Bernard was the oldest in a family of eight boys and two girls whose predecessors had lived in the same area in Bavaria for at least three hundred years. His father, Abraham, began poor but prospered as a wool

*Most information concerning Bernard Goldsmith is from an 1889 interview with Goldsmith conducted in Portland by Hubert Howe Bancroft and contained in *The Chronicles of the Builders*, Bancroft Library, University of California, Berkeley.

merchant. Bernard went to school until age thirteen, worked briefly in his father's business and, restless and somewhat dissatisfied, left for America at the youthful age of fifteen. Many years later in 1889, Goldsmith described his feelings about leaving Germany and his trip to America to the famous historian, Hubert Howe Bancroft:

When I was a young boy, I worked hard all the time. The inducement for me to come over was this: I was the oldest of eight boys and I did not like things over there. In 1848 there was a general revolution and general dissatisfaction ... and I ... just made up my mind that I would come here; that was all.

I came over in an emigrant ship and we were seventy-two days at sea. Steamers were not as plentiful then as now and passage was quite costly. That is the reason I came among the emigrants.... My father furnished me the money to come over here. I had a couple of

Bernard Goldsmith fought in the Battle of Big Meadows on the Rogue River in June, 1856. Courtesy, OHS.

Barely five feet tall, Bernard Goldsmith, mayor of Portland from 1869 to 1871, was the most prominent and prosperous Jew in Oregon well into the 1880s. Courtesy, OHS.

hundred dollars when I landed in New York City. When I arrived I was glad enough to feel that I was in a free country and was a free man.... Afterwards, occasionally, with the first year, there were some days when I felt very depressed, feeling homesick, but I was satisfied with the country from the moment I set my foot on it.

Bernard landed in August, 1848, and stayed with an aunt, uncle and four cousins in New York, where he apprenticed in his cousin's jewelry store to learn the watchmaker's trade. He worked as a salesman for the store, earning forty dollars per year in addition to board and lodging. Apprenticeship with relatives was common among Jews in Bavaria and for newly arrived young men in the United States. Bernard changed his name to Goldsmith, which his relatives had already done in order to relate more easily to their English-speaking clientele.

By 1850, Bernard was off to California with the meager funds he had saved. But when he arrived in San Francisco, Goldsmith did not have the ten dollars needed for transport ashore and was forced to stay on board until the captain had no choice but to ferry him in his own boat. Despite the tumult of Gold Rush San Francisco, Goldsmith was able to locate Michael Reese, an old friend of his father's, who staked him to dinner and fare to Sacramento, where he worked as a clerk for several months. From there he traveled on to Marysville, laboring as a stevedore for ten to twelve dollars per day. When he had saved enough to buy a horse and three mules, he started a pack train between Marysville and Rich Bar on the Feather River.

With the eight thousand dollars he accumulated packing supplies to the gold camps, Goldsmith invested in a wholesale jewelry business in San Francisco with a brother recently arrived from the East. Although they had close business ties to similar establishments run by cousins in New York and Boston, for reasons which are not clear Goldsmith lost all of his money. Flat broke, he left San Francisco and headed north to Crescent City with a stock of goods he had obtained on credit. He did well in the general merchandise business there and opened a second store in Yreka which was run by a brother, then a third along Althouse Creek in Southern Oregon which was managed by yet another brother. In 1858, he replaced his brother in Althouse, managing the store there himself. It was during this period that he became friends with Sigmund and Seligmann Heilner.

As had Sigmund, Bernard Goldsmith became involved in the Indian Wars in Northern California and Southern Oregon. He was a lieutenant in Judge Roseborough's cavalry, which was responsible for protecting the Crescent City area in the spring of 1855. Indians came down from the north, taking possession of the roads and burning some houses. Goldsmith and his company brought settlers to the now-fortified town and persuaded local Indians that they would not be harmed if they would relocate to the island in Crescent City Harbor where they could be "guarded." Six to eight thousand Indians surrounded Crescent City until its inhabitants were relieved by the arrival of federal soldiers. Goldsmith volunteered for further service under Colonel Buchanan's command and was with him at the Battle of Big Meadows on the Rogue River in June, 1856. After initial skirmishes, the settlers maneuvered a large mountain howitzer into place, firing five or six times. Exploding shells were new to Southern Oregon and surprised and frightened the Indians who surrendered shortly thereafter.

A second outbreak of hostilities was prevented by Goldsmith, who had established good relations with many of the Indians. Several delegations of Indians approached him to report abuses by the Indian Agent; they threatened an uprising unless conditions improved. Goldsmith asked them to hold off and promised to secure better treatment. He immediately traveled to San Francisco to meet with the Superintendent for Indian Affairs in California, Colonel Henley, who agreed to redress the Indians' grievances and thus prevented a second uprising.

In 1859, after a year in the wilderness along Althouse Creek, Bernard Goldsmith went back to Germany to visit his family. Before returning the following year, he met with E. D. Cohen, the Heilner brother also in Germany at the time, to ask whether he would object to Goldsmith's approaching Sigmund to suggest that they go into business together. Cohen said that he did object, since Sigmund was already his partner. When Bernard returned to Althouse, he sold his interest in his store there to his brother, Isaac, went briefly to the Fraser River in British Columbia, where gold had also been discovered, but returned south to Portland, where he settled in 1861. It is interesting to note that, as Althouse Creek declined in the early 1860s, it became known as "Goldsmith's deserted village."

At twenty-eight years of age, Goldsmith was, by 1861, already a man of substantial wealth derived from his stores in Southern Oregon and California. In Portland, he again bought a jewelry store and attached to it an assay office, through which he bought gold dust. Goldsmith was able to bring several of his brothers to Portland to assist him, later purchasing a wholesale dry goods establishment for them to operate.

Unlike most of Portland's early Jewish merchants, Goldsmith also branched out into numerous speculative activities. He undertook the raising of substantial herds of cattle in Wasco County, and claims, in his 1889 dictation to Hubert H. Bancroft, to have been one of the largest cattle ranchers in Oregon. He was responsible for importing Durham stock into the state and, according to the *Oregonian*, did more to improve the breed of beef cattle than any other man in Oregon. During the Civil War, he filled large government contracts for horses, mules and supplies and contracted to carry the mail by

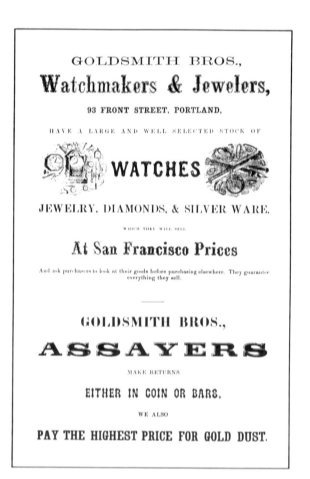

Advertisement from the *Portland Directory*, 1865.

stagecoach from The Dalles to Rock Point, Utah.

In 1868, Goldsmith was involved with others in shipping the first cargo of wheat from Oregon to Liverpool on the sailing ship *Sallie Brown*. At first English millers did not like the Oregon wheat, because its natural fullness appeared swollen to them. In a short time, however, they became accustomed to the differently textured but high quality wheat from the Willamette Valley, and this initial venture bloomed into a thriving trade. Goldsmith was also one of five original incorporators—another was Philip Wasserman, a Jew who followed Goldsmith's two terms as mayor of Portland with two of his own—of the Oregon and California Railroad, which they brought within six miles of East Portland before selling to a consortium headed by Ben Holladay. Goldsmith was one of five, again including Wasserman, to establish the first national bank on the Pacific Coast. Later purchased by Henry Corbett and Henry Failing, it became the First National Bank of Oregon. Goldsmith participated in speculative mining ventures in silver, lead and gold, and at various times owned considerable real estate in Central Oregon, Linn County and Portland. He purchased a valuable piece of land in West Portland ("Goldsmith's Addition") for $15,000, and later turned it over to one of his brothers after its value had increased to more than $1.25 million.

Perhaps Bernard Goldsmith's most visionary undertaking was the building of the locks and canals at the falls on the Willamette River in 1872. Before the locks were built, boats had to stop above and below the falls, transshipping all goods by wagon team in the early days and later by a small tramway, which was both expensive and time-consuming. Goldsmith and his associates secured $200,000 from the state legislature to construct the locks, but the contractor failed to complete the project within budget, and after backers refused further funds, Goldsmith completed the work at his own expense. The final cost amounted to over $400,000, and unfortunately his difficulties were just beginning.

The People's Transportation Company, which had previously enjoyed a shipping monopoly commanding exorbitant rates, refused

Philip Wasserman followed his close friend and fellow Bavarian immigrant, Bernard Goldsmith, as mayor of Portland (1871-1873). Courtesy, JHSO.

to use the locks, so Goldsmith was forced to build his own boats. He founded the Willamette Locks and Transportation Company, whose boats were able to navigate from Astoria all the way to Eugene and charged half what it had previously cost to transport goods on the river. But two rivals, People's Transportation Company and Oregon Navigation Company, consolidated and forced Goldsmith to build newer and faster ships. Ultimately, he was unable to compete and sold out to his rivals at great loss. He was the only loser, however, for Oregon and the Willamette Valley benefited greatly from the alternative transportation, which prevented the railroads from obtaining a monopoly along this key route—the pattern wherever alternatives did not exist. Goldsmith considered the building of the locks his major public achievement, of more importance than his service as mayor.

In the first decades after settlement of Oregon, standing for local public office was seen as the duty and responsibility of those who had achieved prominence. Order and public peace as well as necessary services for vigorous growth were essential to the commercial development of frontier towns. In that spirit, a number of Jews served in key roles throughout the state. In Portland, seven Jews served on the common (city) council in the 1860s and 70s; three occupied the post of city treasurer; and one was the city attorney. Two Jewish merchants became mayor of Portland: Bernard Goldsmith (1869-1871) and his close friend and fellow Bavarian immigrant, tobacco merchant Philip Wasserman (1871-1873).

Most Jews nationally, and Goldsmith and Wasserman locally, belonged to the Democratic party before the Civil War. But because they strongly opposed slavery and supported Lincoln—to whom Jews felt particularly drawn by his character, self-deprecating humor and sense of humanity—Jews shifted to the new Republican party, maintaining allegiance to it well into the twentieth century. Thus Goldsmith ran for mayor on the Union Republican ticket, but reverted to the Democratic party after Ulysses S. Grant's second election. Jews did not trust Grant because he had expelled them from the Tennessee Department for "war profiteering" during the Civil War, an order immediately countermanded by President Lincoln.

Bernard Goldsmith's accomplishments in two years as mayor were relatively modest: the purchase of City Park (now Washington Park) and his support of an ordinance requiring shade trees to be planted by store owners along city streets. The purchase of the first forty acres for City Park at five hundred dollars per acre was controversial, and the mayor and council were roundly denounced for having spent too much money when wilderness abounded on all sides. But Goldsmith maintained that the park would be seen in the future as a great asset to the city, and the *Oregonian* wrote upon Goldsmith's death that the "people in these days are grateful in the extreme" for City Park.

Both Goldsmith and Wasserman had to face difficult social issues involving the influx of Chinese laborers and growing anti-Chinese sentiment. In 1869, Goldsmith dealt sensitively with the quarantine of a shipload of Chinese suspected of carrying smallpox. He arranged for their housing in a tent on the outskirts of town and for Chinese firms to feed them until they could enter the city. Wasserman approved a health ordinance requiring that at least 550 cubic feet of living space be allotted to each occupant to alleviate overcrowded conditions among the Chinese, and in June, 1873, vetoed an effort by the city council to prevent Chinese laborers from being employed on city contracts. Wasserman cited the recently passed Fourteenth Amendment to the Constitution and a treaty with China in arguing for non-discrimination and equal protection for the Chinese.

In the spring of 1886, Goldsmith, Wasserman and Ben Selling, an American-born Jew, joined others as special deputies to defend successfully the Chinese quarter from threatened attack by mobs seeking to expel them from Portland. Goldsmith, Wasserman and Selling were more concerned about the civil liberties of the Chinese and other minorities than were many of their non-Jewish colleagues, due in part to their success as merchants who recognized the importance of civic order and also perhaps to their history in Europe as a people who had long suffered discrimination and outcast status.

Bernard Goldsmith was married to Emma Frohman, also a native of Bavaria, in March, 1863. She was a woman "of a great deal more than ordinary ability," according to Judge Matthew Deady, and was for many years president of the Ladies Hebrew Benevolent Association, the principal voluntary organization for Jewish charity dispensed by women. The Goldsmiths had seven children. Bernard died on July 22, 1901, at his home on the corner of Quimby and 24th Avenue in Northwest Portland. He had been the most prominent and prosperous Jew in Portland well into the 1880s.

The Story of Aaron and Jeanette Meier

Aaron Meier was born in Ellerstadt, Bavaria, on May 22, 1831. His father died when Aaron was still a boy, and he worked in the brickyard of an uncle to help his family while attending school. In 1855, at the age of twenty-four, he decided to join his two brothers, Julius and Emanuel, in Downieville, California, where they operated a general merchandise store. Aaron worked in the store as well as peddling goods deep into Oregon territory for two years before deciding to strike out on his own. Taking a steamer to Portland, he opened a dry goods and clothing store in 1857 with partners N. Simon and Nathan Meerholtz at 137 Front Avenue. Barely thirty-five by fifty feet in size, the store was stocked with several hundred dollars worth of merchandise. By 1857, Portland's population had grown to about thirteen hundred, and the city already had forty-two stores selling dry goods and groceries.

Aaron returned to Ellerstadt in 1863 to visit his mother, leaving his shop in the hands of a partner. While in Germany he married Jeanette Hirsch, twelve years his junior, whose father, Moses, was a grain buyer and well-known to the Meiers. Aaron also acquired fourteen thousand dollars, which was his share of the family estate. Returning to Portland with his new wife, Meier stopped in New York and spent much of his inheritance on merchandise. But the first of several setbacks awaited him in Portland, where he learned that his partner had bankrupted the store the previous year and that a number of merchants in Eastern Oregon had reneged on payments for merchandise he had brought west for them. Meier virtually had to begin over again.

He reopened for business across the street at 136 Front Avenue in larger quarters that measured fifty by one hundred feet. He hand built shelves with rough boards and constructed counters from packing boxes covered with calico. Aaron and Jeanette lived in an apartment nearby, and she brought hot lunch to him each day. Their first child, Fannie, was born in 1865, the year following their return from Germany. Before their second child, Abe, was born, Aaron had purchased a lot at Third and Columbia and built a two-story house for $350. There Abe, Julius and Hattie were born, though Hattie died in infancy.

These were very hard years for Aaron and Jeanette. Funds and credit were difficult to come by. As Jeanette recalled in 1920:

Everything seemed to be going wrong. We needed money, oh, so bad, we needed money. Mr. Meier kept saying over and over that if we had a few thousand dollars our troubles would be over. At the bank our credit was strained almost to the breaking point. My husband went to friend after friend, but none could help, at least none did. Finally we went to a Mr. D. P. Thompson, almost a stranger, and Mr. Thompson said, "Yes, I will see you through," and he did. He let Aaron have all the

Aaron Meier, the founder of Meier & Frank department store. Courtesy, OHS.

money he needed, and it was the turning point in our business affairs.

As the store began to prosper, more help was needed, and, as did so many Jewish merchants of the day, they brought relatives over from the old country. In this case, they brought the Hirsches—Jeanette's half-brothers, cousins and nephews from the marriage of her father, Moses, to his second wife. As Harold Hirsch, Jeanette's great-nephew, recalled in the 1970s, the less fortunate members of the family were brought over "partly because of family feelings of sympathy and love and partly because they could get darn cheap, trustworthy labor that way." In fact, the work ethic was so strong that when Harold's father, Max Hirsch, asked to take a few days vacation to accompany friends to Wilhoit Springs, the sharp response was "What do you want a vacation for? You just came!" This was seven years after he had begun working for the store.

(Max finally left as Meier & Frank's superintendent in 1907, and with Harry Weis purchased the Willamette Tent and Awning Company from Oregon pioneer Henry Wemme, whose last will and testament would play a key, cameo role in helping to make Aaron and Jeanette's youngest son, Julius, governor of Oregon. The firm, which became known as Hirsch-Weis, later anglicized its name to White Stag. Initially they made canvas for ships and tents, horse covers and waterbags for Alaskan gold prospectors. Harold Hirsch started the company's formal sportswear lines during the

The first Meier & Frank store, built in 1874 after Aaron Meier's small store burned down in the great fire of 1873, which destroyed much of downtown Portland. Courtesy, OHS.

Depression and built the company into a major manufacturing concern. In 1966, Warnaco, a large Connecticut clothing manufacturer, accumulated sufficient stock to incorporate White Stag as a Warnaco unit, and in 1987 it closed all White Stag operations in Portland.)

In 1870, on a buying trip to San Francisco, Aaron Meier met Emil Frank and invited him to Portland to work as a clerk in his store. In 1873, Emil Frank became Aaron's partner. That same year, a major fire destroyed much of downtown Portland, including the Meier store. Once again,

---

A. Meier.   E. Frank.

MEIER & FRANK,
Wholesale and Retail Dealers in
GENERAL MERCHANDISE,
133, 135 & 137 Front St., Cor. Yamhill, Portland, Or.

An early advertisement found in *West Shore* magazine, July, 1877. "E. Frank," who became a partner in the store in 1873 after Aaron Meier met him on a buying trip in San Francisco, is Emil. Courtesy, OHS.

Grandmother Drain had a darning needle, and it was the only darning needle among the settlers in Pass Creek Canyon. Grandmother Drain's darning needle was one of the most cared-for possessions in the community, because it was the only one, and clothes had to be patched and mended until new ones could be secured, and who knew when that would be? Women in the lower canyon shared the needle for a day or two, then women up farther would take turns using it to catch up on the family mending.

All went well until the day Mrs. Chitwood sent the needle back to Grandmother Drain's by Jimmy. Jimmy was eight years old, and he was a responsible boy—boys had to be responsible and do their share of the work.

Mrs. Chitwood put a long red ravelling through the eye of the needle and knotted it, then she put the needle into a potato so that Jimmy could carry it safely to the Drain cabin.

Jimmy walked through the canyon trail in the spring morning sunshine which filtered through the tall firs. He paid no attention to rabbits and squirrels that crossed the path in front of him. He scarcely looked up when bluejays scolded. He stopped for a moment when a doe raced a few yards down the trail as though being chased, but he did not leave the trail. He was on an errand with the

only darning needle in Pass Creek Canyon. But when a mother bear with two cubs came into sight, he jumped from the trail and hid behind a service-berry bush to watch them.

Jimmy stood up again and went back onto the trail. He walked a little, thinking of the bears and wishing that sometime he might have a cub all his own, without a mother bear. Then he remembered the darning needle! He looked down at his hand. The potato and the needle were gone!

Everyone was worried, but no one scolded Jimmy except his sister. All the men and women, and children, too, began looking for a red ravelling near a stump under a service-berry bush. Suddenly Jimmy left the others. He said nothing but walked through a bramble of bracken. When he came out, he went straight to his mother and handed her the potato with the red ravelling hanging from it. "It was by the stump," he said.

"Why, Jimmy," replied his mother, "you are a woodsman, and a reliable boy, to find what you lost. Give it to Grandmother Drain. Quick! before you lose it again."

Everyone, and that was about twenty-five people, came together to share the joy of finding the needle. Then the men went back to trimming logs, the women went home to get their suppers, and the children went back to their play.

This early folklore was told and retold by oldtimers about Aaron Meier in the days when he peddled goods in the Oregon Territory.

Meier had to start over, this time returning to the other side of Front Avenue, where his first store had been located. The new store was the first Meier & Frank and covered an entire block.

Emil's brother, Sigmund Frank, followed him from San Francisco in 1873 and immediately made a strong impression on Aaron and Jeanette. Sigmund had been trained in music in Germany and had taught piano and violin in New York to earn funds to come west. Only twenty-three years old in 1873, he was full of ideas and energy. The Meier and Frank dynasty became firmly established with the celebrated marriage of Sigmund to Aaron and Jeanette's oldest child, Fannie, on December 8, 1885.

The children of this marriage, along with Meier's sons Abe and Julius and their children, would play key roles in building Meier & Frank into a preeminent commercial enterprise until they fell into bitter rivalries after Jeanette's death that ended in the sale of the store. Sigmund replaced his brother, Emil, as the principal partner in Meier & Frank in 1887. The following year Emil went into business with

The darning needle was found, and it was kept all that summer and into the fall, but one day when Grandmother Drain was sewing, the head of the needle broke off, and all the women had to make neat piles of clothing to be mended, hoping that before long someone would come from Fort Vancouver or the East with a needle. Each time women were together they talked of their sewing and hoped that another needle would soon be provided.

One day, about Thanksgiving time, a peddler with a mule came over the pass and down through the canyon. The children playing school on some logs saw him and ran to tell their mothers a visitor was coming.

The mothers, one by one, hurried to see the goods the peddler had brought and to hear the news of people to the east. Several hurried to buy combs. One bought a china doll's head. Two women enthusiastically bought dress goods before they thought of needles and thread to sew it with.

Then one of the mothers said, "Oh, do you have any needles? We'll have to have a needle."

"Oh," said Mrs. Chitwood, "how could we forget when it is the one thing we need most—a good needle with a large eye! We need one at least, now that Grandmother Drain's needle is broken." Mrs. Chitwood told the story of the lost darning needle, glancing occasionally at Jimmy who was stroking the mule's neck and pretending not to notice.

Those standing around talked, too, and the peddler listened. Then he reached into his inside pocket.

"My people do not celebrate Christmas," he said, "but I suppose you good people will soon be having a holiday with presents. Are you going to give any presents, sonny?" asked the peddler.

Jimmy looked up quickly, "Oh, yes sir, that is, I guess I will."

"Well," said the kind-faced man, "suppose you and I give the ladies of Pass Creek Canyon each a Christmas present right now, shall we?"

Jimmy looked puzzled. The peddler opened the thin package he had taken from his pocket. "Here are some darning needles, all I have, but I believe there will be enough for every family in the canyon to have one."

No one said anything for a moment, then there was a gasp of astonishment. The women smiled to each other, "He's a good man."

The peddler and Jimmy passed out the needles to those gathered around, and the next day Jimmy delivered the rest of the needles up and down the canyon.

The peddler left, and no one saw him again for many months, but that was just the first of many kindnesses shown the women in Pass Creek Canyon by Aaron Meier who later founded the store of Meier & Frank in Portland.

These events in 1852 or 1853 are recounted by Mary Drain Albro in *With Her Own Wings*, ed. Helen Krebs Smith (1948).

Louis Blumauer, the first Jewish child born in Oregon, forming Blumauer and Frank, a large wholesale drug company which was later sold to McKesson Robins.

Through much of Aaron's life, and particularly after his death at the age of fifty-eight in 1889, Jeanette, who would live for another thirty-six years, was a powerful force at Meier & Frank. A short, stout German matriarch, Jeanette held court at first in the back of the store and later, when she would be called "Tante Jeanette" and "Grandma Meier," in the upstairs sitting room of her home. The many direct and more distant relatives who held positions in the store were "told" how the store was to be managed; when arguments broke out, Jeanette was the final and absolute arbiter. Harold Hirsch remembers Sunday night family gatherings as a young child:

Not only were they social meetings, but they were business meetings. I can recall sitting at the children's table and listening while my great-aunt, Jeanette Hirsch Meier,

Jeanette Hirsch Meier (right), Aaron's wife, with Fannie Meier, their eldest child, and Sigmund Frank. Fannie and Sigmund firmly established the Meier & Frank dynasty in 1885 with their celebrated marriage. Sigmund replaced his brother, Emil, as a partner in Meier & Frank in 1887. Jeanette lived for thirty-six years after Aaron's death in 1889 and was the guiding force behind Meier & Frank. Courtesy, Gerry Frank.

got up at the head table and told each of these men exactly what they were going to do and how they were going to do it. When there were arguments, "Tante Jeanette," as we called her, would "bang their heads together." It is interesting that, practically from the year she died, the family began to fall apart and individuals to go their own way.

Jeanette Meier went to the store every day and is said to have paid minute attention to the smallest detail. She determined, for instance, that the feather dusters so common at the turn of the century would no longer be used, since they "only moved the dust around;" a dust cloth

would take their place. Sigmund Frank was formally the chief officer of Meier & Frank from Aaron's death until his own in 1910, and he did provide solid management. But while Aaron and Jeanette's oldest son, Abe, took over as figurehead president until 1930, it was Jeanette who by force of personality and constant surveillance guided Meier & Frank from a country store to the largest department store in the Northwest.

In the early years, many of the store's best customers were farmers who came by boat or wagon to shop once or twice a year. Great efforts were made to welcome them, with the men offered free tobacco and talk of politics and the women coffee, candy and the latest in fashion from San Francisco and the East. Early ledgers show that much of the firm's business was based on credit; accounts were either paid in cash or settled by the payment of so many eggs, potatoes, pickles, salmon—whatever could be bartered profitably. Because so much produce was taken as payment, Meier & Frank opened a grocery department in its basement to sell these goods to the general public.

The store that had been built after the great fire of 1873 was outgrown by the mid-1880s; a new store, measuring one hundred by two hundred feet, was built in 1885, this time on Taylor between First and Second Avenues. Another calamity occurred in 1894, when the flooding Willamette inundated Meier & Frank and much of downtown beneath three feet of water. But the store stayed open, using rowboats to bring customers to plank walks constructed along the sales counters above the water.

In 1898, Meier & Frank erected the first major "uptown" store on Fifth Avenue between Alder and Morrison. It was a five-story, modern building with two elevators and various mechanical innovations new to the West Coast, and it was nearly seventy times larger than the first store Aaron Meier built forty years earlier. As business increased dramatically, a ten-story annex was added to the Alder Street store in 1909, and only five years later the Fifth Avenue store was demolished to make way for the present sixteen-story, terra-cotta structure handsomely

Salespeople at Meier & Frank during the great flood of 1894 stand on the west side of First Avenue between Taylor and Yamhill streets. Courtesy, OHS.

designed by A. E. Doyle. One of Portland's first skyscrapers, the new store was the fourth largest department store in America when it opened.

In 1910, Abe Meier, as the oldest male member of the clan, became president and Julius, his younger brother, general manager. Abe had little managerial savvy but he was affable, handsome, widely liked, and he served as the "greeter" at Meier & Frank, a custom common to the great department stores of the day. Harold Hirsch reminisces:

Abe Meier was the early public relations man of the family. He was the "greeter." He never had a desk, I understand, but he stood by the front door as you walked in, he greeted you by name and then sent you to the proper sales person or department. He knew you and your buying habits, your bargaining ability, or lack of it, fairly well. He knew whether you were a sharp trader or a pushover. After having said hello to you very politely he would call to the back of the store—let's say to my father, "Max! Mrs. Smith is here! Take her down the middle aisle and show her the wood stoves; she's interested in a new wood stove." Taking her down the middle aisle meant, "She's a sharp cookie and watch your buttons, kid, when you trade with her." If he said, "Take her down the left-hand aisle," that meant she was a pushover. They had all these signals worked out. The object was to sell "with profit." Sometimes they would sell something too low and at other times they made it up by selling at a higher price. The key was the guy on the floor who met the housewives and shoppers at the front door, knew their traits, and could send the cue to a salesperson, usually a member of the family, who could read the code. The man at the front door was very valuable.

The *Oregon Daily Journal*, October 15, 1914. Courtesy, OHS.

Spectator, September 7, 1929. Courtesy, OHS.

As the Meier & Frank Company produced fortunes for its owners, some members of the family enjoyed an increasingly opulent style of life. Each Sunday, Jeanette presided over sumptuous family banquets, served with all the finest appointments, and she also encouraged the children and grandchildren to pursue luxuries appropriate to their newly won status.

Lloyd Frank, Sigmund and Fannie's eldest son, spent most of his time and effort seeing that "Fir Acres," a vast English Tudor manor (now Lewis and Clark College) in Southwest Portland was built and furnished to his taste. He spared no detail and was obsessed for years with its decoration.

Lloyd's only brother, Aaron Frank, lavished as much care on his horses. Often given to a quick temper and vindictive harshness, Aaron's personal failings intensified after his finest horses were lost in a fire. To many, Aaron seemed jealous of his youngest uncle, Julius, who stood directly in front of him in the family hierarchy.

Julius was a man who might well be envied —he was attractive, charismatic, witty; even his mother Jeanette could not resist his charm and denied him nothing. Julius was a lawyer and, in addition to being general manager of the store until 1930 and its president from 1930 until his death in 1937, he was involved in numerous civic pursuits. He promoted Portland's Lewis and Clark Exposition in 1905 and became known as the "father" of the Columbia River Highway. In 1930, the charismatic Julius Meier was elected governor of Oregon in a dramatic series of events described in Chapter 22.

In 1937, Aaron Frank took the helm of Meier & Frank and ruled autocratically but with considerable effect. The store gained a national reputation and was considered by many the finest department store west of Chicago. Through this period, Aaron Frank was closely tied to city politics and became, in historian Kimbark MacColl's judgment, "Portland's most influential business leader in the 1940s and '50s."

In 1925, when Jeanette Meier died, her will had expressed the "earnest wish and prayer" that her heirs carry on in harmony "the great enterprise initiated by my husband ... the Meier & Frank store." But her wish was not to be fulfilled. In 1964, when Lloyd Frank's childrens' trusts terminated, Aaron lost control of a majority of Meier & Frank stock and the dam broke. Years of family resentment and frustration at Aaron's willful management exploded, and Lloyd's widow and daughters joined forces with Julius Meier's widow and children. Led by Jack Meier, Julius' son, they controlled more than half of the shares of common stock outstanding and, therefore, the board of directors. They removed Aaron as president and Gerry, his son, who was vice-president and Salem store manager, from membership on the board.

As a result, Aaron, Gerry and their immediate family, who controlled just over 20 percent of the stock, decided to sell it at fifty dollars per share to Edward William Carter of the Broadway-Hale chain, thereby gaining, in addition to ten million dollars, the power of a major national chain to wield in their family dispute. Jack's group desired a tax-free merger with May Department Stores, but they were blocked by the requirement that two-thirds of the shares approve such a transaction; Aaron's block, together with the 20 percent of the shares that had been sold to the public in 1937, prevented the merger.

In response, Jack's forces sold rights to purchase their shares for fifty-six dollars apiece to the May Company, the offer good until December 1, 1966. The local family feud was now a national battle; both sides vied for additional shares, which skyrocketed during the battle from twenty to over sixty dollars a share before the fight was over.

Portland was fascinated with the conflict. Long stories appeared daily in both the *Oregonian* and the *Oregon Journal*, and even New York and its financial community followed the saga in the *New York Times*. Finally, the deadlock was broken: as the December, 1966, option deadline approached, Carter and Broadway-Hale stores sold their shares to May Company

The modern Meier & Frank, completed in 1932, as seen from the corner of Fifth Avenue and Morrison Street. Designed by famous Portland architect A. E. Doyle, the handsome terra-cotta structure was one of Portland's first skyscrapers and the fourth-largest department store in America when the east section of the building was opened in 1914. Photograph by Walter Boychuk. Courtesy, OHS.

for sixty-three dollars each. The store that Aaron Meier had struggled to begin more than a hundred years earlier, that Jeanette had forcefully guided to prominence, and to which so many family members and others had contributed, was now part of an impersonal national chain. It was a fate that many other family-owned department stores would meet as nationwide conglomerates paid huge sums for local stores after World War II.

3

Other Jewish Pioneers and Pioneer Communities

Beginning in the early 1850s, Jewish pioneers, nearly all of German background, followed just a step behind the discovery of gold or the settlement of farm communities. They spread to rural outposts throughout Oregon, and from there peddled necessities to isolated families in the wilderness beyond. These Jewish traders were important suppliers and small storekeepers for the newly emerging territory; their services and skills were badly needed, since there was no other way for farmers and miners to obtain the essentials to sustain themselves on the frontier. For the Jews, it was wonderfully liberating to be free of age-old oppressive edicts and to be in a wild, free territory where they were needed and respected and, above all, judged by the pioneer ethic: intrinsic worth.

Aaron Rose

Early Oregon Jews left a substantial legacy virtually everywhere they settled. Roseburg, the seat of Douglas County, was named for Aaron Rose, who took up a land claim of 640 acres on the present town site on September 23, 1851.

Rose was unusual in two respects: he was born in America, in Ulster County, New York, on June 20, 1813, not in Germany, and he was raised to be a farmer. At the age of twenty-four he emigrated with his parents to Coldwater, Michigan, where he farmed until 1851. Then he and his wife and two children made the six-month overland journey to settle in the Oregon Territory at the mouth of Deer Creek. He immediately built a house, which was also the first roadside inn in the Roseburg area, serving primarily miners and others traveling to the mining camps. In 1854, the county seat was moved from Winchester to Aaron Rose's farm, where a town site was surveyed that was first called Deer Creek and the following year, Roseburgh (later simplified to Roseburg), to honor its founder. Rose donated the sites for the town's public

Aaron Rose. Roseburg, Oregon, the seat of Douglas County, was named for Aaron Rose, who settled at the site of the future community in 1851 after crossing the plains from Michigan with his family. Courtesy, OHS.

Pioneers and pioneer stockmen of Morrow County. Harry Heppner (the large figure to the right of the town inset) was born of an ancient line of rabbis in Prussia. He founded Heppner, Oregon, seat of Morrow County, with his partner Colonel Jackson Morrow (shown to the left of town). Courtesy, OHS.

buildings and contributed one thousand dollars to erect the first courthouse. His primary occupation was farming, which he carried on with considerable success, but he later also opened a butcher shop and a general store, and bought and sold horses.

Aaron Rose was involved in many of Roseburg's earliest public activities. He was elected to the territorial legislature in 1855-56. He helped build the wagon road from Roseburg to Coos Bay. And he was responsible for damming the South Umpqua River, which then powered the city water works as well as a woolen and flour mill. When the Oregon and California Railroad came south, Rose was instrumental in having the right-of-way pass through Roseburg. He then platted a substantial addition to the city, half of which he donated to the company for establishing its depot in town. Aaron Rose lived the remainder of his life in Roseburg, where he died in March, 1899.

Henry Heppner

Across the state, on the prairies of northeastern Oregon, a second Jewish pioneer would give his name to mark another Oregon county seat, that of Morrow County. Henry Heppner was born on March 25, 1831, to a long line of rabbis at Pleschen in the province of Posen, Prussia. Heppner received a German education and was taught Hebrew at an early age. A friend reported that he "was a fine Hebrew scholar, but it took a college graduate to read Henry's English." Heppner emigrated to New York in 1858 and moved on to Shasta, California, where he clerked in a store for several years. He periodically ran stocks of goods to the mining camps in Canada, Idaho and Montana, and briefly opened a store in Corvallis before settling at The Dalles, where he ran regular mule pack-trains to Canyon City and then on to Idaho.

Several years later, when Heppner had built up a large pack-train of mules, hostile Malheur Indians captured the entire train en route to Canyon City. It was later reported that the Malheur chief "ran the mules off into a Blue Mountain meadow where the grass was knee-high, and in one moon had them hog fat and shot and turned into dried elk meat." Heppner, well liked in The Dalles, was staked to a new pack-train, but it met a similar fate when it was ambushed by Snake Indians who ran off all twenty-nine mules while the five men in charge departed hastily in the opposite direction. Fortunately, this occurred on the return trip when the train was empty. Outfitted with yet another train, his backers suggested the Meacham Road to Idaho, well north of hostile Indians. Heppner made a number of successful trips, repaid his backers, and built considerable wealth.

On July 4, 1872, Heppner rode up Willow Creek and camped at the site later to bear his name. A few scattered families herded sheep in the creek bottoms, but Henry was impressed with the fertile valley at the confluence of three creeks and believed it would make an ideal townsite. While in La Grande that year, he met Colonel Jackson Morrow, a merchant, and they entered into a partnership in 1873 to open the first merchandise store at the forks of Willow Creek. So began the town of Heppner.

Two tales of the town's naming come down to us: one advanced in the *Heppner Gazette* for February 23, 1905, states that Colonel Morrow had a post office established in town and asked that it be named in honor of his partner. The other, recorded in an early history written in 1889 by Elwood Evans, has it that a meeting occurred in the area to name the town, and the vote was unanimous but for one to name it Heppner. The one dissenter was Henry himself.

Heppner began a forwarding and commission business at Arlington on the Columbia River, turning his Heppner store over to Senator Henry Blackman, his brother-in-law, and Phill Cohn, his nephew. In 1878, with the advent of Indian hostilities, he donated the materials to build the fort at Heppner and provided for those who had to take refuge. He helped to build the schoolhouse, roads and, with Colonel Morrow, drove the last spike on the Heppner branch for the Oregon Railway and Navigation Company in 1888. He became known as "Old Hep" in town. He never married, but his sister, Mrs. Henry Blackman, and his nephew, Phill Cohn, lived in Heppner with him. When he died on February 16, 1905, a large number of people from Heppner came to his funeral in Portland, where Rabbi Stephen Wise is said to have delivered a beautiful eulogy. Henry Heppner is buried in the Beth Israel cemetery.

Jacksonville

The first Jewish religious services in the state of Oregon are believed to have taken place in 1856 in the gold mining town of Jacksonville, where a group of Jewish merchants gathered at the Odd Fellows Hall to celebrate Rosh Hashanah. The bustling, colorful town of Jacksonville had grown up overnight after two miners returning to California noticed a glint of yellow while camping along Jackson Creek. Within a year there were over one thousand miners in Jacksonville. Swedes and Irish, Turks, Germans and other Europeans, Americans from all over the country, a number of Chinese and several

In 1854, John and Herman Brunner established the first Jewish business in Jacksonville. Courtesy, Southern Oregon Historical Society (SOHS).

blacks all converged on Jacksonville to seek their fortunes. Jews came too.

The miners needed almost everything, and the Jews (mostly from San Francisco) became their primary suppliers. The first Jewish business was J. A. Brunner and Brother. By 1854, John and Herman Brunner had constructed one of the first brick buildings in Jacksonville. Still standing today, it served not only mercantile needs but as a shelter during the Rogue River Indian uprising, when the entire town took cover behind its brick and iron doors. Other Jews opened dry goods and grocery stores and supplied mining equipment; several were clerks and bookkeepers. Miners and farmers regularly came to these Jacksonville stores from a radius of fifty to a hundred miles to outfit themselves and live it up before returning to the wilderness. At the height of its importance, in the late 1850s, Jacksonville was the largest town between Portland and San Francisco.

The Sachs Brothers Temple of Fashion provided the latest from San Francisco and the East as the numerous Sachs brothers used their branch stores in San Francisco, New York and Germany to bring new styles to Jacksonville. They also served as agents for the Pacific Insurance Company, the only chartered insurance company in Oregon at the time.

Max Muller ran one of Jacksonville's dry goods stores. He arrived in 1855 at the age of nineteen, traveling from Bavaria by way of New York, and then on to Nicaragua and California. He clerked for a few years, opened his own saloon in Ashland, and then returned to Jacksonville, where he remained throughout his life. He served on the Jacksonville Board of Trustees after the city's organization in 1860, and was later president of the trustees, city treasurer, county treasurer and postmaster for eighteen years, when his store served as the Post Office.

Herman Bloom, a colorful Jewish merchant, opened his "one price only" store in 1861, charging a single price for all goods to attract customers. Morris Mensor's New York Store sold general merchandise from the old Brunner brick building on South Oregon Street. Fletcher Linn, an old-time resident, re-

Matilda and Morris Mensor, early Jewish pioneers in Jacksonville, ran the New York Store and had seventeen children. Photographs taken by Peter Britt. Courtesy, SOHS.

members that one of the Mensor boys, Isaac, advertised the store's wares during Sunday afternoon strolls, "dressed in the best style of the day, with high white collar … and the latest model hat and jauntily swinging his cane.…" Morris and his wife Matilda had seventeen children—nine sons and eight daughters—and all lived in a small cottage on California Street. They had been invited to Jacksonville by their relatives, Abe and Newman Fisher, the proprietors of one of the earliest Jewish firms, who had fourteen children themselves. The Jewish community of Jacksonville was exceptional because much of it consisted of members of the same immediate family.

When the Jews of Jacksonville observed the High Holidays, Elias Jacobs closed his store and acted as their rabbi. Circumcisions and *bar mitzvahs* were conducted in Jacksonville, but weddings were celebrated in San Francisco. There was little contact with Portland.

The Jews were seen as Europeans and were assimilated and well-accepted in Jacksonville, while others, such as the Chinese, suffered there as they did throughout the West. The Chinese did much of the backbreaking labor of the camps, had discriminatory taxes levied against them, and only rarely engaged in mining. When they did, they usually gleaned from abandoned mines. A sense of the oppression that existed can be surmised from an editorial in the *Oregon Sentinel*, Jacksonville's Republican newspaper, of September 1, 1866:

It seems an unwise policy to allow a race of brutish heathens who have nothing in common with us, to exhaust our mineral lands without paying a heavy tax for their occupation. These people bring nothing with them to our shores, they add nothing to the permanent wealth of this country and so strong is their attachment to their own country they will not let their filthy carcasses lie in our soil. Could this people be taxed as to exclude them entirely, it would be a blessing.

Hostility and discrimination were also expressed both officially and in daily life against blacks, Kanakas (native-born Hawaiians), and the Takehma Indians, whose land was appropriated to build Jacksonville and its environs.

Gustav Karewski, who had come to Jacksonville in 1860 from Prussia, was one of the first to recognize that farming would have to replace diminishing gold returns, so he turned from general merchandise to selling farm implements and machinery. He purchased the Rogue River flour mill and managed a farm at one end of town and a peach orchard at the other. When Bernard Levy died in 1869, his widow, Joanna, appointed Gustav administrator of his estate. Joanna was thirty-five and Gustav in his early forties; they fell in love, married, and had four daughters.

But many of the younger Jews were leaving by the early 1860s as gold faded. By the late 1870s, the community was in full decline: mining had petered out, and the railroad passed some distance away. The merchants in town were hurt by the railroad's arrival in Southern Oregon, since their substantial stocks had been priced according to stage and steamer costs, and with declining population they were no longer able to maintain their businesses. Everyone returned to San Francisco save the Men-

The gravestone of Annie Fisher in the Jacksonville cemetery. There are approximately thirteen gravestones in the Jewish section. Courtesy, JHSO.

sors, Mullers and Karewskis, who remained throughout their lives in Jacksonville. Gustav and Joanna's daughter, Stella, who never married, inherited the Karewski estate and died at the age of seventy-five in 1936. She was the last direct descendent of a Jewish pioneer family to be buried in the Jacksonville cemetery. Today, Jacksonville is a National Historic Landmark visited by over a hundred thousand people each year; several Jewish homes and storefronts remain, the Brunner Building serves as the Public Library, and the Jewish section of the Jacksonville cemetery is maintained by the Jewish congregation in Medford.

Eastern Oregon

Baker

As in Jacksonville, Baker City (later just Baker) in Eastern Oregon became a booming trade and commercial center when gold was discovered in the region during the 1860s. A century after Sigmund Heilner and his wife, Clara, set-

tled in Baker in 1874, there were five descendants of some of the earliest Jewish settler families still residing there: the Heilners, Baers,
Adlers and Levingers.

Sam Baer arrived shortly after Sigmund
Heilner and established the Baer and Otten-
heimer General Store, which was later called
the Baer Mercantile Company. He married Rosa
Hirsch, from the well-known Hirsch family in
Salem, who died while still a young woman.
Baer then married her sister, Sally. Elizabeth
Baer, their daughter, attended Wellesley Col-
lege and then returned to her hometown to
teach math and German at Baker High School.

Carl and Laura Hirsch Adler traveled to
Baker from Germany by way of the Horn and
Astoria so that Laura could be close to her sister,
Rosa, and (after Rosa's death) to her other sister,
Sally. The families always remained close, living
in two large houses on the same street. In 1877,
Carl Adler opened Adler's Crystal Palace, which
sold books, musical instruments and jewelry.

Sanford Adler, who died in 1981 at age
eighty-eight, and his brother, Leo, who still re-
sides in Baker, are the two second-generation
members of the Adler family who remained in
Baker. They ran the family store after their father's death, and Sanford was postmaster for
more than twenty years. Leo, who like Elizabeth
Baer never married, was ten years old when he
started delivering the *Saturday Evening Post* in
Baker. He parlayed those early magazine deliveries into the largest and oldest wholesale magazine distribution business in the West.

Louis Levinger, the youngest of thirteen
children, was born in 1864 in Augsburg, Germany, and emigrated to the States at the age of thirteen. He worked with a brother in Eureka before opening drugstores in Oregon City and
then Portland. He moved to Baker in 1898 and
again established a drugstore that also sold candy and baked goods and became for a time the
state's largest independent drugstore. It is still
open for business in Baker. Henry Levinger, the
younger of Louis' two sons and a resident of
Baker today, went to Stanford University and
then studied pharmacy before returning to Baker to run the family store.

Carl Adler's Crystal Palace opened in 1877. Courtesy, JHSO.

Carl and Laura Adler with their children Theresa and Leo (Sanford, a third child, is not shown) in Baker, Oregon about 1897. Courtesy, JHSO.

There were at one time over twenty Jewish families in Baker; five of their children remained in the mid-1970s, although none of the grandchildren chose to stay. The families had been close to each other and had annually rented the Elks Hall to hold High Holiday services. Baker is thus one of the few gold-mining towns whose Jewish merchants and their children remained long after gold had disappeared.

Burns

Kaufman Durkheimer came to Portland in 1865 and, as did so many others, became a merchant, operating a secondhand furniture store for seven years. He emigrated from the province of Baden in Germany to Philadelphia in 1837, and when he arrived in Portland already had a wife and four children with three more to follow. While it is the tales of successful merchants that are usually recounted, Kaufman was one who did not do well and was barely able to support his large family. The children went to work at an early age and Julius, the second child, born in 1857, drove a horse-drawn wagon during his school years to help support the family.

In 1874, shortly after he quit school at seventeen, Julius left home to hire out as a bookkeeper and night watchman at Baumberger and Frank, a Jewish general merchandise store in Baker City. He saved room rental by moving

Burns, Oregon, in 1884, five years before Delia and Julius Durkheimer moved there to open a general merchandise store. Julius became mayor of Burns in 1895. Courtesy, OHS.

blankets from the stock shelves to the sales counter and sleeping there each night. With his savings, Julius was able to open several small businesses in Baker. In June, 1887, he sold his Redfront Store in Baker and opened a new general store in Prairie City, fifty miles to the southwest, and a year later he opened yet another store thirteen miles further west in the gold town of Canyon City. The Canyon City store did very well. Help was needed, and three of Julius' brothers, all bachelors, responded to his call. Mose, the eldest, was put in charge at Prairie City with Sam as assistant, and Sig stayed in Canyon City to help Julius. The year 1889 proved a banner one for Julius. He purchased yet another store in the town of Burns, which had been founded just five years earlier, and returned to Portland to marry Delia Fried, a schoolteacher and the daughter of Moses Fried of Marion County. That same year, a group of businessmen tendered an excellent offer to Julius for his Canyon City store, and the Prairie City store was sold to Mose, who operated it until his death in 1919. Julius and his new bride moved to Burns.

Burns was a small assemblage of wooden shacks set in the sagebrush with two saloons, a blacksmith shop, a livery stable, a Chinese laundry, a weekly newspaper and Durkheimer's General Merchandise Store. Burns served a huge area of sheep and cattle ranches. But it was 150 miles from the railroad, and communications were minimal, consisting primarily of biweekly mail deliveries by saddle horse. Julius made annual buying trips through Portland to San Francisco, and all his supplies had to be brought in or out of Burns by early November, before the heavy snows made freighting merchandise impossible. Julius constructed a new building for his store and a new house for himself and his wife.

Life was not easy in frontier Burns. Coal oil lamps provided the light; there were no sewers or plumbing; and the nearest doctor was many miles away in Canyon City. It was also a rough town. The story is told of two feuding sheepherders who met by chance in Julius' store and, without uttering a word, drew their pistols and shot each other to death in front of the stunned

The Durkheimer General Merchandise Store in Burns, built in 1891. The sixth man from the left, ready to move a loaded hand truck, is Julius Durkheimer. The Lodge of the Independent Order of Odd Fellows met upstairs. Courtesy, OHS.

proprietor. Despite the hardships and like so many other Jewish merchants in Oregon towns, Julius became involved in the civic affairs of Burns. He served on the school board and was elected mayor in 1895.

Some time before Delia was ready to give birth to their only child, Sylvan, she returned to Portland to be near her parents and medical attention. When she returned to Burns, she employed Scarface Mary, a well-known local character and one of the few women in Burns, as Sylvan's nursemaid. Scarface Mary, reported to have been either a Modoc or Paiute Indian and a consort of Captain Jack, always wore a red bandana to cover her lost eye and scarred cheek, reputedly suffered when struck by an arrow.

Julius had promised Delia at the time of their marriage that within ten years they would return to the relative comforts of the Willamette Valley where she could look after her aging parents. Thus, in 1896, Julius sold his business in Burns, and they returned to Portland with their young son to move in with Delia's parents and two bachelor brothers. Julius purchased a one-third interest in Wadhams and Company, a wholesale grocery business that had been established in 1866. Wadhams and its successor have remained in the family, managed by Julius' son, Sylvan, and then by his grandson, Stuart.

La Grande and Pendleton

While Baker was the primary, early commercial center in Eastern Oregon, there were Jewish traders and shopkeepers in many of the small settlements east of the Cascades. Isaac Boskowitz and his wife, Sarah, traveled by boat up the Columbia and then by stage to Union, Oregon, where they opened a general merchandise store. Isaac and Sarah had five children, but their store did not prosper and they moved to La Grande, where Isaac served as city treasurer. Their youngest son, Anselm, was sent to Portland at the age of twelve to live with his grandmother, Adelaide Bloch, and her family. Anselm

Isaac and Sarah Boskowitz settled in Union, then in La Grande, Oregon, where Isaac was a merchant and city treasurer. Their youngest son, Anselm, later became an important figure in the Portland Jewish community. Courtesy, Edward Aiken.

would later assume key roles in B'nai B'rith and in the establishment of the Anti-Defamation League nationally and in Oregon. In Pendleton, Moses Baruh opened a drugstore whose soda fountain was said to be a sensation for miles around. Many of Moses' customers were Umatilla Indians, and he became proficient enough in their dialect to serve as a go-between and court interpreter on their behalf.

The Willamette Valley and the Coast

In the Willamette Valley, and along the Coast, Jews also assumed merchandising roles, although they supplied farming communities rather than mining camps. In Marion County, between Molalla and Silverton, the crossroads where Moses Fried established his donation land claim in 1865 is still known as Fried's Corner. It is reported that Fried missed the steamer *Brother Jonathan* on which he had booked passage from San Francisco because his horse became ill and his wagon was delayed. With his wife and three children, Fried took another vessel the following week, only to learn when they reached Portland that the *Brother Jonathan* had gone down in a storm off Coos Bay with most passengers lost. Moses' general store at Fried's Corner was not successful, and he moved several times before finally finding a better situation in Hubbard, where he operated for seventeen years. Each year during the High Holidays, Moses would close his store for two weeks while he and his family traveled to Portland by boat to attend services at Beth Israel. In 1880, at the age of seventy, Moses sold his business and retired with his family to Portland, where he died in 1898.

Albany

Like Moses Fried, a single Jewish family or several families settled in each of the growing towns in western Oregon. In Albany, in 1878, a Hebrew congregation was formed primarily for the purpose of establishing a Jewish cemetery. Barely a *minyan* was assembled by calling on men from as far away as Corvallis, Harrisburg and Eugene. The "Israelites of Albany and Vicinity" met at the dry goods store of Senders and Sternberg to form the congregation, and Leon Senders was elected its first president.

Little is known of the early Albany community. Members of the Senders family, from Oldenburg in Prussia, particularly Leon and his brothers and cousins, were leaders of the small Jewish enclave. Leon, born in 1855, arrived in Albany in 1861, and later became a horse trader, importing stock by boat through Yaquina Bay and then overland to Albany where he sold them from a large barn owned by the family. Leon and his wife, Lena May, who came from Bavaria, had four children; their youngest, Albert, served as mayor of Albany from 1940 to 1944. In 1906, the Senders family began a grain

Leon Senders in 1878. The Senders family came from Oldenburg in Prussia and were leaders of the early Albany Jewish community. Courtesy, JHSO.

ששון ושמחה תשיגר

בשלישי בשבת שכנה ימים לחדש תמוז שנת חמשת אלפים ושש מאורת
ועשרים וארבע למנין שאנו מנין כאן בער אלבאני במדינת ארעגאן איך החתן
ר יהודא בן ר יוסף הנודע בשם Leon Senders אמר לה להדא בתולתא לאה בת
ר משה אריה הנקראה Lena May הוי לי לאנתו כדת משה וישראל
ואנא אפלח ואוקיר ואיזון ואפרנס יתיכי כהלכוה גוברין יהודאין דפלחין ומוקרין
וזנין ומפרנסין לנשיהון בקושטא ויהיבנא ליכי מהר בתוליכי כדחזי ליך
ומזוניכי וכסותיכי וסיפוקיכי ומיעל לותיכי כארחה כל ארעא וצביאת
מרת לאה בתולתא דא והות ליה לאנתו ועל דא קבלי עליהון החתן
והכלה דין אחריות שטר כתובתא דא כחומר כל שטרות דנהגן בבני
ישראל ובמדינת ארעגאן ובדא הכל שריר וקים

העדים

החתן Leon Senders
      Josel Sternbag
      Alexander Blueher

הכלה
Lena May

Julius Eckman
המסדר הקדושין

Wedding certificate of Leon Senders and Lena May signed in Albany on the third day of the week, the eighth day of the month of Tamuz in 5624 (1864). Note that Julius Eckman, rabbi of Temple Beth Israel in Portland, officiated. Courtesy, Bruce Senders.

company dealing in oats, wheat, barley and hops. The business grew into one of the major enterprises in Linn County with grain elevators in Tangent, Tallman and Albany. The Jewish cemetery, begun in 1878 and maintained through the years by the small congregation, still exists today as part of the Masonic cemetery.

Eugene

Born in New York City in 1840, Samson Friendly was an early settler in Eugene. After clerking for two years in California, Friendly opened a general merchandise store and a warehouse that handled hops, wool, wheat and oats. He was president of Eugene's board of trade, served on the city council, and in 1893 was elected mayor. He is best remembered, however, for his involvement with the University of Oregon.

In 1893, the state legislature decreed that

Isaac and Bertha Zwang Senders pose with their children in the early 1880s. Isaac and Bertha provided the land for the Jewish cemetery in Albany. Courtesy, JHSO.

Samson Friendly was mayor of Eugene from 1893 to 1895. He is best remembered for helping to establish the University of Oregon, where he served as a regent for twenty years. Built in 1893, Friendly Hall, the University's first dormitory, is named in his honor. Courtesy, University of Oregon (UO).

any city designated as the site for the new University of Oregon would have to furnish the necessary land and a building. Samson Friendly became a central figure, raising funds during the week so that the builders could be paid each Saturday. In 1876, the state approved the finished building, which was named for Judge Matthew Deady. Friendly served as a regent of the university from 1895 to 1915, built the millrace, and was so popular among students for supporting their endeavors and his enthusiastic attendance at football games that they successfully petitioned the university to name its first dormitory Friendly Hall.

Samson and his wife, Mathilda, had three daughters and lived in a large home at Eleventh and High streets with the Friendly name engraved in stained glass over the front door. When his daughters grew up, he bought them a horse and carriage and before each excursion proudly ordered the carriage from the livery stable in the Germanic English of the day: "Please send me mine team."

Goodman Bettman came to Eugene in 1868 at the age of twenty from Bavaria. He then moved for a time to Portland where he met his wife, Bertha Simon, who lived with her parents on a twenty-one acre farm on what is today SE Division, between Twenty-first and Twenty-sixth avenues. Her uncle, David Simon, owned forty-two adjoining acres along Powell Boulevard and was the father of Joseph Simon, who became a United States senator and mayor of Portland.

Goodman Bettman returned with his wife to Eugene in 1879; they lived on what is now West Fifth Street and ran the Bettman General Merchandise Store at Eighth and Willamette streets. The store contained one of the only safes in town and was used by numerous farmers, as the Wells-Fargo Express Company closed its safe when the train left each afternoon. Goodman was honored by being asked to carry the American flag at the 1873 laying of the cornerstone of Deady Hall. He was also a Royal Arch Mason. It was rare for Jews to join this branch of Masonry, as its rites are based on a belief in Christianity. Bettman said he did not understand the difference between rites, but

The daughters of Samson and Mathilda Friendly are from left: Carrie Friendly (Harris), Theresa Friendly (Wachenheimer; the mother of Fred Friendly, well-known as former vice-president of CBS) and Rosalie Friendly (Hayes). Courtesy, UO.

made it clear he did not believe in Jesus, where-upon a Christian friend is said to have retorted, "You believe in Jesus just as much as we do." In 1897, the Bettmans and their four sons moved to Portland, where Goodman was involved in the retail drug business for many years.

A dozen or so other early Jewish families resided in Eugene during the nineteenth century. They included Charles and Sarah Lauer. Sarah was the sister of Samson Friendly and lived with her husband at the corner of Sixth and Willamette streets. All but one of their four children graduated from the University of Oregon. Abraham Goldsmith was proprietor of a tobacco store and Wolf Sanders owned a clothing store, both on Willamette Street. E. Schwarzschild ran a book store; the Baums, a toy store; and the Washauers maintained a large orchard and acreage in South Eugene. Rabbis from Portland, particularly Jacob Bloch of Beth Israel, who had relatives in Eugene, would travel the Willamette Valley to officiate at weddings and occasional holiday services.

Astoria

While Astoria has never had a large Jewish community, over the years it has elected three Jews to its highest office. Isaac Bergman, known in town as "Uncle Ike," and Herman Wise, Astoria's postmaster for many years, were both born in Germany and settled in Astoria in the 1870s. Bergman was a butcher and rancher in the Gray's River district, while Wise was a clothier and hatter who owned Uncle Sam's Cheap Cash Store in Astoria and later a branch in Seaside. Each served two terms as Astoria's mayor—Bergman from 1898 to 1902, and Wise from 1906 to 1910. Astoria's third Jewish mayor, Harry Steinbock, who is a pharmacist and still alive today, was elected to four terms (1959-1974). He decided not to run again because, he said, "Sixteen years was long enough for anyone in public office."

Toward the end of the nineteenth century, many children of the pioneer Jews who had settled in small rural communities moved to Portland or other larger cities. The economic opportunities for the storekeeper and entre-preneur had diminished with the coming of the railroads and large corporations selling mass-produced goods. In Portland, the Lewis and Clark Exposition, held in 1905, ushered in a period of rapid growth, and the Jewish community, itself burgeoning, offered warmth and a sense of community to new arrivals from the countryside.

Portland

As we have seen, Bernard Goldsmith and Aaron Meier were important early Jewish figures in Portland, but there were many more. Only a few of the most prominent can be mentioned here. Among these were the founders of the largest and most important Jewish business establishment in nineteenth century Portland—the wholesale dry goods firm of Fleischner, Mayer & Co., established in 1875. The firm's three principal founders, Louis Fleischner, Jacob Mayer and Solomon Hirsch, were central figures in Jewish life in early Portland. Their families and business relations were closely interconnected, as was typical of the major German Jewish business establishments of the day.

Jacob Mayer was the first of the three to arrive in Portland. Born in Bechtheim in Germany, he sailed for New Orleans, where he landed in 1842 at the age of sixteen. There he remained for eight years, marrying and starting a family which would later number six children. But the lure of gold in California prompted him to go west. After crossing the Isthmus of Panama, he boarded the *Sarah and Eliza* for San Francisco. It was one of those not uncommon, near-tragic journeys. One hundred days out of Panama, water and provisions were virtually exhausted; shark and pelican were the only food; and a half pint of water was rationed to each passenger per day. Then a Boston ship was sighted. It provided food and water, but at a price. Mayer had to pay eight hundred dollars, all that he had, for a barrel of sea biscuits for the remaining twenty days until landfall in San Francisco.

Jacob Mayer   Louis Fleischner   Solomon Hirsch

Leaders of Portland's early Jewish community and founders of Fleischner, Mayer & Co. Courtesy, left and right, Beth Israel (BI), and center, Gaston, *Portland, Oregon: Its History and Builders* (1911).

Mayer established the second dry goods store in San Francisco with a cargo of merchandise he had shipped previously, and he soon became involved in the Jewish life of the city. He was instrumental in organizing Ophir Lodge, the first B'nai B'rith lodge on the Pacific Coast, and founded the First Hebrew Benevolent Society of San Francisco.

Mayer came to Portland in 1857 to open his City of Paris dry goods store. He was a charter member of Congregation Beth Israel and later its president; at times he performed marriages when a rabbi was unavailable. Apparently, the first couple that he married raised a large family and Mayer liked to tell a story about them. One day, the mother of the family came to town with her eleven children to have them photographed and was told by the photographer that the price was five dollars a dozen. "I'll come back when the twelfth is ready," she replied.

Mayer helped to found B'nai B'rith and the First Hebrew Benevolent Association in Portland, as he had in San Francisco. Later, he helped to start the Oregon Historical Society. He reached the pinnacle of the Masonic Order

in 1888, when, as a 33rd degree Mason, he became Oregon Grand Master. In 1875, he merged his business with L. Fleischner & Co. to create Fleischner, Mayer & Co. His oldest daughter, Josephine, married Solomon Hirsch, a partner in the firm. His son, Mark, managed Fleischner, Mayer's New York office after the death of Alexander Schlussel, one of the firm's original partners, in 1891.

After Jacob Mayer's death in 1908, Abigail Scott Duniway, Oregon's famous women's rights advocate, remembered him with the highest praise. In her autobiographical history, *Path Breaking*, she recalled a turning point in her life fifty years earlier, when, struggling to support an invalid husband and young children, she set out to Portland with thirty dollars to buy stock for a millinery shop which she hoped to open in her home town of Albany:

The late Jacob Mayer, Esq., the original dealer in such goods as I wanted, was doing good business ... and I went to him, introduced myself and stated my need, explaining the state of my finances. "Won't some of your friends go security for you?" he asked, with a businesslike air that sent a chill to my heart. "My husband went broke by going security," I replied, with a shake of my head, "and I vowed long ago that I would never copy his mistake." "How much stock do you want?" he asked, in a tone that reassured me a little. "About a hundred dollars will do for a beginning," I said tremulously. "Nonsense!" was the hearty response of the experienced merchant. "You could carry home a hundred dollar's worth of millinery in a silk apron. Let me select you a stock of goods!" To my surprise the bill amounted to twelve hundred dollars. "I'm afraid to risk it," I said anxiously, as I produced my little wad of thirty dollars to offer in payment. "Never mind," he said, "you'll need that money to get some articles at Van Fridagh's retail store. Take this stock home and do the best you can with it. Then come back and get some more."

Abigail Scott Duniway paid her debt to Mayer in three weeks and her next order totalled three thousand dollars. She would never be poor again and went on to become one of Oregon's most illustrious citizens.

Louis Fleischner, born Levi Fleischner in 1827 in the town of Vogelsang, Bohemia, lived an adventurous life in the years before becoming a senior partner in Fleischner, Mayer—a life dramatically portrayed in a children's book of historical fiction, *Northwest Pioneer: The Story of Louis Fleischner* by Alfred Apsler. Louis left Germany at age fifteen and changed his name from Levi shortly thereafter. He spent a short time in New York, longer in Philadelphia, then headed west in 1849 with his brother, Jacob, who had recently joined him, to seek their destiny on the Pacific Coast. They were unusual among Jews in choosing to travel overland; most believed the water route through Central America or around the Cape safer than braving

Fleischner, Mayer & Co., located at 25/27 Front Avenue (on the site of current Fire Station No. 1). Established in 1875, the company was reputed to be the largest wholesale dry goods store west of the Mississippi. Courtesy, Kathleen Ryan.

potentially hostile Indians and the hardships of at least six months in a covered wagon. But the Fleischners interrupted their journey for three years to open a general store in Drakeville in Southeastern Iowa before deciding to make the final trek to Oregon by ox team and wagon.

The year 1852 was reputed to have been one of the most difficult for those who crossed the plains, and so it proved for Louis and Jacob. Disease killed most of their cattle and many of the other emigrants died of cholera. The harrowing journey ended at Albany, a town of several homesteads founded three years earlier along the Willamette River. There they established one of the first general merchandise stores in town, which became known in that part of the valley as the "Fleischner place." Louis received the title "Colonel," by which he was known for the rest of his life, when he volunteered and fought in the Rogue River Indian War in Southern Oregon.

After returning from the militia, Louis, always restless, left the Albany store to Jacob, who had married Fannie Nadler in 1858. Louis carried supplies by pack train to the gold mining camps at Orofino and Lewiston in Northern Idaho. He returned to Portland in 1864 and joined Solomon Hirsch and Alexander Schlussel in forming a partnership which purchased the wholesale general merchandise operations of the Haas Brothers. They called the new firm L. Fleischner & Co., the forerunner of Fleischner, Mayer & Co. He was elected state treasurer in 1870, served four years and was credited with correcting abuses involving earlier state loans of public funds. Louis Fleischner was also the indomitable spirit behind the building of the beautiful, twin-spired Temple Beth Israel that was completed in 1888 at Twelfth Avenue and Main Street. He remained a bachelor, and toward the end of his life returned to Europe for a visit to his childhood home in Bohemia; in a hospital in Tachau, a few miles from his native village, he endowed a bed to be forever used by the people of Vogelsang.

Solomon Hirsch, the last of the three major partners in Fleischner, Mayer & Co., was also born in Germany, in Württemberg in 1839. (He was not related to the Hirsch family involved with Meier & Frank.) In all, five Hirsch brothers came to America: the four oldest settled in Salem; Solomon, who became the best-known of the brothers, arrived in the United States at age fifteen and, after spending several years in the East as well as at Silverton and Dallas in Oregon, settled in Portland in the fall of 1864 to become a partner in L. Fleischner & Co.

Solomon Hirsch was an important figure in the Oregon Republican party. Twice its chairman, he was elected to three terms in the state senate, was once its president, and, in 1885, fell but a single vote short—his own—of being elected by the legislature to the United States Senate. He was widely respected as one of the most ethical public servants in an era when political chicanery was common. In 1889, while visiting Vienna with his partner, Louis Fleischner, Hirsch received notice from President Harrison of his appointment as ambassador to Turkey—a major post, since the Court of the Sultan controlled the far-flung Ottoman Empire. Hirsch remained in Turkey for three years before returning to Portland. Five years later, President McKinley asked him to be ambassador to Belgium, but he declined. Hirsch passed away a few years later on December 15, 1902.

Fleischner, Mayer & Co. salesmen at the turn of the century. Courtesy, the Goldsmith Company (GC).

4

Extraordinary Business Success

By any standard, the Jewish merchant pioneers in Oregon achieved remarkable success. Not all of them by any means, but an exceptional number did amass considerable wealth in relatively few years, and nearly all began with little or no capital. Many could be mentioned specifically, but the experience of Sigmund Heilner, the Meiers and Franks, Bernard Goldsmith, the early rural pioneers and the principals of Fleischner, Mayer & Co.—albeit some of the most successful—demonstrate common patterns and approaches which produced extraordinary prosperity for numbers of Oregon's Jewish merchant pioneers.

By their exclusion from most professions, Jews had been forced in medieval Europe to enter trade and finance. Persistent discrimination had taught them to adapt and innovate. Therefore, by the time a German Jewish middle class emerged in the early nineteenth century —the class that produced nearly all of Oregon's Jewish merchants—a code of hard work, respectability, moderation and devotion to family was firmly in place. And after centuries of official restrictions on Jewish economic activity, the desire for a better life was keen.

The young Germans left for America with a rich network of relatives and friends—many of whom had already emigrated or would follow —who shared not only a set of mores but a sense of community and common blood. It is this sense of shared identity that created the trust and confidence on which the loyalties so necessary to successful commercial relations were built in the New World. Jews brought their craft and entrepreneurial skills to America where, in contrast to the fear of Jewish competition they had encountered in Europe, their skills and energy were welcomed by the growing country. For those who came west—and that in itself demonstrated a willingness to accept risk—the unhindered possibilities for prosperity were truly exhilarating.

And so they came, with determination, energy and valuable skills, blending easily into the mix of religious and ethnic groups that made up the frontier. Most were young, single males who often came with brothers or cousins and apprenticed with relatives in the East or California before arriving in Oregon. They were mobile and probed from place to place, seeking opportunity within the broad network of Jewish businesses owned by relatives or friends.

The prevailing pattern was similar throughout the United States: the peddler on the newest frontier accumulated enough money to establish a retail store, which then either expanded and specialized or developed into a wholesale supplier for other retail outlets and finally, in a few instances, emerged as a financial empire. Not many Jewish merchants reached the pinnacles achieved by Fleischner, Mayer & Co. (at one time reputed to be the largest wholesale dry goods house west of the Mississippi), or Meier & Frank department store, or even the more personal accumulation of wealth by Bernard Goldsmith or Sigmund Heilner. But a great many became successful retailers and shopkeepers, and very few did not become at least solid members of the middle class.

The 1860 national census listed 146 merchants in Portland, of which approximately one-third were Jews and nearly all owners of their own businesses. It is interesting to note that there were no Jewish professionals. Even by 1880 there were only five. The German Jewish immigrants were largely traders with minimal education. Nearly all Jewish women were listed in the census as "keeping house" or "living at home."

While retail and wholesale trade predominated, some Jews were involved in manufacturing. Ralph and Isaac Jacobs established the Oregon City Woolen Mills in 1865, and lived in stately mansions side by side on West Park Avenue in Portland. Levi Hexter and Levi May manufactured sheet metal and stoves, while Fishel and Roberts, who employed twenty-six people in the early 1880s, and Fleischner, Mayer, who later employed over three hundred, manufactured clothing. By 1880, Jews dominated Portland's clothing industry and owned significant shares of general merchandising, furniture, tobacco and wholesale supply establishments. While Jews such as Bernard Goldsmith, Philip Wasserman, Julius Loewenberg,

Ralph Jacobs came to America with his brother Isaac from western Poland in 1867. They acquired controlling interest in the Oregon City Woolen Mills, which became the largest Jewish manufacturing concern in Oregon. Courtesy, JHSO.

Stately mansions of Ralph (left) and Isaac Jacobs, built in the 1880s on SW Park between Montgomery and Mill streets, one of the most fashionable addresses in Portland. Courtesy, JHSO.

Joseph Simon and Solomon Hirsch were involved in speculative enterprises, most early Jewish merchants were quite conservative in business practice, and preferred to restrict themselves to trade and, at times, the purchase of land, wheat or cattle.

When employees were needed for expansion, relatives were sent for—Jeanette Meier brought the Hirsches to America, and Julius Durkheimer called his brothers to Eastern Oregon. Branch stores were opened in the hinterland and often served as apprenticeships for young family members. Ben Selling, who managed Akin, Selling & Co., a boot and shoe store in downtown Portland in the 1880s, found work for his young cousin, Julius Wertheimer, at the store's Pendleton branch. Selling was perturbed, though, when Wertheimer seemed more interested in women and cards than in learning business. In 1885, he transferred him to Joseph, Oregon, in order "to get you away from bad company and try and make a man of you.... You are not up in the country for your health nor for pleasure but to make and *save* money."

Often members of major commercial families would intermarry, the most famous such union being that of Fannie Meier and Sigmund Frank. Meier & Frank, like the Fleischner, Mayer enterprise, employed an extensive network of relatives in managerial positions and obtained employment for many other Jews in their Portland stores and in the rural outlets they supplied. As members of the first generation aged or died, the second would often replace them as principal partners, which occurred through three generations at Meier & Frank. At Fleischner, Mayer, two sons and a son-in-law of Louis Fleischner's brother, Jacob, succeeded Louis. Jacob Mayer's son, Mark, succeeded him, and his eldest daughter, Josephine, married the third principal partner, Solomon Hirsch. Families provided shelter and employment for their relatives, and offered them immediate access to successful business and social circles. After a period of years, relatives often would spin off new enterprises, such as Max Hirsch's White Stag or the Goldsmith Company, which

emerged after the demise of Fleischner, Mayer in 1930.

But starting these new businesses was not always easy. Although Jews confronted relatively little anti-Semitism on the frontier, persistent racial stereotypes made it difficult for them to obtain credit. The principal credit-rating agency in the United States was R. G. Dun and Company, a forerunner of Dun & Bradstreet, whose reports on Jewish-owned businesses identified Jews specifically and, often replete with offensive stereotypes, found them "untrustworthy." For instance, Aaron Meier was described as "shrewd, close, calculating, and considered tricky." The Jews responded by developing intra-family and Jewish network credit arrangements. Funds were borrowed from large family-connected enterprises in San Francisco, the East or even Germany. In frontier towns family businesses in San Francisco or Portland often provided credit, supplied a stake of goods, or

A tea party with the grandchildren of Jacob Fleischner includes Louis Goldsmith (left) and Archie Goldsmith (standing). Louis and Archie Goldsmith sold dry goods for Fleischner, Mayer & Co. for many years. With its demise in 1930, Archie Goldsmith and Brother (later the Goldsmith Company) was successfully launched. Courtesy, GC.

Lipman, Wolfe & Co. building, designed by A. E. Doyle and built in 1912 on the half-block between Washington and Alder streets on Fifth. Adolph Wolfe, the store's founder, left Germany in 1864 at age sixteen to join his uncle, Solomon Lipman, in Sacramento. In 1880, Lipman sent Wolfe to Portland to open a new store which flourished as Lipman, Wolfe & Co. Courtesy, OHS.

set up a relative in a branch store. Bernard Goldsmith borrowed capital from a friend of his father in San Francisco, and he always maintained business relations with the family firm in Munich. Thus, sophisticated trading and credit networks were established, and family connections were instrumental in fostering Jewish business success.

Jews were also innovative in devising new business techniques which would appeal to their customers. An interview with Sylvan Durkheimer, the son of Julius, describes a revolutionary commercial strategy that his father helped introduce in Eastern Oregon to assist the cattle, sheep and grain ranchers. Farmers nearly always needed annual advances to buy their animals or seed crops until the harvest, but few of the storekeepers had the capital to grubstake most of their customers. However, because of the credit network within the Jewish community, Durkheimer and others were able

to negotiate annual settlement agreements with their wholesale suppliers that allowed them to extend the same terms to their customers. Durkheimer attributes the election of so many popular Jewish merchants to key leadership positions in frontier towns to the gratitude of the farmers.

Jews also helped to pioneer other merchandising approaches: many provided the rudimentary banking service of maintaining a safe in their stores before banks were common; they allowed installment buying; they introduced set prices, particularly at larger stores such as Meier & Frank; and offered money-back guarantees. Jews were the leading general merchants in most of the small towns in Oregon and a major commercial force in Portland. They pursued their goal of prosperity and respectability with energy, creativity and singlemindedness. Within a single generation, their success was remarkable.

5

Jewish Community Life

Congregations Beth Israel and Ahavai Sholom

The young Jews who came to America left behind not only the formal restrictions of German states, but the traditional hierarchical authority of the family and synagogue as well. In America, and particularly on the frontier, individual Jews could decide for themselves what values they would maintain and how they would express them in their new communities.

At first, there were few religious concerns for the young single males who were constantly traveling the frontier, but the ever-present dangers of accident or disease did raise the issue of burial. The earliest Jews who died in Portland were buried in the non-Jewish Lone Fir Cemetery opened in Southeast Portland in 1854; their coffins were floated across the river on logs, and then carted up to the cemetery. But so strong was the desire to provide a traditional burial site that the first Jewish institution in Oregon appears to have been the Mt. Sinai Cemetery Association, which was incorporated by an act of the territorial legislature on January 10, 1856. Marking the beginning of an organized Jewish community in Portland, land was purchased in Caruthers Addition close to Portland.

In 1854, shortly after Mrs. Weinshank had opened her boarding house for Jewish bachelors, a second Jewish woman arrived in Portland, the new wife of Simon Blumauer. Blumauer had returned to New York City in 1853 and had married Mollie Radelsheimer, who was also from Bavaria. Their first son, Louis, was the

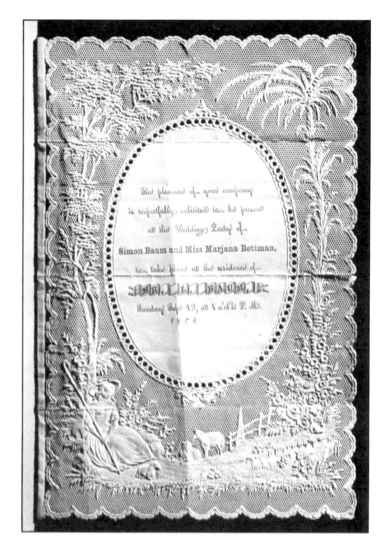

Simon Baum and Marjana Bettman were the first Jews to be married in Oregon. The ceremony took place in Burke's Hall in a bare upstairs loft over a livery stable and blacksmith shop where Beth Israel first held its services. Courtesy, BI.

first Jewish child to be born in Oregon. By 1858, more women had arrived, and a Jewish wedding was planned between Simon Baum and Marjana Bettman, members of early pioneer families. A congregation to provide for the ritual and ceremonial needs of a growing Jewish community had become essential.

On May 2, 1858, a group of eight men met at the National Hotel in Portland to discuss forming a congregation, and on June 13 of that year, with twenty-one original members present, it was resolved:

To organize a congregation for the worship of the One, only, everlasting God, according to the ancient ritual of the Jewish Faith.

Congregation Beth Israel, the first Jewish congregation in Oregon, was thereby founded with Leopold Mayer as its president. Services were held every Friday evening and Saturday morning in Burke's Hall on First Avenue in a

Leopold Mayer, first president of Congregation Beth Israel, founded in 1858. Courtesy, BI.

bare upstairs loft over a livery stable and blacksmith shop. In this same room, on September 19, 1858, Simon and Marjana were married by the Reverend Samuel Laski, who had been engaged as reader by the congregation and was most likely a self-educated layman.

Beth Israel received help and inspiration from Temple Emanu-El in San Francisco, which had been established nine years earlier. Beth Israel adopted its constitution and purchased the new Temple's first Torah and shofar from Emanu-El in time to conduct the High Holiday services in 1858.

The loft on First Avenue was situated above the noisy jumble of riverfront warehouses and stores, and Beth Israel quickly outgrew it. The board of trustees purchased a lot on the corner of Fifth Avenue and Oak Street—although some members objected that it was too distant from town—for $750 from Benjamin Stark. In 1861, the first synagogue building was consecrated, a small structure in the Gothic style with an English Gothic front portico which the *Oregonian* found "quite an ornament to that part of the city." The following year, the Mt. Sinai Cemetery Association was absorbed by Beth Israel.

In its early years, the congregation was served by a series of learned laymen: Reverend Laski; the twenty-eight-year-old German-trained Reverend Herman Bien; and Reverend Herman Bories, who made his living as a shoe and boot maker. Each remained for only a relatively brief time, and more often than not departed in conflict with the congregation. In 1863, Julius Eckman left the editorship of the *Weekly Gleaner* in San Francisco to become the first ordained rabbi to lead Beth Israel, but he too remained only three years, returning to San Francisco due to the bitterness that had developed between him and the young congregation. For the first decades of Beth Israel's existence, the congregation experienced recurrent turmoil over whether the traditional German service should be reformed and adapted to the new conditions of frontier America. Traditional and reform factions divided the congregation, and one of them was usually hostile to its current religious leader.

To appreciate the roots of this discord, it is necessary to understand changes in Jewish religious doctrine that were occurring in Germany and elsewhere in America. Jewish practice in Germany at the beginning of the nineteenth century was similar to that in Poland, where each aspect of life was governed by 613 *mitzvoth* (commandments). But Moses Mendelssohn, along with the impact of the Enlightenment, brought the authority and utility of many of the commandments into question. Mendelssohn challenged the traditionalists with the proposition that one could be both a good Jew and a rationalist within the rapidly changing world brought about by Napoleonic reform.

In 1819, the Reform movement was born, when fifty prominent Jewish intellectuals met in Berlin to alter the traditional structure of Judaism. They attempted to separate the essential, universal precepts of Judaism from the laws and customs rooted in historical practice, to separate Biblical imperative from rabbinic interpretation. In this way, as they saw it, the core could be maintained while forms were allowed to adjust to changing circumstances. In Germany, this was primarily an attempt to stem the tide of conversion, intermarriage and non-belief among Jews. Curiously, the Reform movement never gained the support in Germany that it found in the fertile ground of secular and innovative America.

In the 1840s and '50s, traditionalism still dominated, but congregations in America began to experiment. They simplified services, offered family pews, recited some prayers in English, presented choral music and sermons, and generally gave the service greater order and decorum. Isaac Leeser of Philadelphia championed the traditionalists; moderate reformers were led by Isaac Mayer Wise of Cincinnati, who was primarily concerned with a revised service; the radicals were led by David Einhorn of Baltimore and New York, who with his followers set out the "Pittsburgh Platform" in 1885, proclaiming Judaism a "progressive religion" concerned with reason and social justice. Although compromise developed in Reform Judaism toward the end of the century, in the years after Beth

The first Beth Israel synagogue was built on the corner of Fifth Avenue and Oak Street. Courtesy, OHS.

Israel was formed in Portland, German Jewish congregations throughout the country were in turmoil. The strife centered primarily on reform of the traditional ritual, the German *Minhag*.

Julius Eckman was already an accomplished rabbi when he arrived in Portland in 1863. Born in Posen in 1805, he served as rabbi of Temple Emanu-El in San Francisco after holding a number of other pulpits in the United States. He founded the first Jewish newspaper in the West, the *Weekly Gleaner*, in 1856, and also worked to restore the ancient Jewish congregation of Kai-Fong-Fu in China. In 1863 Beth Israel appeared ready to explore modest reform. But despite the rabbi's formal training under Leopold Zunz at the University of Berlin— one of the principal sites of radical reform thinking—he was inclined to change only limited aspects of decorum, not traditional religious interpretation. Antagonism grew between the rabbi and the congregation, and when the congregation formally decided, over Rabbi Eckman's opposition, to align with the Board of Delegates of American Israelites (a national movement to unite Judaism around moderate reform and to protect Jews against acts of anti-Semitism), the rabbi departed, returning to San Francisco to edit a new newspaper, the *Hebrew Observer*.

Isaac Schwab was recruited from Bavaria to serve as rabbi and *chazzan* in 1867, but discord worsened, with congregational factions vying for control and nearly always in conflict with their religious leader. Meetings became so heated that fines had to be imposed on unruly members. The congregation split over renewal of Schwab's contract, and in the ensuing tumult, he, too, resigned.

A second congregation, Ahavai Sholom, was formed in Portland in 1869. Due to the absence of records for the new congregation prior to 1884, it is impossible to determine whether it grew out of the ideological conflict at Beth Israel or from the arrival of more Orthodox Jews from Prussia and Poland. Nathan Goodman, from Posen in Prussian Poland, who had been a member of Beth Israel, was the first president of the new congregation, but it appears that most of its initial membership had not been previously affiliated.

Hostility to Beth Israel's minimal steps toward reform was reflected in an anonymous letter from one of Ahavai Sholom's new congregants that excoriated the older congregation for "mimicking third-hand here, the fashionable congregational life of the merchants of New

Rabbi Julius Eckman became the first ordained rabbi at Beth Israel in 1863. He also became the first rabbi of Congregation Ahavai Sholom, when it was founded in Portland in 1869. Courtesy, Rabbi Joshua Stampfer.

Ahavai Sholom synagogue was located on Sixth Avenue between Oak and Pine streets and served the congregation for thirty-five years. Drawing by Robert C. Harder. Courtesy, JHSO.

York, which borders on nihilism and gentilism." Rabbi Eckman, in San Francisco after resigning from Beth Israel, was immediately hired by Ahavai Sholom, which exacerbated the differences between the two congregations.

On December 5, 1869, the new Ahavai Sholom synagogue, located near Beth Israel on Sixth Avenue between Oak and Pine streets, was dedicated. In front of a large gathering, Rabbi Eckman carried the Torah seven times around the synagogue, thus fulfilling the ancient custom, as the rabbi told those assembled, to symbolically assure that the synagogue and Torah would be at the center of each congregant's life. Rabbi Eckman's two-year tenure was on the whole harmonious, because neither he nor his new congregation desired the reforms that had caused so much dissension at Beth Israel. Older and weaker, the rabbi returned to San Francisco once again and passed away a few years later in 1877. He was followed by Robert Abrahamson, *chazzan* and rabbi, who served Ahavai Sholom from 1880 into the twentieth century. Born in Poland, Rabbi Abrahamson preserved the traditional orientation of the new congregation.

At Beth Israel, however, the decade of the 1870s would prove to be the most divisive in its history. Reverend Schwab was replaced in 1872 by the young Mayer May from Bavaria, twenty-four years old and a fervent proponent of reform. He assumed his duties as rabbi, *chazzan* and Hebrew schoolteacher, and within a year was forcefully advocating replacement of the *Minhag Ashkenaz* with the Reform prayer book *Minhag America*, developed by Isaac Mayer Wise in Cincinnati. Traditionalists persuaded the congregation to oppose May's desire, but then reversed themselves after he addressed a passionate letter to the semi-annual meeting of the board of directors:

How is it possible for any minister to do good where there is such a lack of good spirit? ... Regarding our service in the House of Worship I am sorry to state that by a great many there is no interest whatever taken because they very seldom need any, and again others trouble themselves too much about it. The one wants an alteration [reforms in the

The confirmation class at Congregation Beth Israel, 1878. Rabbi Mayer May sits at the center of the class. Courtesy, BI.

service], the others don't. The third wants Minhag Ashkenaz as our Constitution provides; the fourth wants the alterations that have been made by my worthy predecessor.... I stand in the midst of a chaos of forms and it is very difficult to discern whether to go to the right or to the left.

I ... would advise the worthy congregation either to adopt Minhag America, the land we are living in, or if you don't like to depart [from] the book which your great-grandfathers found suitable in Spain and Germany in times entirely different from ours, let us at least have Minhag Ashkenaz as it has been newly adopted.... I have begged the worthy congregation to give me a plan of the alterations you have made and how you want your services conducted in the future, even if you don't desire any other Minhag than Minhag Portland. It is my sincere wish to do right and to please my congregation with the hope you will accept this with the love and honest intentions as it is given to you. I remain

Your obedient servant,

M. May

The young rabbi was frustrated by congregants who were religiously unversed and often non-observant, yet stubbornly resistant to reform of ritual. Most of the members of Beth Israel were business leaders in the community and their zeal was reserved primarily for business, not religious observance. They did have views on reform that spanned the range of opinion from those who were inclined to Americanize the service such as Bernard Goldsmith and, to some extent, Jacob Mayer, to those such as Abraham Waldman who staunchly defended traditional practice. Controversy raged back and forth until it came to a head in 1879, when four conservatives charged May with a wild assortment of offenses, including

referring to the married women of his congregation as ladies of easy virtue, ... acting as a libertine and rake during a visit to San Francisco, ... threatening to join the Unitarian Church in the event Mr. Philip Selling were reelected president [of Beth Israel], and so on.

A committee, which included Solomon Hirsch, Bernard Goldsmith, Simon Blumauer and other responsible members of the congregation, conducted an investigation which generally exonerated the rabbi, although they

Temple Beth Israel, erected in 1889 at Twelfth Avenue and Main Street. The *Oregonian* called it, "the handsomest temple to be found in the Northwest." Courtesy, JHSO.

found that he did "say some indiscreet things about the ignorance of the congregation." May was rehired for another term of two years, but bizarre events in the following year finally terminated his acrimonious and extraordinary tenure.

On October 1, 1880, Rabbi May became engaged in a doctrinal argument with congregant Abraham Waldman on Front Avenue opposite the sheet metal and stove works of Hexter and May. They had a history of conflict, and this time Waldman lost his temper and knocked May to the ground. May drew a pistol from beneath his coat, fired twice at Waldman, but missed his target both times. Shortly thereafter, May resigned his pulpit, the congregation tendered him twelve hundred dollars as the remainder of his salary, and he left Portland.

During the turbulent 1870s, Beth Israel membership declined, despite a substantial increase in Jewish population in Portland. Relative peace was finally established with the appointment of Jacob Bloch in 1884. Born in Bohemia, Rabbi Bloch was primarily a scholar who brought, at last, a quiet dignity to the pulpit at Beth Israel. As time passed, the tenets of Reform Judaism came quietly to the congregation, *yarmulkah* and *tallis* slowly disappeared, a choir was begun, and in 1895 the *Union Prayer Book*, the successor to *Minhag America*, was adopted. By the mid-1880s, membership was again increasing, creating the need for a new and larger synagogue.

In 1889, an imposing new synagogue for Beth Israel was erected at Twelfth Avenue and Main Street with dramatic Moorish and Byzantine motifs. It was semi-Gothic and had large stained glass windows and two soaring towers topped with exotic onion domes. The *Oregonian* called it "the handsomest temple to be found in the Northwest." It had cost seventy thousand dollars, largely raised under the dedicated leadership of Louis Fleischner, who himself contributed the first thousand dollars and the cost of the interior frescoes. Tragically, this ornate and beautiful building was destroyed in 1923 by a fire apparently set by an arsonist, who was never apprehended.

The synagogue's *shammes* of forty-seven years, Theodore Olsen, a lifelong Christian, risked his life in the fire in a vain attempt to save the Torahs. He did rescue prayer books, records and whatever he could carry from the burning synagogue. Honored on his twenty-fifth anniversary at the Temple, Olsen said in his heavy Norwegian accent:

I am very proud to be a shammes. To be a shammes is a great honor. I have tried to do my work with that thought in mind and nobody could be happier than I am to have such a big responsibility.

At his request, Olsen was buried in Beth Israel's cemetery. After the fire, the congregation accepted the offer of the First Presbyterian Church to use its facilities until their third and present synagogue—a majestic domed Byzantine structure—was completed four years later in Northwest Portland.

Temple Beth Israel was destroyed by an arsonist's fire in December, 1923. The synagogue's devoted *shammes*, Theodore Olsen, risked his life trying to save the Torahs. Courtesy, BI.

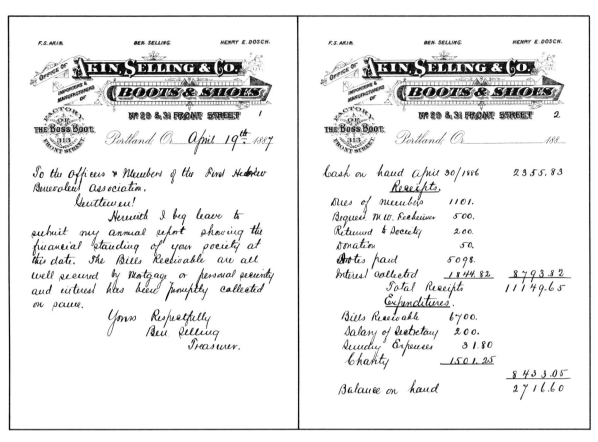

Ben Selling had broad authority as treasurer of the First Hebrew Benevolent Association to assist those in need, particularly new immigrants to Portland. Courtesy, JHSO.

Charitable Institutions

In the rough and tumble of frontier towns, religious and cultural ties helped provide a measure of comfort and security to Oregon Jews. But since the formal organizational structures of Europe did not exist, the settlers had to form voluntary associations to meet their needs. They had established a congregation to address spiritual and communal necessities and a cemetery society to bury their dead. Now, basic tenets of Judaism required that they develop the means to care for those in need.

In its first years, Beth Israel itself had provided charity, particularly for burials, but in 1859, the First Hebrew Benevolent Association was established, separate from the congregation, by Jacob Mayer and other members as well as non-members of Beth Israel. It was formally

incorporated in 1863, and was supported by Jewish merchants.

Records for the organization do not exist prior to 1884, but at that time the Association had $17,000 to loan, and 170 members had paid dues. Capital was loaned out to both Jews and non-Jews, often to help immigrants get started in business. The Association charged 6 to 10 percent interest, which was dispensed as charity during the 1870s and early '80s by Louis Fleischner, the moving force behind the organization in those years, and later by Ben Selling. The Association helped pay for hospital and nursing care, funerals and general assistance to needy coreligionists without regard to affiliation. In 1889, a salaried loan officer, Benjamin Cohen, was hired to handle the growing demands placed on the Association by an influx of immigrants from Eastern Europe and to assist Jewish victims of pogroms in Europe.

In 1864, the wives of Portland merchants formed the first Jewish women's organization in Oregon, which they incorporated in 1874 as the First Hebrew Ladies Benevolent Society. The organization assisted "ladies of the Jewish Faith" who were poor or ill by providing money, clothing and other necessities. Members made regular visits to the sick and bereaved and cared for children in need.

At first men served as president and secretary of the society, while the remainder of the board was composed entirely of women. But in 1879, Mrs. Cecile Friedlander became secretary, and the women's authority increased. By 1884, they required that any expenditures by the president be approved by the board. This led three months later to Edward Kahn's resignation after ten years as president. Women fully controlled the organization from then on under the strong leadership of Emma Goldsmith, the wife of Bernard Goldsmith. Membership in the society more than doubled in ensuing years.

The Founding of B'nai B'rith

As Jewish merchants became settled in Portland, achieved success in business, and began to raise families, a desire grew for a fraternal organization to provide fellowship as well as health and life insurance. B'nai B'rith (Sons of the Covenant) had been founded in New York City in 1843, in a coffee house on the Lower East Side by German Jewish immigrants. It was modeled on the popular Masonic and Odd Fellows orders with all their accoutrements of secrecy and regalia. In 1866, nineteen Jews, all members of Beth Israel and led by Jacob Mayer, met at Templar's Hall at Front Avenue and Alder Street in Portland to found Oregon Lodge 65, the first B'nai B'rith lodge in the Northwest and the second on the Pacific Coast. A charter was granted by District Grand Lodge No. 4 in San Francisco. The initial membership numbered thirty, nearly all established, stable merchants in the city. But one founder of the lodge, Bailey Gatzert, who had come to Portland in 1862 from San Francisco to begin a business, left in 1869 to open a branch of Schwabacher Bros. & Co. in Seattle. He became Seattle's mayor four years later. Many still remember the sternwheeler named for him, the fastest on the Pacific Coast, plying Northwest waters early in this century.

Oregon Lodge 65 was open to all Jewish men. Its membership was drawn from the entire community and does not appear to have been affected by the religous conflicts occurring at Beth Israel. Attempts were made, however, to begin a second lodge in the mid-1870s by younger, less well-established individuals who did not want to pay insurance claims for the older members of Lodge 65 and preferred to socialize with members closer to their own age.

Charles Friendly, cousin of Samson Friendly of Eugene, was one of the early presidents of B'nai B'rith Lodge 65 in Portland. He was also the fourth president of Beth Israel, an organizer of the First Hebrew Benevolent Association and a commission broker in the hides and leather business. Courtesy, JHSO.

A Purim party at Beth Israel in 1898. Closely associated with B'nai B'rith Lodges 65 and 416, Beth Israel served the religious and social needs of the German Jewish community. Courtesy, OHS.

Although members of Lodge 65 resisted strongly, a charter was granted for a second lodge, North Pacific Lodge 314, in 1879. Its membership included a number of unmarried men, most of them young merchants, and it added both white collar workers and craftsmen in the years that followed.

In the 1890s, two additional B'nai B'rith lodges were formed, reflecting the rapid changes and social stratification that had begun to occur in the Jewish community. In 1891, Portland Lodge 416 was established, largely by American-born, second-generation German Jews, and in 1897, Sabato Morais Lodge 464 was founded by Eastern European immigrants and named for the recently deceased and renowned Orthodox rabbi of Philadelphia.

A Young Men's Hebrew Association (YMHA) was organized in Portland in 1880 by German Jews. The YMHA sponsored lectures, debates and cultural events, and maintained a library and reading room. It was financially supported by older, established members of the community, but it was used primarily by the young. The YMHA was disbanded in 1894, however, apparently due to limited resources.

6

Civic Involvement in the Broader Community

The Enlightenment had brought new ideas and hope for full civic participation to Jews and all minority peoples in Europe, but throughout much of the nineteenth century they were perennially frustrated. In America, however, and especially in the West, where the need for public participation was great, the early Jewish pioneers wasted little time in fully involving themselves alongside respected Christian leaders.

The family and newly formed Jewish institutions helped to provide cultural identity and security in the personal lives of the Jewish pioneers. And fortunately, involvement in the Jewish community and full participation in public life were not as incompatible as they had often been in Europe. The pioneers, small as their numbers were, had earned the right to participation in the broader community, and they were eager to accept the challenge.

Nowhere were they more involved than in the political life of the communities in which they settled. Merchants were respected central figures in frontier towns and had a stake in the conduct of peaceful, orderly civic affairs. For it was only in such communities that economic growth could be nurtured. Literate and sober, Jews were quick to accept social responsibility, and a tradition of the Jewish merchant as protector of civic order began to grow. Scarcely a public office existed in Oregon which Jews did not fill at one point or another. This was true throughout the West—even in towns with the romantic names of Deadwood and Dodge City —but nowhere was it more true than in Oregon. Even as early as 1879, the *Hebrew Sabbath*

School Visitor of Cincinnati reported in its May edition:

> *The Israelites of Oregon, contrary to their brethren in California, appear to play quite a lively part in public affairs. Although their number is limited and quite out of proportion to the Gentile population of the State,*

Aaron Fox with his sons. Fox served as Troutdale's first mayor from 1907 to 1909. Courtesy, Troutdale Historical Society.

Edward Hirsch of Salem, state treasurer from 1878 to 1887, was one of five early pioneer brothers, including Solomon who was appointed ambassador to Turkey. Courtesy, OHS.

Jews fill a large number of high public offices, many of the incumbents holding them for several terms, presenting thereby an unmistakable proof that the manner in which they have acquitted themselves of their duties has met with the full approbation of their constituents.

Throughout Oregon's hinterlands, Jews were often the most prominent shopkeepers in frontier settlements, and they were elected in unprecedented numbers to local posts. Indeed, many were elected mayor in cities and towns throughout Oregon.

Jews not only served in local office, where their economic roles brought them naturally to the fore as city fathers, but at all levels of the state and federal government in Oregon. Jewish state senators and representatives are too numerous to list, but those who occupied leader-

ship posts included: Ben Selling, who served as both president of the senate (1911) and speaker of the house (1915); Solomon Hirsch (1880) and Joseph Simon (five terms: 1889-1891 and 1895-1898) who both served as president of the senate; and recently, Vera Katz, who has been speaker of the house, and Shirley Gold, who has been house majority leader (in the 1985 and 1987 sessions).

Julius Meier was governor of Oregon from 1930 to 1934, and Neil Goldschmidt, former mayor of Portland, began his term as Oregon's second Jewish governor in January, 1987. Two Jews have served as state treasurer: Louis Fleischner (1870-1874) and Edward Hirsch

Neil Goldschmidt, in 1976 during his tenure as mayor of Portland (1972-1979). He also became governor of Oregon in January, 1987. Goldschmidt continues a long tradition of Oregon Jews who have held high public office, which currently also includes United States Congressman Ron Wyden, state house speaker Vera Katz and house majority leader Shirley Gold . Courtesy, Neil Goldschmidt.

(1878-1887).

There have been two Jewish United States senators: Joseph Simon (1898-1903) and Richard Neuberger (1954-1960). Ron Wyden is currently a member of the United States House of Representatives.

The list cited above includes only major officeholders, not the many who served in local posts such as city commissioner or on water or transportation boards. Jews were also involved in a range of non-political activities that enriched the public life of their communities. Sigmund Heilner, Bernard Goldsmith and Louis Fleischner fought in the militia. Others, like Edward Hirsch in Salem, Sanford Adler in Baker and Herman Wise in Astoria, served for many years as postmaster. Many others helped establish, then volunteered for the local fire brigade, since fires were the greatest danger to early frontier communities, which were constructed almost entirely of wood.

Typically, Jewish politicians have been politically progressive, concerned with civil liberties and involved in the reforms of their day. Ben Selling, the most prominent Jew of his generation, and Julius Meier, governor of Oregon during the great public power disputes, will be discussed at length later; let us turn now to an early and not so liberal politician, one of the most important Republican figures in the state for thirty years, Joseph Simon.

Born in Germany in 1851, Joseph Simon was brought to the United States when only a year old and to Portland at age six. He left school to help in his father's store when he reached thirteen, but in 1870, when business was slow, Simon apprenticed in the most prestigious law office in Portland, Mitchell and Dolph. In September, 1872, after reading law for two years, he became one of three Jewish lawyers admitted to the Oregon Bar. Simon became a major corporate lawyer, representing and acting as corporate secretary to the Oregon Railway and Navigation Company, which was the dominant force in Portland's business and political life, and was run by the Ladds, Corbetts, Failings, Lewises, Weidlers and C. A. Dolph, Simon's mentor and law partner.

JEWISH MAYORS OF OREGON TOWNS AND CITIES

Albany
Albert G. Senders, 1940-1944

Astoria
Isaac Bergman, 1898-1902
Herman Wise, 1906-1910
Harry Steinbock, 1959-1974

Burns
Julius Durkheimer, 1895-1896

Dufur
Al Roth, dates unknown

Eugene
Samson Friendly, 1893-1895

Gervais
M. Mitchell, dates unknown

Harrisburg
B. May, dates unknown

Heppner
Henry Blackman, 1887-1890

North Powder
H. Rothschild, dates unknown

Pendleton
Reuben Alexander, 1892-1894
N. Gorfkel, dates unknown

Portland
Bernard Goldsmith, 1869-1871
Philip Wasserman, 1871-1873
Joseph Simon, acting mayor, 1877; mayor, 1909-1911
Neil Goldschmidt, 1972-1979

Prineville
William Wurzweiler, 1904-1906

Seaside
William H. Galvani, about 1928

Troutdale
Aaron Fox, city's first mayor, 1907-1909

President William Howard Taft (in top hat) campaigns in Portland in 1911 with Joseph Simon sitting at his side. Simon was a dominant figure in the Oregon Republican party and served as a United States senator from 1898 to 1903. He was in the second year of a two-year term as mayor of Portland when this picture was taken. Courtesy, OHS.

With the help of Dolph, Simon was appointed secretary of the Multnomah County Republican convention at age twenty-six and went on to become Republican county chairman and state party chairman from 1880 to 1886. His friends called him "little Joe" while his opponents referred to him as "the Boss" because, in the words of Portland historian Kimbark Mac-Coll he was "the most powerful political force in Oregon politics from 1880 to 1910." After holding office on Portland's city council (1877-1880) and in the state senate (1880-1891, 1895-1898), he was elected to the United States Senate in 1898.

But in contrast to the bitter struggles in Oregon Republican politics in the 1880s and '90s, which pitted Simon and his allies (Henry Corbett, the Dolph brothers, Jonathan Bourne, Jr., Solomon Hirsch and others) against the faction supporting courtly, colorful United States

Senator John Mitchell, Washington D.C. seemed remote and unengaging. Simon wrote to Jonathan Bourne, Jr.:

I find conditions in the Senate much different from what I expected.... I am not particularly impressed with life at Washington. I would infinitely prefer to be home.

And return he did after one term. Home again, Simon was elected mayor of Portland in 1909, despite considerable political opposition. During his career, he was so immersed in law practice, politics, and various investments in real estate and mining, that he never became significantly involved in the Jewish community. He did, however, provide free legal services to Beth Israel, to the First Hebrew Ladies Benevolent Society and to the Portland Chapter of the National Council of Jewish Women.

In 1882, Joseph Simon sponsored legislation that set up the first professional fire department in Portland, and in 1885 he created a three-member citizen board of police commissioners—two of the first three were Simon and Bourne—to oversee the Portland Police Department and, as a by-product, to help consolidate Simon's own political power.

David Solis-Cohen and Joseph Teal, Jr., two Jewish Republican lawyers identified with liberal reform, strongly opposed the "Simon machine." Solis-Cohen was appointed a police commissioner in the 1890s, under the banner of eliminating "politics" from the police department. He also supported nominating candidates by election rather than by party caucus and advocated civil service reform to control government patronage, the organization of labor unions and women's suffrage—all issues challenging entrenched Simon Republicans.

David Solis-Cohen was an unusual man who made exceptional contributions to Portland and its Jewish community. He was born in Philadelphia in October, 1850, to a mother from the famous Sephardic family, Solis, who agreed to marry David's father, Myer Cohen from Poland, on the condition that they hyphenate their last names so that the "loftier" Solis could be retained. David's early teachers were Rabbi Isaac Leeser of the Spanish-Portuguese congregation and Rebecca Gratz, an early social welfare advocate from a well-known family and reputedly the model for Rebecca in Sir Walter Scott's novel *Ivanhoe*. Rabbi Sabato Morais was a close friend of the family.

Solis-Cohen came to Portland in 1878, a devoted Jew and a man of broad, liberal education. He was a lawyer, merchant and banker, and also a gifted poet, author and speaker. He was widely sought as an orator on major occasions by both Jewish and non-Jewish audiences. He delivered the keynote address at the laying of the cornerstones of Beth Israel temples in 1889 and again in 1927, and also spoke at important events at Ahavai Sholom. He belonged to both congregations, and helped them resolve earlier animosities. In 1880, he wrote and produced the musical *Esther* at the Metropoli-

tan Theater, dividing the twenty-five-hundred-dollar profit equally between Beth Israel and Ahavai Sholom.

Solis-Cohen was a romantic who fervently believed that the democratic ideals in the Declaration of Independence and the Constitution were the fulfillment of ethical principles enumerated in the Torah and Talmud. He was a felicitous blend of American and Jew who felt—as did so many of the Jewish pioneers—that a Jew could be an American, participating fully in the building of a pluralistic society, and yet remain true to Judaism. He was an enthusiastic member of fraternal orders, Jewish and non-Jewish alike —B'nai B'rith, the Masons and the Elks— because he believed that their message of brotherhood helped to promote a humane and

David Solis-Cohen descended from a famous Philadelphia Sephardic family. He came to Portland in 1878 and made exceptional contributions as a lawyer, merchant and banker. He was also a gifted poet and author, and a widely sought-after public speaker. Courtesy, JHSO.

progressive society.

Jews like David Solis-Cohen were involved in many aspects of Oregon's cultural life, but others also made cultural contributions, particularly in the field of music. Simon Harris organized an amateur music society and was its first conductor in 1875; seven years later, after returning from his native Prussia, he founded the Orchestral Union. Sigmund Frank, a professionally trained violinist, was also involved in Portland's early musical life. Along with the many private recitals *de rigueur* for accomplished young people of the day, these early musical ventures led to the founding of the Portland Symphony Orchestra in 1895.

The Portland Library Association was established in 1865 with Judge Matthew Deady as its first president. Bernard Goldsmith served on the first board of directors, and a Jewish lawyer named Morris Fechheimer, who arrived in Portland in the late 1860s, became an important figure on the board (to which he had been nominated by Deady), serving until his death in 1886. A Jewish literary society was launched in 1873, but was later disbanded when many of its cultural functions were assumed by the YMHA.

7

The 1880s: German Jewry Reaches Its Peak

The single young men who first came to Oregon in the 1850s had grown by the 1880s into a prosperous and well-established Jewish community. From a single Jew identified in Oregon in the census of 1850, census records show a Jewish population in Oregon of one hundred in 1860 (there were 183,080 in the United States) and 868 by 1877 (226,042 in the United States). In Portland, where as early as 1860 approximately half the Jews in the state resided, the Jewish population comprised between 4 and 6 percent of the general city population in the years between 1860 and 1880.

As the community grew and attained financial security, the young pioneers married. At first their wives came from Jewish communities in San Francisco, the East and Europe, but by the 1880s, children of families that had grown up in Oregon were providing marriage partners for each other. But due to renewed immigration of single individuals from Bismarck's conservative regime in Germany—Jeanette Meier's nephews, Leopold and Max Hirsch, and Sigmund and Moses Sichel, the nephews of Solomon Hirsch, for instance—along with the inclination of some Germans to remain single—

The Ehrman brothers—Solomon, Myer, Joseph and Edward—with their wives in 1892, in the finery of successful German Jews of the day. The family founded Mason, Ehrman & Co. in 1885 with William Mason (later mayor of Portland), and the business grew to be one of the largest grocery wholesale houses in the Northwest. Courtesy, JHSO.

more than 30 percent of Oregon Jews remained unmarried.

The German Jews desired to integrate fully into the life of Portland and the frontier settlements throughout Oregon, and they lived easily with Christian neighbors of similar economic status. In the 1850s and '60s, most Portlanders lived near the city center, but by the mid-1870s and 1880s, many of the successful Jewish and non-Jewish proprietors were moving "uptown" to newer areas near Park Avenue and further west, while younger people and newcomers remained downtown until they too were able to afford to move away from the river.

The families of Abe Meier, Sigmund Frank, the Jacobs brothers and Ben Selling lived in the South Park Blocks area with the Corbetts, Bensons and Dolphs, and all of them sent their children to the Portland Academy or the Ladd School. Some of the most successful Jewish families erected great mansions: Philip Wasserman and Bernard Goldsmith, longtime friends who lived next to each other, and the Jacobs brothers with their adjoining Florentine villas. None was more splendid than Julius Loewenberg's thirty-two-room mansion, built in 1893 at the east entrance to Washington Park and modeled on a Prussian castle Julius had admired in boyhood (it was razed by subsequent owners in 1960). Others began to build in the new areas of Northwest Portland along Nineteenth and nearby avenues that had become fashionable.

The households of successful Jews were sometimes quite grand. Joseph Teal, Jr., a lawyer and one of the wealthiest Jews in Portland,

Sigmund Sichel with his wife Sarah (rear left) and daughters Ruth (rear right) and Marion, at their home on NW 23rd between Irving and Johnson, about 1906. Sichel came to Portland from Germany in 1873 with the help of his well-known uncle Solomon Hirsch. He served in the state senate and as president of Beth Israel, and was successful in the cigar business. Courtesy, JHSO.

though married to a non-Jew and not closely associated with the Jewish community, had living under his roof his wife, five children, a clerk from Ireland, four relatives of his wife, and three servants—a black woman, a white woman and a Chinese man. While intermarriage had been fairly common in colonial America, as Jews became more numerous in the mid-nineteenth century, it became rare and was strongly opposed by Jewish religious leaders. In Oregon, intermarriage occurred more frequently in outlying areas, although most Jews came to population centers to find spouses. In Portland, only Joseph Teal, Jr., Benjamin Cohen and a few others married non-Jews. And marriage between German and Polish Jews was virtually unknown during this period.

In the years before 1870, a number of German Jews in Portland participated in cultural and charitable activities sponsored by the broader German community, which comprised a quarter of Portland's foreign-born population. Many were members of the German Aid Society, begun in 1869 to help needy German immigrants, and some belonged to the earlier German *Turn-verein* (a social and athletic society founded in 1858), which elected three Jews as president before its reorganization in 1871.

When Jews arrived in Portland, it was usually their second or third place of residence in the United States. They had some familiarity with English and, desiring to become part of Oregon life, they used English, not German, for most business transactions and for the minutes of the Jewish organizations they formed. By the 1880s, while they maintained pride in their German heritage, the German Jewish community was well-integrated into Oregon life. Many had been born in America, and ties to Germany were gradually diminished.

An indication of how fully the Jews of Oregon were accepted by the communities in which they lived is provided by their participation and leadership in the fraternal orders that were so popular in America in the 1860s. Many Jews in the commercial elite joined the Masons and Odd Fellows, often rising to hold office; a few, such as Joseph Simon, David Solis-Cohen and Jacob Mayer, who became grand master of Oregon's Masons in 1888, reached the highest levels in these prestigious organizations.

While Jews moved freely within Oregon society, were generally well-respected and even honored by their fellow citizens, there were occasional expressions of anti-Semitism. The earliest came from Thomas J. Dryer, founder and publisher of the *Oregonian*. Angered by the defeat of his bid to enter the territorial legislature in 1858, Dryer attacked Germans because he believed they had opposed his candidacy, and aimed his vitriolic bombast primarily at the German Jews:

The Jews in Oregon, but more particularly in this city, have assumed an importance that no other sect has ever dared to assume in a free country. They have leagued together by uniting their entire numerical strength to control the ballot boxes at our elections.

They have assumed to control the commercial interest of the whole country by a secret combination. . . . The history of the Jews is but a history of a great variety of ways and means adopted by them to obtain money and power. They as a nation or tribe produce nothing, nor do nothing unless they are the exclusive gainers thereby.

Do you know of a Jew who ever drove an ox team across the plains, or engaged in an Indian war to defend the homes and firesides of our citizens on this coast, or on any other frontier?

Dryer continued to spew invective, but other Oregon newspapers, long in battle with Dryer and the *Oregonian*, counterattacked. Salem's *Oregon Statesman* called him "an ignoramus ... a man without integrity or honor. . . . Jews stand preeminent as men of honesty and integrity." Dryer, said the *Statesman*, is no more than "an irresponsible libeler" whose "object was to proscribe men on account of their birthplace and their religion." Portland's *Weekly Times* also came to the defense of the Jews—who, in fact, did not cast their votes for the same candidate in any election. Much heat was generated by these charges and countercharges, which undoubtedly sold newspapers and may have reflected their mutual animosity more than it did any persistent strain of anti-Semitism in Oregon.

Aside from Dun and Company's stereotyping of Jews in credit investigations, there are few other indications of anti-Semitism until the mid-1880s, when Ben Selling lamented the "many Jew-haters in Oregon." He was concerned at the time with defeating Judge Waldo, a candidate for the Oregon Supreme Court who had said that he "never knew a Jew to come into court with a straight case." Selling influenced many, especially his coreligionists in Oregon's small towns, to oppose Waldo, who was ultimately defeated.

While Jews shared neighborly relations, membership in fraternal orders and strong political and business ties with Portland's gentile elite (Goldsmith, Simon and others also shared directorships on the boards of major Oregon corporations), it seemed appropriate to non-Jews—and apparently to Jews also—that the social clubs of Portland society should exclude Jews from membership. The Arlington Club, founded in 1867 by the leading non-Jewish businessmen of Portland, was a place, then as now, where decisions crucial to the future of the city and state were discussed informally in a relaxed and convivial setting. Jews were simply not offered membership. While it is unclear how Jews reacted to that fact, there is no record of Jews seeking membership or of their unhappiness at being excluded. Jews in society's upper echelons who might be eligible for membership apparently felt that they had sufficient access to non-Jewish brethren—some as close

The Concordia Club at Sixteenth Avenue and Morrison Street, about 1908. The *Jewish Tribune* called it the "handsomest club structure in Oregon" and described its lavish interior, which included a billiard room, German room, card rooms, smoking room, library, apartments and a "magnificent ballroom." Courtesy, UO (Angelus Collection).

as Dolph, who shared a powerful law partnership with Simon for many years, but not Arlington Club membership—through business, political and fraternal ties. As social discrimination and class distinctions began to emerge in towns and cities across the country in the 1880s, the German Jews followed suit by establishing their own exclusive enclaves.

They established the Concordia Club, which was organized initially in 1878 by less

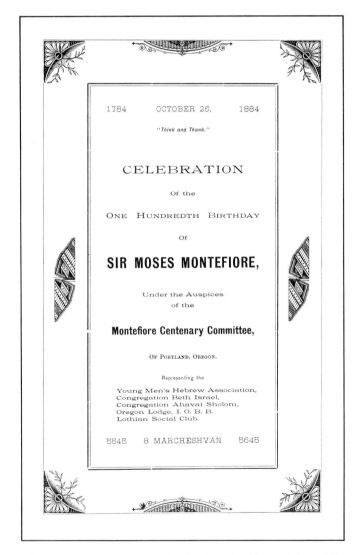

1784   OCTOBER 26,   1884

"*Think and Thank.*"

CELEBRATION

Of the

ONE HUNDREDTH BIRTHDAY

Of

SIR MOSES MONTEFIORE,

Under the Auspices
of the

Montefiore Centenary Committee,

OF PORTLAND, OREGON.

Representing the

Young Men's Hebrew Association,
Congregation Beth Israel,
Congregation Ahavai Sholom,
Oregon Lodge, I. O. B. B.
Lothian Social Club.

5545   8 MARCHESHVAN   5645

The celebration program for the hundredth birthday of Sir Moses Montefiore, the renowned Jewish philanthropist from England. Held at the New Market Theater, the celebration was crowded with luminaries. The occasion also celebrated the extraordinary success achieved by German Jews in just over three decades in Oregon. Courtesy, BI.

established merchants but within a few years attracted the cream of Portland's younger German Jewish society—the men who would establish B'nai B'rith Lodge 416 in 1891, as well as the sons of prominent families like the Meiers, Franks, Blumauers, Mayers, Fleischners, Wolfes, Sellings and Goldsmiths. Concordia Clubs were organized in many cities across the country, probably in partial reaction to exclusion from elite gentile clubs, and with new immigrants beginning to arrive, these clubs expressed a sense of class pride and superiority.

When the Concordia Club was reorganized in 1887, all of its members were successful in business and German in origin; the Jacobs brothers and Julius Loewenberg, early pioneers and wealthy Portlanders who were born in Poland, were not members. The club was primarily patronized by the second generation of German pioneers, while older community leaders either did not join or held only nominal membership. Concordia at first rented rooms, but later built its own lavish hall, first at SW Second Avenue and Morrison Street and then at Sixteenth Avenue on Morrison Street. Like the Arlington Club, it was a social club where business matters might be politely discussed and where a continual round of grand balls and gala events were held.

On Sunday, October 26, 1884, the Jewish community of Portland held a major citywide event to celebrate the one-hundredth birthday of the Jewish philanthropist from England, Sir Moses Montefiore. This occasion was also a chance to rejoice in the satisfaction and well-being that Jews in Oregon had achieved in just over three decades. Services were held at Beth Israel in the morning, and the celebration itself in the evening at the New Market Theater, the largest in downtown Portland. Ben Selling reported to a friend that "the New Market Theater was jammed. Hundreds were turned away and the affair was equal if not superior to any ever before held in this city."

The audience included both Jews and non-Jews, with leading dignitaries from both communities honored on the stage. Major addresses were given by David Solis-Cohen, the finest

Jewish orator in Portland, as well as by Thomas Lamb Eliot of the First Unitarian Church and A. L. Lindsley of the First Presbyterian Church, two of the leading ministers of the day. It truly marked the success and acceptance of Oregon's Jewish community.

Oregon's German Jewry had come a long way in the span of a single generation. The economic instability of the early years and the religious strife of the 1870s were behind them. The small shops of the 1850s had bloomed into sophisticated wholesale, retail and specialty enterprises. Not all Jews were wealthy, but most had attained stable middle-class status and few were poor.

In 1889, Isaac Markens, a journalist from New York, noted in a series of historical sketches entitled *The Hebrews in America*, that:

The prosperity of the Hebrew colony at Portland, Oregon, is attested by their wealth, which, in proportion to their numbers, is more widely distributed than in any other section of the Union, and by their prominence in public affairs.

Jacob Rader Marcus, one of America's most distinguished Jewish historians, described the importance of the early German Jewish community in Oregon during a 1938 address commemorating the eightieth anniversary of the founding of Beth Israel:

In no other state in the Union has the Jew adjusted himself to his environment better than Oregon.... There is no other state in which the Jew reached such high positions in the political life of the commonwealth.... The foundations were laid strong and deep by the pioneers who built the Jewish community.

Jews in Oregon had built a well-wrought social and cultural support structure which met the needs of the community and gave them a sense of their unique identity within the melting pot of a rapidly growing frontier state. Further, they had done it without the authoritarian traditions that prevailed in Europe. They had built their community institutions themselves, and they exuded the pride and confidence of a self-reliant people on a new frontier.

Although the Jewish pioneers insisted on developing uniquely Jewish cultural institutions, they were well-accepted in Oregon society. It was their state as much as anyone else's. They built it alongside their Christian neighbors, contributing their efforts to virtually every aspect of early Oregon life. The Jews adapted easily, fashioning their religious and benevolent institutions to fit a frontier context. Their essential political and economic interests—commercial success in a thriving, stable setting —were very similar to those of other Oregonians. The Jews of Oregon had found a comfortable home.

But as the ironies of history would have it, just as the German Jews had arrived at the height of success and stability in the 1880s, events were beginning to occur in Eastern Europe that would shock and alter Oregon's Jewish community and change the face of American Jewry forever.

PART II

THE COMING OF THE JEWS
FROM EASTERN EUROPE

1890-1920

8

Background, Passage and Arrival

Avraham and Goldie Sharffrenko and family in Kobischa, Russia, before emigrating to America. Morris Sharff (front right) lived most of his life in Portland. Courtesy, Blanche Sharff.

Jewish Life in Eastern Europe

On March 1, 1881, Alexander II, the czar of Russia, was felled by an assassin's bullet, precipitating profound changes for the Jews of Eastern Europe and massive waves of emigration to the United States, including Oregon. For centuries, the Jews had lived in Eastern Europe (Russia, Rumania and Austro-Hungary) subject to the tyranny of czars and to the violence of Christian peasants mistreated by their rulers. Jews occupied the roles of trader and artisan to which they had been relegated since the Middle Ages. They were restricted in Russia (including much of modern Poland) to a relatively small area called the Pale of Jewish Settlement (approximately 380,000 square miles in Eastern Russia between the Baltic and Black Seas). In the villages (or *shtetls*) and towns of the Pale, they lived as best they could in wooden houses with mud floors, large families often crowded into a room or two. Here the archetypal character was the *luftmensh*, the person who managed to "live off air," to scrape together a living however possible. In this difficult environment, the Jews created a rich culture centered on the family, where every aspect of life was infused with religion. The bitterness of poverty and the ever-present possibility of violence were softened by the pleasure derived from ritual and community and the learning of Torah and Talmud.

Serfdom endured in Russia until 1861, and in Rumania until 1864, and it was only in the middle of the nineteenth century that the lands of Eastern Europe slowly emerged from feudalism. Changes were inevitable, as the peasant-based economies of Eastern Europe eroded under the pressures of industrialization and mass production, and the Jews dependent on that economy became increasingly impoverished. After the 1860s, young Jews began drifting from the *shtetl* and seeking opportunities in the larger cities of Warsaw and Lodz, Odessa and Vilna. Once in the cities, the long-harbored hope for the coming of the Messiah turned some of these youth to the pursuit of socialism and Zionism.

Official reaction to the Jews prior to 1881 alternated between repression and tolerance, between forced attempts at Russification and ghettoized segregation. Hundreds of edicts were promulgated that regulated Jewish life, including economic and religious activity, military service and place of residence.

In 1881, with the ascension to the throne of Alexander III, who was advised by the fanatic and powerful Konstantin Pobedonostsev, official Russian policy became virulently anti-Semitic, its goal to convince the peasants that their problems were caused by the Jews. Under this new regime, devastating pogroms took place in hundreds of towns between 1881 and 1884, and a series of even more terrible massacres occurred between 1903 and 1906 in Kishinev, Odessa, Bialystok and elsewhere.

Celia Blumenthal was eighty-five years old and living at the Robison Jewish Home in April, 1986, when she described for the *Portland Jewish Review* her horrifying memory of the terrible pogrom in Kishinev on Easter Sunday, 1903:

I was just a little tot then. They murdered a man right in front of my eyes. He was an old man just walking up the street, a Hasidic man with a long beard and pe'ot [sidelocks], and a velvet hat. Along came a soldier on his horse; he got off and, just about three feet away from me, took out this big saber and sliced the man's throat. He just fell at my feet, and I ran inside and hid behind a table. I was screaming and crying and my mother couldn't control me. That was a picture that I've never forgotten.

Zabludow, a town in Russia's Pale of Jewish Settlement. Flora Marcus of Portland remembers that in the Russian town of her childhood, "We all lived in one room; the cow even had better accommodations than we did." Courtesy, YIVO Institute for Jewish Research (YIVO).

The government produced and distributed anti-Semitic tracts, including the infamous forgery, *The Protocols of the Elders of Zion*, which was concocted by a Russian secret police official. The May Laws were passed in 1882, restricting movement even within the Pale and leading to the expulsion of Jews from many areas; in 1891, twenty-two thousand Jews in chains were led from Moscow and St. Petersburg to the Pale.

Emigration to America

In the years that followed the May Laws, life in Eastern Europe became intolerable. One third of the Jews left in search of the *Goldeneh Medina* (the golden land), America. Whole families left. But the routes from Russia were treacherous, and often required illegal border crossings into Austro-Hungary and then on to Vienna or Berlin and finally German or Dutch port cities. Jewish families often traveled long distances on foot, stretching what little money they had to cover both food and transportation. In Hamburg, Bremen and Rotterdam, thousands tried to find passage to America, standing

Immigrants on the Atlantic liner *S.S. Patricia*, about 1906. Courtesy, LC.

Between 1881 and 1910, 1.5 million Jews emigrated from Eastern Europe—over a million from Russia (including Congress Poland), 280,000 from Austro-Hungary and 67,000 from Rumania. Upwards of a million more would come by 1924, when immigration to America was severely restricted. Non-Jews were also part of the swollen tides of immigration, but while the general population of the United States increased 112 percent between 1881 and 1920, the Jewish population increased 1,300 percent. Before 1881, a few of the early Jewish settlers had come from Posen in German Poland and other Eastern origins. But by 1928, 3 million of the 4.2 million Jews living in the United States had come from Eastern Europe. In Oregon the story was the same: the 868 Jews counted in 1877 had swelled to 9,767 in 1918, an increase of over 1,000 percent, caused almost entirely by the immigrant waves from Eastern Europe.

At first sight, it would appear that the immigrants from Eastern Europe were unlikely to adapt to America's ways. They were poor, hungry and ill-clothed, and many of them were illiterate. Those with the least *yihus* (status derived

in long lines by day and sheltering in parks, railway stations and wherever possible at night. The lucky ones who secured the precious piece of paper would then crowd into steerage below water level for two to four weeks of seasickness, little air and hundreds sharing a toilet before reaching that dreamed of moment when the Statue of Liberty was sighted and New York City came into view. But their anguish was not yet over, for the immigrants had to face the *Trernindzl* (the isle of tears), Ellis Island and the dreaded inspections—especially eye examinations for trachoma. If they did not pass—and in 1904, twenty thousand did not—they were sent back to Europe on the next boat. Harry Mesher was suffering from inflamed eyes before leaving the Ukraine. When he and his family arrived at Ellis Island, the doctor began to inspect his eyes, but Harry recalls:

> *I wouldn't let him. He turned away to talk to somebody and I remember distinctly my sister Bessie gave me a shove on to the next doctor who looked at my throat and that's how I made it. If he had seen my eyes they would have sent me back to Russia.*

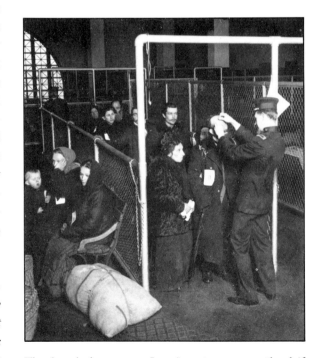

The dreaded eye exam. Immigrants were sent back if they were found to have eye problems. Courtesy, LC.

Hester Street was a ferment of activity. Most immigrants to Oregon who came from Eastern Europe spent their first weeks in America on New York's Lower East Side. Courtesy, LC.

from lineage, learning and wealth) tended to be the first to emigrate, while those from larger cities, with more education and resources, followed later. The Eastern European immigrants spoke little English, and brought with them the boisterous Yiddish polemic of the *shtetl* and *heder* (Jewish elementary school). Religious orthodoxy was central to their lives but foreign in America, particularly to the Jews already established here. Politically, many of the newcomers were inclined toward socialism and Jewish nationalism, ideas that might be seen as radical and dangerous in America.

But they came with passion and yearning and a surge of energy long suppressed by the tyrannies they had fled. They were eager to try on the new, to see what fruits secularism had to offer. Yet they understood well who they were as Jews, and exhibited none of the ambivalence of some of the German Jews who had preceded them. As the Yiddish song went: *Vos mir zenen zenen mir, aber iden zenen mir* (Whatever we may be, we may be, but Jews are what we are).

They came with dreams about what the modern world might be, but they also came with solid roots in a rich family and religous life and with the instinct—long nurtured in a hostile world—to fight and survive. This they did, and much more. In a single generation, the Eastern Europeans adapted, obtained education and became an important part of every community they settled in, reaching prominence in virtually all walks of life. America offered the opportunity; the Jews from Eastern

Market day in Krzemieniec, one of the oldest towns in Eastern Poland and close to Chartoriysk, the town from which the Director, Schnitzer and Rosenfeld families came to Portland. Courtesy, YIVO.

such as the Directors, Schnitzers and Rosenfelds, who had all arrived from the town of Chartoriysk and surrounding *shtetls* near the everchanging border between Poland and Russia, had already settled in Portland.

Another group, including the Menashes, Policars, Hassons, Babanis, Benvenistes, Russos and others—Sephardic Jews descended from the Jews of Spain—came from Marmora in Turkey and the Isle of Rhodes, where their families had settled after escaping the Spanish Inquisition centuries earlier. Toward the end of the nineteenth century, the decline of the Ottoman Empire and military conscription resulting from Turkish wars prompted many Jews to seek new lives in the West. A large Sephardic community settled in Seattle, while a smaller contingent came to Portland.

Inspired by the *Am Olam* movement in

Europe had the burning desire, inner resources and persistence to make the most of it. But it was not always easy.

Many immigrants spent their first weeks in America in the ferment of New York's Lower East Side. Life was both confusing and intoxicating to these new arrivals, who found their Old World rabbinic orthodoxy, Yiddish culture and secular ideologies confronted with the potent mixture of a new language and values. For Jewish immigrants, the Lower East Side had the strangeness of a new country and yet the familiarity of a teeming Old World *shtetl*. But while New York remained the center of Jewish life in America, many sought their destiny elsewhere.

Arrival in Oregon

Most Eastern European immigrants destined for Oregon stopped on the Lower East Side before traveling by train across the country to Portland. Others, however, came more directly because relatives or families from their villages,

Uncle Fuchs (also called "Vetter Fox") was the first member of the Director, Schnitzer and Rosenfeld families to arrive in Oregon. He helped to bring over many family members. Courtesy, JHSO.

The Central Square (the *Calle Ancha*) of the Jewish Quarter in Rhodes. Courtesy, Diana Golden.

Odessa and Rabbi Joseph Krauskopf's Natural Farm School in Pennsylvania, both of which believed in the importance of returning to the land as an essential part of Jewish renewal, some families came to Portland only after trying their hand at farming for a period. Joseph Nu-

delman, for example, emigrated from Odessa and organized farm colonies in Canada and near Settlement Wechsler, in North Dakota, before coming to Portland in 1892. The Brombergs, Lautersteins and Calofs also arrived from North Dakota. Leon Swett came to America from Odessa with the *Am Olam* group, which started a utopian agricultural commune in Douglas County, Oregon, known as New Odessa. But since Leon had a young family, with four children, he decided instead to farm near Buxton in Washington County with his sons Zachary and Isaac. Zachary later became grand president of District No. 4 of B'nai B'rith, and Isaac graduated from law school in Portland in 1896 and became an influential Zionist and lawyer for the underprivileged.

Often families were reunited in Portland through the work of the Industrial Removal Office (IRO), set up in New York in 1900 by the Baron de Hirsch Fund to disperse Jewish immigrants throughout the country. Nationwide depressions in the 1890s and in 1907 had caused widespread unemployment and resentment of immigrants competing for jobs. To ease these tensions, the IRO began to relocate Jews out of

In 1883, Joseph Nudelman and other families from Odessa, Russia, tried to establish a farm colony in North Dakota near Settlement Wechsler. Severe winters and only one good crop in nine years forced the Nudelmans to leave in 1892. They settled in Portland, as did the Brombergs, Lautersteins and Calofs. Courtesy, Eugene Nudelman, Sr.

The Nudelman family house in Wellington, Nevada, (Joseph and Fanny Nudelman at end of porch) in 1895. Joseph tried founding another rural colony in Nevada but finally returned to Portland permanently in 1902. Courtesy, Eugene Nudelman, Sr.

New York and other overpopulated Eastern cities. Over seventy thousand persons were sent to fifteen hundred communities between 1901 and 1917. Eight hundred and fifty-eight of them settled in Portland.

Ben Selling and Sig Sichel were the volunteer IRO representatives in Portland. Based on urgency of need, availability of jobs and ability to help repay the loans, Selling and Sichel recommended who should receive assistance from New York's central office. The IRO paid the cost of transporting unemployed workers if a job was waiting for them, but families were asked to contribute to the cost of bringing relatives. The Hebrew Benevolent Association, whose funds were also administered by Ben Selling, helped provide transportation. Selling nearly always recommended reuniting families. Records indicate for instance that an eighteen-year-old widow from Kishinev was brought to live with her grandmother, Zlata Nudelman, who ran a boarding house on Sheridan Street, and that sixteen-year-old Annie Weiss was brought from Philadelphia to join her mother,

Freda, who was able to contribute a small part of her railway fare.

When Jewish immigrants came to Portland, they usually settled in South Portland on the west side of the Willamette River, between the river and Fifth Avenue and between Harrison and Curry streets. Housing was cheap there, and new immigrants sharing a common history and culture were able to live together for mutual support, walking to *shul* and the kosher stores that dotted the neighborhood. In Portland, Eastern European Jews created anew the family and communal setting that had been so important and familiar to them in the old country. With resilience and ingenuity, they created a vibrant culture in South Portland. Warm, intimate and full of life, it retained its vitality for more than half a century. When they initially came to Portland, though, as happened in New York and other cities and towns across the country, the new arrivals caused shock and consternation among the established German Jews, a reaction which was more than reciprocated by the Eastern Europeans.

Discord Between German and Eastern European Jews

Jews arrived in Portland from Eastern Europe carrying their worldly possessions in gunnysacks and old valises. The men were swarthy and often bearded, the women dressed in the old ways. They were frightened and poor but strangely defiant and proud. The resident, decorum-loving German Jews cringed at their sheer numbers and their "backwardness" and orthodoxy. They wondered whether the Eastern Europeans could ever become Americans and whether the success they had fought so hard to achieve would be undermined and tarnished by these new arrivals. To the Germans, they appeared "clannish" and as the immigrants crowded into South Portland, it acquired the feel of a European ghetto.

The German Jews worried that the new immigrants would never want to assimilate, and found their manners noisy, assertive, feisty and argumentative, reflecting the tone of their Yiddish theater which was filled with melodramatic passion, agony and wild laughter. German Jews, who conducted their business with a handshake, their honor being their word, felt that good taste and culture were embodied in music by Brahms and Beethoven, not the Eastern Europeans' garish entertainments. Furthermore, they could not even understand the language the immigrants spoke.

But perhaps worst were the political ideas some had brought—socialism, anarchism, Zionism—which German Jews considered upsetting and dangerous. German pioneers had learned to play "the game" politically in America. They believed that if the Eastern Europeans adapted quickly to democratic and American ways, they too could be successful. But they feared that the immigrants' Zionism would undermine everything, creating dual loyalties and bringing into question their desire to be full Americans. In short, the newcomers were embarrassing, and the established Germans were afraid that gentiles might lump them together

and withdraw their camaraderie and support. Their goal was to stay clear of the new Jews and, at the same time, to provide charity and to Americanize them as soon as they could—if that were possible.

The newly arrived Eastern Europeans were, on the other hand, shocked and dismayed by the assimilated ways of the German Jews, who seemed *goyish* to them. The immigrants were astonished at the Reform accommodations of Beth Israel, whose Americanized ritual appeared to be a betrayal of Judaism. Even Ahavai Sholom did not seem appropriately Jewish. It would be better to give up religion entirely, the immigrants believed, than water it down to look like Christianity. The established Jews did not appear to be proud to be Jews; they seemed instead to be Americans or Oregonians or businessmen or anything before they were Jews.

Eastern Europeans found the German Jews conservative, stodgy, pompous and always ready with advice. It appeared that the German Jews wanted to help them—*tsedakah* or righteousness, the duty to help, required it—but the Eastern Europeans suspected that they were more concerned about how they appeared in the eyes of the gentiles than in the eyes of God. Even the IRO and the Hebrew Benevolent Association, which did provide help, were perceived as paternalistic by the recent immigrants, who felt they had to prove themselves to get assistance. The immigrants were determined that they would not simply adopt the models set out for them by German Jews, but would forge their new lives in their own way.

This conflict was extreme in New York and a number of other large cities, but in Portland it was much softened by the sensitivity and commitment of several extraordinary Jews: Ben Selling and Ida Loewenberg, second generation pioneers who had grown up in Portland; and Stephen Wise, the young rabbi who came to Beth Israel from New York in 1900.

9

Three Exceptional Individuals

Ben Selling, Beloved Philanthropist

Ben Selling was a German Jew born of pioneer parents in San Francisco in 1852. At ten he was brought to Portland, where his father, Philip Selling, ran a general merchandise store at First

Ben Selling's clothing store at Fourth Avenue and Morrison Street is decked out for an Elks convention in Portland, 1912. Courtesy, UO (Angelus Collection).

Avenue and Yamhill Street. After studying at Beth Israel's Religious School, Ben attended the Portland Academy, but did not graduate because he was needed in his father's store, where he clerked for some years. In 1881, he launched his own enterprise, a wholesale boot and shoe business with F. Akin and H. Dosch that was called Akin, Selling & Company. He was later involved in the Moyer Clothing Company, and owned his own clothing store, "Ben Selling, Clothier," at Fourth and Morrison.

Although these businesses thrived, Ben Selling was different from most other successful German Jewish businessmen. What set him apart was his profound desire to help others, which he practiced on many occasions, not with a superior sense of noblesse oblige, but with simplicity and caring. He was a rare individual. Always the person called upon to raise funds when need arose or tragedy struck, Selling always responded. His solicitations were seldom denied, since he was the first to give generously.

Selling carried himself modestly despite his political and financial success and seemed to spend nearly all his time organizing charitable efforts. One historian notes that during the First World War, Selling bought a large number of Liberty Bonds, but "wore the same business suit for three years." Julius Nodel, rabbi of Beth Israel from 1950 to 1959, describes in his valuable book *The Ties Between* a "steady stream of indigent students, bankrupt businessmen, itinerant beggars . . . Old World rabbis and numerous others [who] found their way into his cluttered little office which consisted of only a desk

Ben Selling breaking ground for the Sephardic synagogue, Ahavath Achim in 1930. Selling, the preeminent Jewish philanthropist of his day, was particularly beloved by the Sephardic community. Courtesy, JHSO.

and an extra chair tucked away in a tiny corner of the balcony of his store."

Eastern European Jews responded to him, even loved him. It was Selling's personal qualities that enabled him to provide a vital bridge between the old and the new Jewish communities. His greatest efforts were directed toward relieving Jewish suffering in Eastern Europe. Under Selling's leadership, Portland raised more per capita for survivors of the Kishinev pogrom than any other city in the country. During the First World War, a national circular announced that Ben Selling was one of six men in the United States willing to match 10 percent of what their entire state would give to assist Jewish war sufferers.

Selling also raised $10,000 for Chinese flood victims, $4,000 for Japanese famine aid and $100,000 for Armenian relief. To help the war effort he personally bought $400,000 in War Bonds, reselling them to people of modest means for $1 cash and $1 a week. He was always a supporter of Neighborhood House, South Portland's settlement house, founded by the Portland Chapter of the National Council of Jewish Women. For twenty years he was the president and moving force behind the Hebrew Benevolent Association, and he assisted the Jewish Relief Society, B'nai B'rith and a number of other community and national organizations. His energy for organizing benevolent efforts seemed boundless; his son, Dr. Laurence Selling, said that, "Giving was his hobby and his passion."

EVERYBODY KNOWS WHERE BEN SELLING STANDS.

A cartoon from the *Oregonian*, March 12, 1912, during Ben Selling's successful primary campaign against incumbent United States Senator Jonathan Bourne, Jr. Although Selling lost the general election by a narrow margin, he was a widely respected, progressive public figure in Oregon who held many important posts during his life. Courtesy, OHS.

Although much of Selling's charitable effort was anonymous, he was known to have staked a number of individuals, many from Eastern Europe, to enough funds to start a business, and once said that he was proud to have launched a number of his competitors. He was particularly concerned with assisting the unemployed, and in the depressions of 1893 and 1907 established the Working Men's Club, located at 271 Front Avenue, which served over 450,000 meals for five cents apiece. When asked why he had founded the Club, which by 1914 was serving 800 meals a day, Selling wryly replied:

I did it to save money. Last year I must have wasted three or four hundred dollars because I didn't go at the thing right. A man would ask me for the price of a meal, and I'd give him twenty or twenty-five cents. There was no place where he could get a decent meal for less. Now I can give him a ticket to the Working Men's Club and he can not only get a meal but a place to sit around and smoke. Instead of costing me a quarter, it costs me a nickel, and I can feed five men for what it used to cost me to feed one.

Ben Selling was also a well-respected Republican who served as both the president of the Oregon Senate and speaker of the Oregon House of Representatives during separate tenures in each body. He was a charter member of the Portland Dock Commission, on which he served ten years. In 1912, he defeated incumbent Senator Jonathan Bourne, Jr., in the Republican primary for the United States Senate, but lost the general election by several hundred votes to populist Democrat Harry Lane, former mayor of Portland.

Though a very successful public official and businessman, Ben Selling has been primarily remembered for his extraordinary generosity. His spirit of giving had a profound effect on healing the rift between Portland's well-established German Jews and the wave of new immigrants. Kimbark MacColl wrote of Ben Selling that, "For a quarter of a century before his death in 1931, [he was] the outstanding Jewish leader in Portland." When he died on January 15, 1931, both houses of the state legislature adjourned immediately, and flags throughout the city were flown at half-mast.

Ida Loewenberg and the Early Years of the Council of Jewish Women

Ida Loewenberg and an early group of remarkable Jewish women began to alter the long-established patterns of patriarchical domination toward the end of the nineteenth century.

They founded both the Portland Chapter of the National Council of Jewish Women and Neighborhood House, the community center so vital to immigrant life in South Portland.

Ida Loewenberg was born in Portland on June 12, 1872, the oldest of four children whose father, Julius Loewenberg, came from Posen in Polish Prussia and whose mother, Bertha Kuhn, came from Bavaria. Arriving in New York at the age of fourteen, Julius Loewenberg came to Oregon several years later and participated in various merchandising and speculative pursuits, including the running of pack trains to the mining camps in Idaho. After marrying in San Francisco in 1871 and settling permanently in Portland, he entered the hardware business, then became involved in insurance and banking as the founder of the Northwest Fire and Marine Insurance Company and the president of the Merchants National Bank.

Ida was born in the Loewenberg home at Fourth Avenue and Stark Street, and moved with the family in 1880 to a fashionable West Park Street address. After schooling at St. Helens Hall, a private Episcopal school, she spent a year with the entire family in Hamburg in 1891-92, where she studied piano while Julius' dream house was being built just below Washington Park. The house, a copy of a Prussian castle that he remembered from boyhood, was outfitted with marble baths and sinks and the finest furnishings from Europe, including the concert Steinway on which Ida had practiced in Hamburg. But with the depression of 1897, Julius became financially overextended, and upon his death in 1899 the family had to move out of the great house and into a hotel.

Only one Loewenberg offspring, Rose, married; Ida, Zerlina and Sydney lived together with their mother until her death in 1927, and the sisters then kept house for Sydney. Since they had to support themselves after their father's death, Ida and Zerlina were two of the first Jewish women of pioneer parents to seek professional training. Ida studied at the School of Social Work in New York, and Zerlina, at the library school run by the Library Association of Portland. For many years Zerlina was much-

loved as the librarian at the South Portland Branch of the public library. In 1912, Ida became the headworker (executive director) at Neighborhood House, where she remained the guiding force for thirty-three years until her retirement on January 1, 1945.

The Portland Chapter of the National Council of Jewish Women was founded in 1896, just three years after the national organization was begun in Chicago by Hannah Solomon and other women who were dissatisfied with their subordinate role in Jewish education and other activities. The Portland Chapter was organized at a public meeting held at Temple Beth Israel and attended by thirty-six women of German Jewish origin, with Mrs. Ben Selling elected temporary chair. Mrs. Solomon Hirsch was elected the chapter's president at its first regular meeting held two weeks later. These early officers had also been leaders of the Ladies Hebrew Benevolent Society, but they were poised to move dramatically beyond the maternal roles they had occupied at the Benevolent Society.

Julius Loewenberg's thirty-two-room mansion, modeled on a Prussian castle remembered from his boyhood, was built in 1893 just below Washington Park. Courtesy, OHS.

Ida Loewenberg

Zerlina Loewenberg

In 1890, Ida and Zerlina Loewenberg were young women of eighteen and sixteen, respectively. In 1946, three years before Ida's death, they had had long careers of public service: Ida as Neighborhood House headworker for thirty-three years; Zerlina as South Portland's librarian. They are shown with their sister, Rose, and her daughter, "Laddie" Goodman Trachtenberg. Courtesy, JHSO.

The early years of the Council were devoted to self-education, Bible study and Jewish history as well as the musical entertainment common to upper-middle-class women of the day. Ida Loewenberg, a charter member, gave lectures on the "Romantic School of Music" and the plight of Captain Dreyfus, the cause célèbre which exposed anti-Semitism in France. Mrs. Max Leopold and Sadie American, national leaders of the Council, came to Portland to encourage the formation of a committee on philanthropy and "free schools" that would teach sewing, kitchen, garden, household and vocational skills.

The charitable orientation of men's organizations such as B'nai B'rith and the Hebrew Benevolent Association were informal and paternalistic in nature, and although beneficent, they depended on the altruism of individuals like Ben Selling and Sig Sichel. Historian William Toll, in his ground-breaking research on Jewish women, asserts that, "The women simply eclipsed the men in their understanding and organization of welfare, and they thereby gained a far larger civic role."* Young women in the rapidly growing organization, which numbered 84 members in 1897 and 233 by 1902, included Ida, Julia Swett, Blanche Blumauer, Mrs. Isaac Leeser Cohen and Salome Bernstein, the sister of David Solis-Cohen. They were anxious to take on larger causes and to provide professional help and education for the ever-increasing number of immigrants in South Portland. They were aware of the settlement work begun in Chicago and the East and, with the young Rabbi Stephen Wise from New York assuming the pulpit at Beth Israel, their initial planning gained momentum.

*See Chapter 2, "Jewish Women and Social Modernization 1870-1930" in William Toll's *The Making of an Ethnic Middle Class: Portland Jewry Over Four Generations*; Albany, State University of New York Press, 1982.

Wise, who would become the most socially active and progressive rabbi of his generation, rolled up his sleeves and went to work with the Council. He suggested study of the latest in reformist literature, Israel Zangwill's *Children of the Ghetto*, and began a religious school with volunteer teachers at the Council's request. In 1902, Wise presented a proposal suggesting that the Council form a "neighborhood guild" to coordinate the activities already begun with professional settlement work. From here, it was only a step to the founding of Neighborhood House in 1905.

Ida Loewenberg became the central figure at Neighborhood House, and with great energy and care she built its programs to serve the new Jewish community of South Portland. Her sister

Zerlina served a similar function in the South Portland branch library, stocking it with both Yiddish and English books and the latest copy of Jewish dailies and periodicals. The immigrants from Eastern Europe were hungry to learn, filling the available tables daily and nearly always carrying more reading home with them. Ida and Zerlina were very much admired in South Portland, and they were important in easing the transition into the strange new world of America for many bewildered residents of the immigrant district. The Council of Jewish Women took the leading role in the Jewish community in initiating civic action and in establishing Neighborhood House itself, which provided the context for Ida and so many others to work together for the well-being of South Portland.

Early presidents of the National Council of Jewish women, Portland Chapter, about 1910. From left: Mrs. L. Altman, Mrs. Ben Selling, Mrs. Alex Bernstein, Mrs. Julius Lippitt, Mrs. Rose Selling, Mrs. S. M. Blumauer, Mrs. Max Hirsch, Mrs. Isaac Swett. Courtesy, JHSO.

Rabbi Stephen Wise,
Passionate Reformer and Zionist

Rabbi Stephen Wise was the third major figure who helped to create understanding between Portland's German and Eastern European Jewish communities. Wise spent only six years in Portland as rabbi of Beth Israel before returning to New York, but in that short time he had a profound impact. His passion for justice and social reform involved him deeply with the problems of living and working conditions in South Portland and throughout the city. In addition, his leadership of the early Zionist movement—so unusual for a Reform rabbi—struck a strong, responsive chord among many Eastern European immigrants, for whom Zionism was already a basic aspiration.

Stephen Wise was born in Budapest, Hungary, in 1874, the grandson of the chief rabbi of Hungary, Joseph Hirsch Weisz, famed for both his Orthodox piety and political liberalism. Wise grew up in New York City, where his father was rabbi of Temple Rodeph Sholem. He studied at City College, Columbia and Oxford universities and received his ordination in Vienna. He was selected as rabbi of B'nai Jeshurun, the Madison Avenue synagogue, at age nineteen.

Six years later, in 1899, Beth Israel approached Wise after he had addressed a meeting in Portland during a tour of the Pacific Coast to raise funds for the fledgling Zionist movement. They were seeking a well-educated, younger rabbi from the East to revitalize the Temple. Wise accepted their offer of a five-year contract at $5,000 per year, a handsome sum in those days and more than twice as much as Wise's predecessor, Rabbi Jacob Bloch, was receiving. On September 7, 1900, when Stephen Wise was installed as rabbi, he delivered a sermon which startled and enthralled the crowded synagogue: "I have but one condition," he said of his new ministry, "I ask it as my right. You will and must allow it. This pulpit must be free. This pulpit must be free." Wise would speak his mind on every issue of importance whether anyone, including the congregation's board, ap-

Rabbi Stephen Wise was Beth Israel's dynamic young rabbi from 1900 to 1906. Courtesy, Jewish Publication Society and Dr. Carl Voss.

proved or not. His character and energy brought new vitality to Beth Israel.

After being installed as rabbi, Wise returned to New York briefly to marry Louise Waterman. Their two children, James and Justine, were born in Portland. Wise always characterized his six years in Oregon as "the happiest years of my life."

Along with David Solis-Cohen and Joseph Teal, Jr., Wise supported the Council of Jewish Women and the largely female-led Consumer League in their fight to outlaw child labor, prevent the legalization of gambling and support women's suffrage. To do so, the pulpit truly had to be free, because Wise and Solis-Cohen were sharply critical of Jews as well as others in the city's business elite who profited from gambling and prostitution. Wise recounts in his autobiography, *Challenging Years*, that the head of the gambling combine in Portland once approached the president of Beth Israel, Solomon

Hirsch, to seek his help in quieting the crusading rabbi. Hirsch replied, "I cannot and I would not try to."

Wise helped elect reform mayor Harry Lane and was asked to be part of his cabinet. Later, Wise was asked to run for the United States Senate as a Democrat. But he refused such offers as inconsistent with his rabbinate. He did, however, accept an unpaid appointment by the governor to the state's new Child Labor Commission in 1903.

A brilliant orator who gave innumerable sermons and lectures on both religious and social issues throughout the state, Wise was frequently asked to speak by Christian ministers, who, led by Unitarian minister Thomas Lamb Eliot, his close friend, were often allies in fighting for social causes. Wise developed strong interfaith relationships which he called upon when he sought help for the cause of Zionism, relationships that would endure long after Wise's tenure in Portland was over.

When Stephen Wise came to Portland, he was already a fervent Zionist. In 1897, he had helped found the Federation of American Zionists in New York and was chosen its honorary secretary; the following year, at twenty-four, he attended the Second Zionist Congress in Basle, where he became friends with Theodor Herzl, who appointed him American secretary of the World Zionist Movement.

Zionist dreams had been kindled during the dark days in Eastern Europe, and the first Jews to settle in Palestine in the late nineteenth century were from Russia. But Zionism was not generally acceptable among Reform Jews in America. B'nai B'rith went so far as to ban discussion of the subject for a period.

In Portland, however, the force of Stephen Wise's personality and zeal made the pulpit at Beth Israel the focal point for Zionist organization, and he carried with him many of the most influential Jews and non-Jews of the city. The Zionist Society of Portland was founded in 1901, with its officers coming from Beth Israel: Judge Otto Kraemer was president and Julius Meier, vice-president. David Solis-Cohen was among its directors and shared with Wise a passionate

commitment to Zionism. He also spoke often on the subject, expressing the view that Zionist aims were not only consistent with, but a fulfillment of American democratic ideals. Isaac Swett, Nehemiah Mosessohn and others of Eastern European origin shared these views and were instrumental in the early growth of Zionism in Portland. Ben Selling, Otto Kraemer and others in the established German community supported the new association, but more from traditional philanthropic impulses toward Jewish suffering in Eastern Europe and a shared sense of pioneer spirit than from political commitment to the cause.

Wise's influence extended to many Christians, who became supporters of Zionism out of sympathy for a devastated, homeless people and because biblical prophesy foretold that Jews would return to the Holy Land before the Messiah came again. A Mr. Campbell actually willed his estate to the Zionist Society in 1902.

Wise always supported Theodor Herzl—even when many fellow Zionists believed that he was impractical and dangerous. He recalls in his autobiography the last time he saw Herzl alive, in Vienna in April, 1904. Putting his arm around young Wise, Herzl said, "I shall not live to see the Jewish State. But you, Wise, are a young man. You will live to see the Jewish State." Wise went on to write:

I thank God that it was given to me to live till that glorious day of May 14, 1948, when out of the centuries of Jewish suffering and persecution, of prayer and hope and labor, the prophesy of Theodor Herzl was at last fulfilled.

Stephen Wise, who had labored so long to bring the state of Israel into existence, would, like Moses, never set foot there, since he was too frail to travel in 1948 and he died the following year.

In 1905, Wise was asked by Temple Emanu-El, New York's "cathedral synagogue" and the most prestigious in American Reform Judaism, to be its rabbi. Wise said that he would accept on the same condition that he had set at Beth

Rabbi Wise left Portland in 1906 and went on to become one of America's most renowned rabbis. In 1933, he addressed an anti-Nazi protest meeting in New York. Courtesy, Jewish Publication Society and Dr. Carl Voss.

a pulpit that is not free can never powerfully plead for truth and righteousness.

Wise rejected the offer of a lifetime contract at an unprecedented salary and founded instead the Free Synagogue in New York, devoted to absolute freedom of the pulpit, pews equally open to rich and poor, direct participation of the synagogue in community social activities, and a commitment to be "vitally, intensely, unequivocally Jewish." The Free Synagogue was also dedicated to fulfilling Israel's destiny. At first derided, within a few years the Free Synagogue grew into a large and influential congregation. In time, Wise became one of the preeminent rabbis in American Judaism and an adviser to presidents, but he always remained committed to the ideals he had fought for in Portland.

Beth Israel prospered under Wise's leadership. Many were drawn to the congregation by the force of Wise's vision and his fine sermons, and he was able to cancel the congregation's entire $30,000 debt by 1903. In fact, Wise was such a proficient fundraiser that Harry Gevurtz, a child when Wise was rabbi, but later president of Beth Israel twice, recalls:

The rabbi was a friend of my father and I remember when he came to my father's store to ask him for some funds for a needy cause. My father saw him, threw his hands up and said "Don't tell me what for, just how much."

Israel, that the pulpit be free. But Louis Marshall, chair of the hiring committee and one of America's most prominent Jews, refused on behalf of the board of trustees. Wise replied, "If that be true, there is nothing more to say." James Seligman, president of the Temple, Daniel Guggenheim and Jacob Schiff tried to coax Wise to change his mind. But Wise formally responded with his famous "Open Letter" to Marshall, which was widely quoted in the American press at the time:

The chief office of the minister, I take it, is not to represent the views of the congregation, but to proclaim the truth as he sees it. . . . How can a man be vital and independent and helpful, if he be tethered and muzzled? . . . A free pulpit will sometimes stumble into error;

Oregon was fortunate to have a man such as Stephen Wise, if only for six years. The Jewish community as a whole—established Germans and immigrant Eastern Europeans alike—were inspired by the ideals that he so fervently espoused: justice through social action and a homeland for the Jewish people. His farewell banquet was attended by a broad spectrum of the Jewish community, influential Christian leaders, the governor, two United States senators and the mayor of Portland. "In the six years of residence in Oregon," Wise wrote in his autobiography, "I had come to love the state and its people."

10

New Odessa

Nearly all Eastern European Jewish emigrants who made their way to Oregon settled in South Portland. However, in 1882, one unusual group of young Jewish idealists from Odessa founded a utopian community near Glendale in Southern Oregon. Nearly two thousand years of persecution and restriction had transformed Jews from tillers of their own land to dispossessed town and city dwellers. But in the oppressive Eastern Europe of the late nineteenth century, the dream of Jewish revitalization through a return to the land was born. In the vanguard was a group calling themselves *Am Olam*, the Eternal People, whose emblem was a plow and the Ten Commandments. They were socialists, dedicated to common property, shared work, brotherhood and harmony pursued in an isolated setting where they could live out their ideals free from the corrupting influences of society.

In 1881, a group of *Am Olam* members, nearly all in their late teens or early twenties, left Odessa for New York. In New York, still wearing their Russian student uniforms, they waited at *Am Olam* headquarters on Pell Street for promised help from Michael Heilprin, an author and scholar who sympathized with their movement. Henry Villard, a business associate of Heilprin and an Oregon railroad magnate, had recently taken over the bankrupt Oregon and California Railroad, and suggested to Heilprin that they establish their commune near the railroad's furthest extension, between Roseburg and Ashland. He also promised to arrange transport for the entire group at twenty dollars per person.

A scout was sent ahead who located 760 acres, 150 of them tillable, with two modest houses, for the sum of $4,800 with $2,000 down. Heilprin helped raise the money among New York Jews—a difficult task because there were not many who were sympathetic and had funds to spare. The first contingent of twenty-five crossed Panama by foot and wagon and then proceeded by coastal steamer to Portland. From Portland they traveled by train and again by foot to their new home.

They were a strange people, speaking Russian and wearing Old World clothes. They knew little about farming, but were generally accepted by neighbors curious about their Russian ways. These neighbors helped them plant their first crops and often attended commune dances and songfests. Several other Jews lived in the area, including Isador and Simon Caro, who had come north from Jacksonville, and Solomon Abraham, a local merchant who signed the articles of incorporation on behalf of New Odessa, the name chosen for the colony.

By the spring of 1883, the commune consisted of forty to fifty people; its president was Peter Fireman (age twenty); its secretary, Moses Frie (twenty-two); its treasurer, Abraham Headman (twenty-three). Married couples had private rooms; everyone else slept in one large space in the upstairs of one of the houses. The commune, largely vegetarian, raised nearly all its own food from its crops of wheat, oats, peas and beans and from a large community vegetable garden. The daily food budget was set at five cents per person to preserve limited funds and

Solomon Abraham, a Jewish merchant and right-of-way agent for the Oregon and California Railroad, founded Glendale, Oregon in 1883. Abraham named the site for his wife Julia (it was later changed to Glendale) and named the streets for his children and friends. He signed the articles of incorporation for the nearby colony of New Odessa. Courtesy, Douglas County Museum (DCM).

prevent extravagance. A visitor described the colony's fare as consisting of "bean soup and hard-baked biscuits of unbolted flour called after the name of that wretched dyspeptic, Graham." Funds were raised for essentials and farm payments by cutting timber—four thousand cords of wood in the first two years—for ties and fuel for the Oregon and California Railroad.

The early years at New Odessa were austere but harmonious. An itinerant farm worker who spent a year at New Odessa reported that there was "never quarrelling, [they were] constantly cheerful, permeated with idealism, and 'labored to save the world.'" Men and women shared tasks equally. When work was completed, there was often music, singing and dancing in the community hall they had constructed.

The pride and joy of the colony, though, was its fine little library of philosophical works,

and perhaps its favorite entertainment was discussion and debate. Many years later, an observer reported having witnessed a heated philosophical discussion that flared up in the kitchen and caused the "oatmeal to burn to a crisp."

One wedding was held at New Odessa. Eighteen-year-old Annuta Glantz married Selig Rosenbluth amid much warmth and merriment, described by a reporter for the *Overland Monthly* of December, 1885:

Yesterday was Sunday, and there was a marriage in the community.... There was an immediate bustle and hurry, and every man in the community tried to find the suit of clothes in which he left Russia. Two or three young girls went into the woods for flowers, and the rafters of the hall, up stairs and down, were soon hung with the flowering branches of the tulip tree.... To Annuta the wild flowers were brought, and her fingers wove them into wreaths for the bride and bouquets for the table. She was attired in a close-fitting black dress without even a ribbon as ornament.

The brothers and sisters had been gathered a few moments on the benches in the dining room, when the bridegroom and bride entered. Both parties were young, perhaps twenty-two; the young man well educated, well read in philosophic and romantic literature, and rather good looking. The bride is noted for her kind disposition.

On the arrival of the bridal party, which included the mother and sisters of the bride, a little ceremony took place, in which the young man and woman were understood to unite themselves in the conjugal relation. After this, both the groom and bride were embraced by their associates, the kissing being entirely different from the kissing done on similar occasions by English or Americans. Each in turn took the groom and bride in his or her arms; the lips were pressed together again and again with a long, deep, and almost solemn emotion.

At quite an early hour, the new couple retired from the scene to the shanty assigned them close by the hall.

Two of the three children born in the colony were theirs.

Sometime after New Odessa was founded, its members invited an older, charismatic non-Jewish émigré from Russia to join the commune. They had met William Frey, also known as Vladimir Konstantinovich Geins, previously and were deeply impressed by him. The son of a Russian general, Frey was an astronomer by training, and a sincere but fanatic seeker who, when he came to New Odessa with his wife and her sister, was taken with Auguste Compte's "Religion of Humanity." Frey was a powerful figure, teaching his intensely held views as well as mathematics.

In 1884, Frey drafted "An Agreement" that was signed by all New Odessa members and dedicated the group to "altruism, self-perfection, common property and moral cooperation." But the commune began to polarize around Frey, on the one hand, and Paul Kaplan, an original member and political radical who resented Frey's continual proselytizing, on the other. Several other commune members were also unhappy because Jewish religious traditions were not being observed. As a result, the following year, Frey left with fifteen followers for London, the center of positivist thought espoused by his hero Compte. The leave-taking was on friendly terms, and a former colonist recalls the parting was so difficult that "tears fell like rain."

In 1885, a fire destroyed the colony's much-treasured library and part of the community building. Idealism had also begun to wear thin. The colonists, young and vital, felt a growing need to return to the world, to learning and careers, and the hope of marriage. They began to leave in small groups, eight to set up a communal laundry on Essex Street in New York. Of the others who could be traced, three became doctors; two, lawyers; two, druggists; one, a dentist; another an engineer; still another a chemist; and one a teacher. Paul Kaplan became a doctor among the poor in New York City, working with Felix Adler and Lillian Wald in the progressive social work movement, and serving as secretary to the Russian Revolutionary Party in America. Peter Fireman, the last-known survivor of New Odessa, died at ninety-four without heirs. He had become a chemist and a millionaire from his discoveries. In 1887, the commune was declared bankrupt, and in February, 1888, the land was foreclosed and returned to its original owners.

Like other utopian communities of the 1880s—Brook Farm and Oneida in the East, the Aurora Colony in Oregon, and other brief attempts to form Jewish communes in Louisiana, the Dakotas, Colorado and Nevada—New Odessa did not last. But it was a courageous experiment in which young Jews attempted (and succeeded for some time) to live deeply held beliefs in a pioneer setting. It may also be seen as an early example of the *kibbutzim* that would one day be founded in Israel by young people of similar background and spirit. As one of the commune's original members plaintively reminisced, "What began as an experiment, ended as an experience."

Robert Rosenbluth, the son of Selig Rosenbluth and Annuta Glantz, was the first child to be born at New Odessa. During a visit with his wife in 1956, he points out the site of New Odessa near Glendale, Oregon. Courtesy, DCM.

11

The Community of Old South Portland

Family Life

New Odessa had been an exciting but unusual experiment, for nearly all Jews arriving from Eastern Europe settled in South Portland at the edge of the central city. There were few Jews living in South Portland before the influx of immigrants after the turn of the century, but within twenty years, the Jewish population of the area had mushroomed to over six thousand people.

By the 1920s, a vibrant Jewish culture had developed, although many Italian families and a scattering of others from diverse ethnic backgrounds shared the immigrant district in relative harmony. The shock of being uprooted from the intimate, communal Jewish life of Eastern European *shtetls* and towns was softened by

Family and friends were always close by in old South Portland. Here, the Herman and Mishka Horenstein family celebrate a holiday. Courtesy, JHSO.

Immediate family at the home of Joseph and Fanny Nudelman, 1916. Courtesy, Eugene Nudelman, Sr.

the close-knit, warm, family-centered neighborhood that Jews created in South Portland. Everything they needed was close by. Relatives and friends lived within a few blocks. *Shul*—of which there were six in South Portland at one time—was a short walk away. Kosher shops dotted the neighborhood, particularly along First Avenue, where most shopping was done, especially before *Shabbes.*

Those who lived in South Portland speak eloquently of life in their old neighborhood. Augusta "Gussie" Kirshner Reinhardt recalls the intimacy:

People chose to live close to each other and it was a wonderful way to live, really, very much as we think of a shtetl because in this small area, anything that anybody needed for good living was available within walking distance. There was the library within a few blocks, there was the synagogue within a few blocks, there were the grocery stores, the

The Blackman family with Molly and young Irv Rotenberg on the stoop of their home on First Avenue next to Mosler's Bakery. Courtesy, JHSO.

laundry, the hospital, the community center, you name it and we had it in our so-called ghetto. It was sweet living and really everybody helped each other.

And Frieda Gass Cohen:

When we grew up in South Portland, that area housed practically every Orthodox Jewish person in the city. There were very few who lived anyplace else. It was really a teeming place for Jews and what an exciting place! They brought up their children there; they educated them; they sent them to Hebrew school.... The children grew up in the neighborhood and more or less stayed in the neighborhood all the time they were growing up. All of my lifelong associations from then until now were made right there. Those people that were my friends at that time, remain my friends now [1975].

What I liked most about my neighborhood was the fact that it was an ethnically Jewish group.... You were at home in ten houses on the block. You could knock on any door or you would not even have to knock;

you could just open the door and walk into so many homes. Everyone in the neighborhood looked out for you. You could send your child out to play and it couldn't get hurt or mistreated because someone else's mother was always looking out to see that nobody hurt it. Everybody knew who you were. We were close to our neighbors.

Yes, our house was literally very close to that of our neighbors. Our windows were right next door to those of Abraham Rosencrantz's. That was all right because he was the chazzan of the Sixth Street Synagogue [Neveh Zedek] and he had a most beautiful voice. In the summer we would open our windows and he would open his windows and we could hear him practice davening. It was a pleasure.

Large families were often crowded into the simple, already aging wooden houses and apartments of the area. Jobs were difficult to come by and were part of the confusing "American" world outside the district, but there were always one's family and friends, the synagogue, and the sense of mutual caring that pervaded the neighborhood and nurtured its inhabitants. Leon Feldstein, whose family came from Rumania in 1907, remembers the early gatherings:

My parents' home was a refuge of happiness for the Rumanian Jewish colony here in Portland. My mother used to play the piano and the guitar. We would sing and we would dance and many times, I remember so vividly, we danced the horah.... It was danced right in our house.... We Rumanian Jews would get together and have what we would call a "mameliga party." A mameliga party consisted of a huge tub of mameliga. Mameliga is corn meal—a hardened corn meal mush.

When my parents had first come to Portland they became acquainted with other Jews who also had come from Rumania.... They understood each other and they talked about the customs of the country in which they had lived. We were all very, very poor. When our family had a party, mama would make a huge vat of mameliga, putting into it, after it

Life in South Portland recreated the closeness and intimacy of the *shtetls* of Eastern Europe. Courtesy, OHS.

Mrs. Bertha Feldstein (to the right) with her mother, Mrs. Rachel Korn, about 1915. They held *mameliga* parties for Rumanian Jews in the early days of South Portland. Courtesy, JHSO.

Jewish. I went to lectures every night. It was wonderful. But here to get a job you had to work on Shabbes; I couldn't work on Shabbes. On Shabbes I had to go to shul. All my life I did and I wouldn't give it up. . . . When I came here it was a hardship. You had to be strong like the Bible says or you could go meshuga.

The sense of family and neighborhood warmth seemed to reach its fullest with celebration of the Sabbath. The smells of *Shabbes* and the neighborhood on Saturday night afterward pervaded Mollie Blumenthal's youth:

Come Shabbes, come Saturday, Mrs. Gurian and her sister, Esther, would come in the house. When they smelled our bagels they would come across the street. Mother would have fresh-baked cookies or fresh-baked bagels, and they would sit in their Shabbes clothes. I can remember this; I can remember the smell; I can remember the odor of Shabbes. You know, the chicken soup and the freshly-baked bread and the gefilte fish, and the house, a very humble home, but immaculate. And these are my recollections; of all these people at our house, always at Blumy's. . . .

We didn't come from an affluent family; I would say we came from a poor family, but you know, we didn't think we were poor. We thought this was our way of life.

And I can remember Saturday nights in South Portland, especially in the summertime, of course. People would come out and they would sit on the stoops of different stores and they would rubberneck people coming down to South Portland to buy kosher stuff. And the butcher shops would open Saturday nights you know. . . . People would be sitting out on their porches, talking to others across the way. If it was a very hot night, somebody would buy the ice cream, somebody would buy the cantaloupes, and they would make cantaloupe a la mode, or they would have watermelon, all in the neighborhood. I love South Portland. It bred an awful lot of wonderful people.

was cooked, a huge amount of gravy, the few pieces of meat which they could afford to buy, and lots of onion and garlic. That was a national Rumanian dish.

But life could also be lonely and difficult, as it was for Israel Boxer, who came from Odessa and then New York, where he had been immersed in Yiddish culture:

In 1907, we came to Portland. I had an older brother, Abe Boxer, who was in the junk business and he wrote to us that Portland was the Goldeneh Medina, that gold grows here on the trees. It was a wild country. I didn't know who to talk to. I cried here for two years; I cried; I couldn't live. No Jewish words you could talk like New York where the Jewish boys from Odessa gathered. We used to sing Jewish songs, Russian songs, recited poetry in

A strong nostalgia lingers for many of those who lived in old South Portland. There, Eastern European Jews found a way to recapture the closeness, vitality and Jewishness of the village life left behind in Europe and yet make their way in the new, strange world of America. The retention of Jewish religious practice and ritual, a sense of tradition and roots and, perhaps above all, family unity, were essential as a base from which to grow. South Portland's Jews would not give up these essential aspects of their Jewish identity, and in that sense resisted "Americanization." But they also had a strong desire to share the benefits so apparent in their new world. Eastern European Jews brought with them the resources of careful saving and sharing necessary to forge a better life. For centuries they had disciplined themselves in self-denial, so it came naturally to parents to sacrifice in order that their children might have better lives than they. The family was typically a strong, stable unit, and each member was expected to contribute to its well-being.

Shopping

The South Portland community was nearly self-sufficient. Aside from jobs which sometimes took people outside, nearly everything essential to life was available within its borders. Within a few blocks were the synagogues, the *mikvah*, public and Hebrew schools, the Neighborhood House with its myriad activities, and many small shops that served the community.

The stores are remembered fondly by many people who grew up in old South Portland. An important part of Jewish life centered in and around the neighborhood shops along First Avenue. There was an air of excitement as shoppers socialized or exchanged the latest news with shopkeepers or friends. The shops were crowded on Thursday and Friday, because Sabbath meals had to be prepared and everything made ready for the Sabbath, when cooking and other work were not allowed. When sundown came on Saturday and the Sabbath was over, most of the neighborhood could be found strolling along First Avenue, just enjoying themselves or shopping for the coming week.

Try to imagine the sounds, the smells, the motion along First Avenue for the several blocks between Grant and Meade streets. Perhaps most former South Portland residents would best remember Mrs. Levine's Fish Market (she was sometimes called Mrs. Levin), which initially was located near First and Sheridan and then a block north at First and Caruthers. Listen! Can you hear Mrs. Levine?

I opened a fish market. See, so the ladies they went to bed early, they knock at my door, five o'clock in the morning. They wake me up to open the store and I have to do that. Then in the night I had to deliver my orders. My daughter Esther was a young girl and my boy also helped. This was my life.... So I had this fish market and two big tanks.... I got a little net and I took out a carp and these ladies told me "she said the head is too big." I took another one, she said "the stomach is too big," so I went, and I was the fish lady.... I had to attend one year eight hundred pounds carp, to sell myself and cut salmon, halibut, black cod, white fish.

And Jack Hecht recalls that, as a boy:

A joy in my life was always going to Mrs. Levine's Fish Market, where the fish were alive in a great big, huge tank, and standing looking down into this tank and seeing all these hundreds of fish swimming around, and they would catch one with a net, lay it on a piece of paper, and rap it on the head with a hammer and that's the fish you took home.

Mrs. Levine and her family lived in the back of the market. Her husband, Ephraim, was one of several *shochets* in the community who slaughtered cattle and chickens in the prescribed kosher manner. He worked across the street from the fish market, next to the small *shul*, Linath Hazedek, where he butchered chickens for five cents apiece. As Besse Harris remembers:

Dora Levine stands in front of her fish market on First Avenue with her daughter, Esther, about 1910. Courtesy, JHSO.

If we were fortunate enough, or rather unfortunate enough, to have to carry the chicken down to Mr. Levine to get it killed, that was another thing. I was really very frightened about carrying a live chicken, so mama very kindly would put it into a gunny sack for me and I would have to hold it out at least twelve inches from my body for fear that he might peck on me if it were any closer. Well, coming back was a much easier process as the chicken was dead already and there was never any fear of any problem. Mr. Levine was very nice. He always took our chickens and he blessed them and drew the jugular vein, but we had to bring them home to get them flicked. The flicking is pulling the feathers out. Well, we had a gas plate in the basement and mother would take ahold of the chicken with its legs in one hand and the neck

in the other and keep turning it and singeing it at the same time. It made it much easier to flick the chickens after they were singed and that's how we did our Friday chicken routine.

Live chickens, like Besse's, as well as fresh fruit, vegetables and other produce were often purchased not in a store but from a peddler's cart. The peddler would go from home to home or simply park mid-street, where he would hawk his wares to anyone within hearing.

The important intersection at First and Caruthers had Louis Leveton's drugstore on one corner for many years. When he died, Korsun's grocery moved into the same space. Across the street was the grocery run by Mrs. Maccoby, whose husband, Moses, taught at the Hebrew school. Next to it were the well-known Solomon Apartments, built by Jacob Solomon whose son Gus became a federal judge, and Dave Schneiderman's pool hall, often crowded with older boys and the neighborhood characters, including its foot patrolman, Mr. Nichols.

Mr. Mosler's bakery was also located on First near Caruthers, and he produced what many would swear were the best bagels they ever tasted. Two other fine bakeries competed for South Portland's business: the Star, run by William Rosumny and Hyman Rotenberg on Second between Arthur and Sheridan, across the street from Ruvensky's Soda Works, and Gordon's Bakery. Louis Rotenberg, Hyman's son, describes a short-lived merger of the bakeries in the late 1920s:

Harry Mosler bakes bread at his bakery on First Avenue near Caruthers. The Mosler Bakery was open for business until it was demolished by urban renewal in the late 1950s. Courtesy, JHSO.

They realized that three bakeries couldn't make it, so by all going together they felt, with less overhead, they could make it. Their temperaments clashed quickly. We had three guys who felt that they could run the whole thing and they just could not get along. I think the strongest of them was Mosler. I am sure the merger didn't last a year. Then it got back to three bakeries and very quickly Gordon disappeared from the picture. Then it was just two and there were always these two here until World War II. About that time my dad went out of the bakery business and then Mosler had it all to himself.

There were other colorful shops along First Avenue. Calistro and Halperin's delicatessen between Caruthers and Sheridan catered to both the Italian and Jewish trade, since its owners came from each ethnic group. Charlie Cottel's drugstore was a popular, non-Jewish store at First and Sherman, where one could get a shake or sundae at the soda fountain or have an eye exam or a bottle of pills made up. Dr. Labby's dentist office and Dr. Wolf's medical offices were upstairs. Simon Director, Isaac Friedman and Joseph Nudelman had kosher meat markets within a few blocks of each other along First Avenue. A little north, at First and Grant, stood Robison's dry goods store, which was really a mini-department store widely used by South Portlanders. It was Mrs. Robison's sons, Charles and Edward, who later donated significant funding to help establish the Robison Home, the Jewish community's modern care facility for the elderly.

The Star Bakery truck making deliveries in 1912 with Ben Medofsky sitting on the fender. Courtesy, JHSO.

There were also movie theaters along First. The most popular were the Gem, at Sheridan, and Berg's, at Grant. Admission was five cents a movie, and families flocked to the silent films, particularly on Saturday nights. Norman Kobin describes Berg's Theater:

They had a theater on First and Grant ... and lived in the Solomon Apartment building. One of their girls who was friendly with my sister, Lillian, was Minnie Berg, who everybody knows became the very well-known opera singer, Mona Pallay. You know it was the days of the silent movies. They had a bathroom, as I recall, up on the stage, so that whenever somebody had to go to the bathroom they would have to walk on the stage and sometimes it would obscure the pictures. In addition to that, they had an old matron ... who would be playing the piano all through the show. The First Avenue Theater was really something.

Some of the best preserved lore concerning any of South Portland's establishments involves Mr. Wolf's barber shop. Originally located across the street from Cottel's Drugs at First and Sherman, Wolf later moved his shop to the edge of Marquam Gulch, an area of the neighborhood itself steeped in legend. Moses "Scotty" Cohen recalls:

I'll never forget one day. There was a barber named Wolf and there was a wooden bridge which wasn't kept up very well which went across the Gulch. The barber shop was right next to the bridge. One day this darn wooden bridge sank down into the Gulch and Wolf's Barber Shop slid down with it. He had a customer in the chair and both of them went down, but neither one of them got hurt. I went down and saw it and there was quite a hole down there. It was sure funny.

Wolf, he'd take his time, he'd give these fellows haircuts and shaves, and he'd work all hours of the night. He'd go to work at eight in the morning and wouldn't be through until eleven or twelve at night. He always made

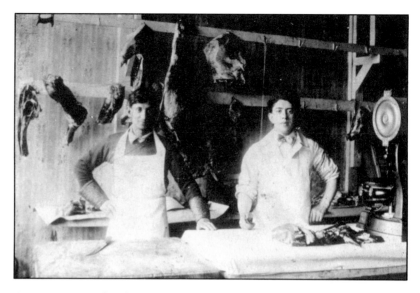

Simon Director (left) with a helper at his kosher meat market, located on First near the kosher meat markets of Joseph Nudelman and Isaac Friedman. Courtesy, JHSO.

Robison's dry goods store at First and Grant served the neighborhood as its mini-department store. Courtesy, JHSO.

appointments with people—many worked, you know; they couldn't get a haircut in the daytime—he'd wait for them until they got off work at night. He was a good barber. He always had a cigar in his mouth, even when he was shaving or giving a person a haircut—he always had a cigar in his mouth, but he never smoked it; he just chewed it.

A house perches precariously at the edge of Marquam Gulch. Wolf's Barber Shop slid into the Gulch while Wolf had a customer in the chair. Neither were hurt. Courtesy, JHSO.

The First Avenue cable car, shown in 1914, was one of the few connections between the immigrant community of South Portland and the rest of the city. Norwegian Olaf Krogstad (right) was for many years the cable car's conductor. Courtesy, JHSO.

In the early days of Jewish South Portland, the horses and wagons of the peddlers were housed in the Gulch, and each morning they could be seen streaming up to begin the day's rounds. Before the Gulch was filled (it is now SW Arthur Street), boys played baseball and other games in it, and stories are told of a hermit called Kasaboo who lived in a shack of cans and pieces of lumber at its bottom, of Umbrella Jimmy, and of Miss McGee, a woman who came out of the Gulch to preach along the streets each day. The Gulch was later used as a city dump for many years, and finally, in the 1930s, it was filled by WPA workers in order to create Duniway Park.

A Separate Community

Life in old South Portland was largely self-contained. People felt more comfortable in their own community with only minimal English and family customs shared by neighbors. The cable car ran from downtown along First Avenue into South Portland—and for many years before the First World War its conductor on the South Portland run was a friendly Norwegian named Olaf Krogstad. But few rode the cable car regularly except those who worked outside the neighborhood. Participation in city politics was minimal; South Portland had its own newspapers, and sometimes even referred to its informal leaders as "mayor."

But Eastern European immigrants also wanted to become "good" Americans. They took classes at Neighborhood House and Failing School, which enabled them to pass the tests necessary to obtain precious citizenship papers. They then began to vote in elections, and they voted regularly, considering it a treasured right often denied them in Europe. Many also followed national and international issues, particularly those related to the Zionist dream of a Jewish state in Palestine. The Jewish immigrants of South Portland were proud of their new home in America and their wonderful new life of freedom and hope.

The close-knit, warm, family-centered community of South Portland always included the old and the young. Courtesy, JHSO.

The Rosenberg grandparents, Abba and Toby

The Mesher grandparents, Benjamin and Dora

Jewish Population and Major Institutions in 1920

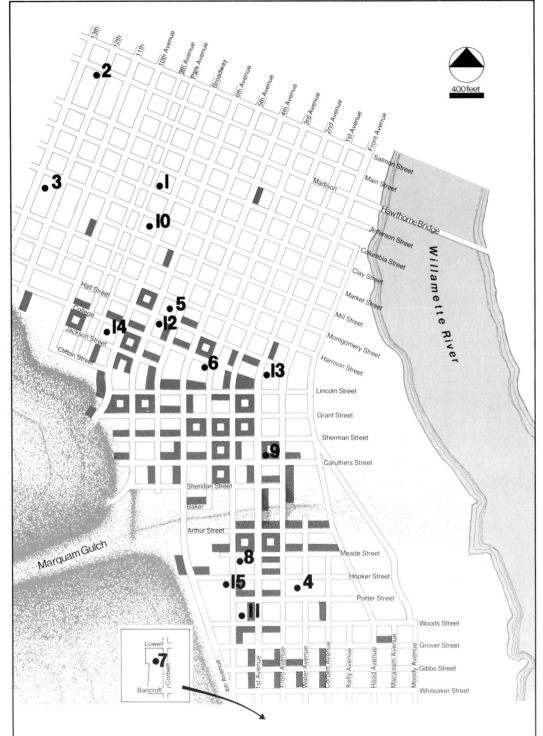

1. Ahavai Sholom

2. Beth Israel

3. B'nai B'rith Building

4. Failing School

5. High School of Commerce

6. Jewish Old Peoples Home

7. Jewish Shelter Home

8. Kesser Israel

9. Linath Hazedek

10. Lincoln High School

11. Neighborhood House

12. Neveh Zedek Talmud Torah

13. Shaarie Torah

14. Shattuck School

15. South Portland Library

Jewish Population (at least one family per side of block) ● Major Institutions

Some of the material for this map was derived from William Toll's *The Making of an Ethnic Middle Class: Portland Jewry Over Four Generations*, page 119.

12

The Synagogues

When the first Jews arrived from Eastern Europe, they found two synagogues in Portland: Beth Israel, which they came to call the *Deutschesha shul*, because it was virtually the exclusive domain of Reform Jews of German background; and Ahavai Sholom, a somewhat more conservative synagogue that the new arrivals called the *Polisha shul*, since it was started in 1869 by immigrants from Poland.

These synagogues were not appropriate for the primarily Orthodox Jews coming from Eastern Europe. They were seen as Americanized, since they had abandoned the basic ritual and practice that Eastern European Jews saw as central to Jewish identity. On the other hand, neither Beth Israel nor Ahavai Sholom was then interested in having these new immigrants as members.

The first synagogue in Portland to meet the needs of the Eastern European immigrants was Talmud Torah, established in 1893 at Third Avenue and Mill Street by Russian Jews from North Dakota. These first Russian immigrants were not as Orthodox as those who came later, so Talmud Torah was organized as a Conservative congregation. The congregation of Talmud Torah met in several rooms above stores downtown until late in the 1890s when twenty-five members contributed $4,500 to purchase the Brethren Church at SW Eleventh Avenue and Hall Street.

Then in 1900, a small group formed Portland's first more Orthodox congregation, Neveh Zedek, and held their services every day in a small store on First Avenue between Mill

Neveh Zedek Talmud Torah synagogue was built in 1911 after the congregations of Talmud Torah (founded 1893) and Neveh Zedek (founded 1900) merged. The new congregation was Conservative and usually referred to as Neveh Zedek. Courtesy, JHSO.

The choir at Neveh Zedek led by Cantor Abraham Rosencrantz (center) about 1915. Courtesy, JHSO.

and Montgomery. In 1902, at the invitation of Talmud Torah, Neveh Zedek merged with them at their synagogue to form Neveh Zedek Talmud Torah. But by 1905, the more Orthodox members were dissatisfied with the merger and decided to join those who were in the process of organizing Shaarie Torah, a strictly Orthodox place of worship. Neveh Zedek Talmud Torah thereafter remained a Conservative synagogue.

In September, 1911, Neveh Zedek Talmud Torah dedicated its handsome stone synagogue with its square central tower and beautiful stained glass windows. All of Portland's rabbis were there, as well as Ben Selling, David Solis-Cohen and other community leaders. Neveh Zedek Talmud Torah (later called just Neveh Zedek) existed for sixty-eight years, then merged with Portland's other major Conservative synagogue, Ahavai Sholom, to form Neveh Shalom in 1961.

The records of Shaarie Torah, the first Or-

thodox synagogue in the Northwest, date from 1902, when services for a small group of congregants were held in a hall at Second and Morrison. Later that year, services were moved to a small building at First and Hall. In 1905, as the congregation expanded under the leadership of its first president, Joseph Nudelman, it purchased a Presbyterian Church then located at Third and Washington, and moved it to the congregation's site at First and Hall. The building was a large wooden structure, shake covered, with a small cupola on its roof and tall windows of stained glass. Here Shaarie Torah grew into the preeminent Orthodox synagogue in old South Portland, known to everyone as the "First Street" *shul*.* With Mr. M. Medofsky, the father-in-law of the congregation's president,

*The older use of "street" rather than "avenue" is retained here because it is contained in a widely recognized proper name.

William Rosumny, as its *chazzan*, services were first held in its new building on Succoth in 1905. The First Street *shul* engaged a number of men who served as *chazzan* and several as rabbi until 1916, when Rabbi Joseph Faivusovitch became the synagogue's charismatic leader for the next thirty years.

Rabbi Faivusovitch left the town of Slutzk, near Pinsk in Russia, to avoid serving in the czar's army; he escaped through China to Seattle. He had originally intended to become a rabbi in New York, but in Seattle he was told there were already too many rabbis in New York, but that they did need a rabbi in Portland. Faivusovitch came down to Portland, was interviewed and engaged by Shaarie Torah. He sent for his wife and daughter, who had been waiting with her parents in Siberia, and when they

Shaarie Torah Synagogue, known as the "First Street" *shul*, was the first Orthodox synagogue in Portland. Services began in this building at First and Hall in 1905. Courtesy, Congregation Shaarie Torah.

arrived, Faivusovitch had already found a house for the family at Third and Caruthers.

Later, Rabbi Faivusovitch changed his name to "Fain" because his eldest daughter, Rachel, complained of having trouble putting the name "Faivusovitch" at the top of every lesson in school. When he became an American citizen in 1921, he intended to change his name to "Fine," but in confusion with Russian mistakenly wrote "Fain," and so it remained.

Shaarie Torah retained the Orthodox forms from the old country. Services were held every morning, women sat separately upstairs, and the Torah reading took place in the center of the synagogue. Manly Labby recalls that his family joined the First Street *shul* because "the customs and life style of the people in this congregation were completely in keeping with the life my family had lived in Russia." His father, Abraham Labby, previously a hat-maker but always interested in the spiritual life, was the *shammes* at Shaarie Torah.

Abraham Lapkowski (who later changed his name to Labby) came to Portland in 1905 from Golta in Russia. He became the *shammes* at Shaarie Torah in 1918 and held this post for over forty years. Courtesy, Daniel Labby.

Rabbi Joseph Faivusovitch (he later changed his name to Fain) was the charismatic religious leader of Congregation Shaarie Torah from 1916 to 1946. Courtesy, JHSO.

The synagogue thrived. By 1921, it had nearly two hundred and fifty members. It also remained strictly Orthodox. Rabbi Fain would only consent to marry two Orthodox partners. In fact, he did not approve of marriage in the synagogue itself, which as he put it, "is a place you go and you *daven* and that's it." Each of his three daughters was married in large gatherings at the Neighbors of Woodcraft hall, and Rachel recalls that over eight hundred people attended her marriage ceremony there. All the rabbis in Portland participated, as well as Rabbi Vogelander of Seattle. Afterwards, a sitdown kosher meal, cooked on big stoves in their basement by her mother and her aunt, Mrs. Runie Hymen, was served to everyone.

Rabbi Fain was called the "Royta Rov" because of his red beard. Small of size, he carried himself with great dignity and was a colorful, charismatic community leader. He traveled throughout Oregon and Washington performing weddings and *b'riths*, and also supervised the proper milling of flour for the Manischewitz Company mills in Tacoma and Spokane. He served as a *shochet* and from time to time came into spirited competition with several other *shochets* in South Portland. He was also a *mohel*, performing circumcisions, a skill he learned

from Rabbi Abrahamson of Ahavai Sholom.

In 1924, a Rabbi Zucker came to Portland. Harry Arnsberg, who was then studying for his *bar mitzvah* with Moses Maccoby at the Hebrew School in Neighborhood House, describes the conflict that developed between the "Royta Rov" of Shaarie Torah and the upstart "Shvartza Rov," the blackbearded rabbi, of the short-lived congregation of Machzika Torah.

My melamed was Mr. Maccoby, who was a very learned teacher and he was a little hesitant about the place where my bar mitzvah would take place as it was an offshoot from the Shaarie Torah, the First Street synagogue. A group of mavericks, including my father, had rebelled against Rabbi Fain who was called the "Royta Rov."...

A new rabbi had come into the city and was a portly looking man with a full head of black hair, and they called him the "Shvartza Rov." These supporters rallied around him and were so ardent that they raised enough money to promote another synagogue in a big house on the corner of First Avenue and Lincoln Street which they called the Shvartza Rov's synagogue.

Mr. Maccoby, who was a very devout, sincere man, did not look favorably upon this new synagogue in competition with Shaarie Torah, but reluctantly came in September, 1924, to the syngagogue and I was able to have my bar mitzvah there successfully. The "Shvartza Rov" later left town and the mavericks came back to become members in Shaarie Torah again and we have had a continuous membership in Shaarie Torah for over fifty years [now over eighty years]. I am happy to say that both my sons had Rabbi Fain for their circumcisions and everything turned out all right.

Shaarie Torah remained at First and Hall in Southwest Portland until 1960, when most of the immigrant neighborhood had already dispersed. Since it needed a larger and more modern building, the congregation built a new synagogue at Park Avenue and Jackson Street.

Harold and Mark Schnitzer co-chaired the building campaign. Tragically, however, within a few years of completion the new structure was threatened by freeway expansion. Harold Schnitzer led a fight at City Hall that managed to delay the freeway for several months, but in the end the synagogue was forced to move, locating at Twenty-fifth Avenue and Lovejoy Street in Northwest Portland. The Schnitzers were again involved in raising funds to build the new synagogue, which still stands today.

The human cost when a synagogue is forced to move—especially an Orthodox synagogue to which the devout walk—is captured by Frieda Gass Cohen:

When my mother used to attend services [at Shaarie Torah] . . . she walked. As we children grew older, we were not averse to riding, but my mother always walked so some of her children walked with her. . . . Then as God would have it, the Shaarie Torah decided that they were going to build a new synagogue and they built the synagogue next door to her, right on the corner by my mother's house. For a few years this was a very convenient arrangement but then it was decided to tear the synagogue down for a freeway and with it they tore down my mother's house. This was the tragedy of her elder years, that she had to give up her home of forty-four years. When Shaarie Torah relocated into the Northwest area we built a home for my parents, again within walking distance of the synagogue and unfortunately, it became within wheelchair distance of the synagogue. My mother, up to the last, would never ride, but at least the house was close to the synagogue.

The choir at Shaarie Torah, about 1919. Courtesy, JHSO.

In later years, as its membership became increasingly assimilated, Shaarie Torah evolved from strict Orthodox to Modern Orthodox or Traditional, and today provides both integrated seating as well as separate sections for men and women who wish them.

Three other smaller Orthodox synagogues were also organized in old South Portland: Linath Hazedek (1914) and Kesser Israel (1916) were formed by Eastern European Jews; Ahavath Achim, following the Sephardic ritual that came down from ancient Spain, was founded in 1910 to serve Portland's small Sephardic community.

The first services conducted at Linath Hazedek, also known as the *Kazatzker shul*, were held in a building at the corner of SW Front and Arthur. The congregation later moved to a storeroom on First Avenue between Sheridan and Arthur and finally to a small, pleasant structure at First and Caruthers. This building had a number of stained glass win-

Linath Hazedek at First Avenue and Caruthers was a small Orthodox congregation founded in 1914 which merged with Shaarie Torah in 1964. Courtesy, OHS.

dows at street level, and was previously known as the Manley Center.

Frances Stein Slifman, whose father-in-law, Hillel Slifman, was the cantor at the *Kazatzker shul*, remembers the excitement of holidays and community life at Linath Hazedek when she was a child:

In those days families would bring their children and they would have live music playing. They would have a violin and a clarinet and a piano and these were all played by Jewish people. I remember our grandmother, my father's mother, used to take all her little grandchildren ... and they would make their circle and they would all dance together. We would have dinners and celebrations for the different holidays.

Jacob Tonitzky was rabbi from the congregation's inception until well into the 1930s. But in 1917, shortly after the move to First and Caruthers, a split occurred in the congregation and a number of members joined the newly formed Kesser Israel. Linath Hazedek remained small through the years. It moved its place of worship to Fifth Avenue where it too, as so many other Jewish institutions, was displaced by urban renewal. As a result, in February, 1964, representatives of Congregation Linath Hazedek and Shaarie Torah carried the sacred scrolls from both synagogues in a procession ending at Shaarie Torah that symbolized the merger of the two congregations.

The first services of congregation Kesser Israel were held in homes and in a small building at 136 SW Meade Street. In 1920, the congregation moved to its present location at the corner of Second and Meade. This handsome wooden structure had originally been built in 1888 as a Baptist Church and had both Romanesque and Gothic features and a large tower at its northwest corner. Kesser Israel thereafter became known as the "Meade Street" *shul*. For most of its history, Kesser Israel has not had a permanent rabbi, although Rabbi Fain served for many of its early years as interim rabbi. Gussie Reinhardt, whose father, Oscar Kirshner,

The frontal page of one of the earliest prayer books used at Kesser Israel (for the study of the Book of Exodus) shows Moses on the right and Aaron on the left, with important rabbis depicted at the bottom. The book was published in Russia in 1898. Courtesy, JHSO.

Kesser Israel is the only remaining synagogue located in old South Portland, and the only strictly Orthodox *shul* founded by Eastern Europeans left in Oregon. Flora Steinberg Rubenstein, who came to Portland in 1921 from Lublin, is one of the few Jews remaining today in the old neighborhood. She lives in one of two little houses at Second Avenue and Arthur Street, the other occupied at various times by other members of her family. In 1973, Flora spoke of her attachment to Kesser Israel:

Our synagogue was little Kesser Israel—it's been here ever since we've been here. My parents used to go there. For one thing it was close, and they liked it because it was the most Orthodox. They have beautiful shuls in

was president of Kesser Israel for forty-one years, remembers its early days:

Papa decided that it would be better for us to be members of the Kesser Israel synagogue.... As a child I can remember lying in bed in the early morning and hearing somebody go through the street hollering, "tsvay tsu minyan, dry tsu minyan," or "ainse tsu minyan" and I can also remember my father going into my brothers' bedrooms and scurrying them and saying "wake up, get to the synagogue." ... Of course, this was all said in

Kesser Israel, founded in 1916 at Second Avenue and Meade Street, is still located there and is the only remaining fully Orthodox synagogue founded by Eastern European immigrants in Oregon. Courtesy, OHS.

Portland today, but they're not shuls like the little shul that I am accustomed to. They are like palaces with the shine and the gleam in the eye. . . . Kesser Israel is my little shul and will be as long as I live. Even though I don't observe the laws, it is God's little house of worship to me. It is.

The first members of the Sephardic Jewish community arrived in Portland around 1910. They came from the Sea of Marmora on the Coast of Turkey near the Greek border, and from the Isle of Rhodes, where their families had lived nearly continuously since their expulsion from Spain in the late fifteenth century. Their langugage was Ladino, a blend of Spanish and Hebrew, which they continued to speak at home in Portland. The groups from Turkey and Rhodes tended to separate into two clans, calling each other *agenos* (strangers), but their common language and ritual brought them together in a single Sephardic congregation.

The Sephardic congregation was named Ahavath Achim or "brotherly love," and was formally established in 1910, when twelve men of Sephardic background held High Holiday services in the old Newsboys Club at First and Hall. The congregation moved shortly after that to Neighborhood House and then to the Lodge Room at the B'nai B'rith Building, the Jewish Community Center, where it met from 1913 to 1930.

Sephardic Jews of the Seattle and Portland communities dressed to perform a Purim play, about 1922. Courtesy, Sarah Menashe.

In 1930, on behalf of the congregation, Isaac Hasson and Ezra Menashe approached Ben Selling for help and advice about building a synagogue. Selling, who had always taken a special interest in the Sephardic community, not only gave several thousand dollars toward its construction, but solicited donations from Julius Meier, Joseph Simon, Isaac Swett and other community leaders. He also introduced the building committee to Harry Herzog, the well-known Jewish architect who had been consulting architect for Temple Beth Israel on NW Flanders Street a few years before. The building fund included money saved from years of traditional auctioning of the right to take the Torah from the Ark during services and from other fundraising events in the Sephardic community. They also received gifts of materials, such as brick facing, roof tiles and a gas furnace donated by Moe Levin.

A brick structure in the Mission style, located at Third Avenue and Sherman Street, it recalled the congregation's Spanish and Eastern Mediterranean roots. The roof was constructed of curved ceramic tiles, and the fine arched entranceway was of marble. While the services were Orthodox in the Sephardic tradition, there was no permanent rabbi. Jacob Maimon, a Seattle rabbi, came for over forty years to Ahavath Achim during the High Holidays to lead services and during Purim to read the *Megillah* (the Book of Esther).

Urban renewal also forced Ahavath Achim to move in the 1960s. The City of Portland exercised its right of eminent domain and compensation was determined by a court. After some debate, the congregation decided to try to move their fine synagogue to a new site on SW Barbur Boulevard. The synagogue was repurchased from the city and insured; in July, 1962, the move was attempted. The building was lifted and transported most of one block, but then it slipped on the flatbed truck, causing major cracks to appear. Fearing imminent collapse, the city sealed the doors; it was necessary to destroy the synagogue shortly thereafter.

The insurance company would only agree to pay half of the building's insured value of a

The congregation attempted to move the Ahavath Achim synagogue in July, 1962, as it was in the path of urban renewal. Moved most of one block, it slipped, causing major cracks which required its destruction. The congregation built a new synagogue on Barbur Boulevard which stands today. Courtesy, JHSO.

hundred thousand dollars, so Norman Kobin was retained as attorney for the congregation, a suit was filed, and, after testimony by Harry Herzog and Rabbi Yonah Geller (who became Shaarie Torah's rabbi in 1960), the full amount was secured. With the condemnation money, the insurance money and several contributions, the present synagogue—with its intriguing Byzantine-inspired rounded roof modeled on synagogues from Turkey and Greece—was constructed and dedicated in 1965. The Sephardic community is diminishing in size in Portland today because its youth tend to marry Ashkenazim and, as they assimilate, follow the old Sephardic ways less and less. As Ezra Menashe plaintively exclaimed to his wife, Joya, in 1975 at the age of eighty-three:

After you and I are gone, they will be all through. The young people don't come to Ahavath Achim. My grandchildren may remember that they are Sephardic, but they don't want to do [things the way] we did. They won't do that.

Congregation Tifereth Israel at NE Twentieth Avenue and Going Street was the only synagogue established on the east side of the Willamette River. Known as the "Alberta" *shul*, it was founded in 1911 and remained a small Orthodox/Traditional congregation until it merged with Shaarie Torah in 1986. Courtesy, OHS.

Only one synagogue was established in the early twentieth century on the east side of the Willamette River. The Eastern European immigrant congregation of Tifereth Israel held its first meeting and services in the home of Mr. and Mrs. Gershon Sherman at NE Eighteenth Avenue and Alberta in 1911. While there were not many Jewish families living in Northeast Portland, those who did were Orthodox, and they required a synagogue within walking distance. On behalf of the congregation, the Shermans purchased a house in 1914 at Twentieth and Going, which was remodeled for use as a synagogue known as the "Alberta" *shul*.

While the congregation never had a resident rabbi, its major religious leaders were the Reverend I. Schochet, who was the synagogue's cantor from its founding in 1911 until the mid-1930s, and Israel Boxer, who served as religious leader and cantor through most of the 1950s and '60s. The congregation sponsored popular second-night Passover *seders* and numerous picnics and social events through the years. Jackie Aderman, whose family belonged to Tifereth Israel for many years, reminisces:

I will forever hear my uncles singing so fervently the prayers in each service, with the cantors, the congregants joining in, and the children's joy at Simchas Torah and Purim. It was a special place, a congregation that was really an extended family whose arms were far-reaching.

In 1952, the Tifereth Israel congregation inadvertently found itself involved in a difficult conflict. Wanting to expand as more Jewish families located in Northeast Portland, the congregation decided to move, and purchased the Redeemer Lutheran Church at NE Fifteenth and Wygant as its new synagogue. The congregation sold its former synagogue, through real estate agent Frank McGuire, to Mount Sinai Church.

Some neighbors were upset when they learned that the Mount Sinai Church was black. The officers of Tifereth Israel, led by its president, Hyman Balk, stated that it was their "moral obligation" to sell to any legitimate buyer, regardless of color. The Portland Jewish community, particularly the Anti-Defamation League of B'nai B'rith, led by its western regional director, David Robinson, came to the support of the congregation and a memorable letter was written by the congregation to the real estate agent which stated in part:

At the time said agreement was entered into, this congregation had no knowledge of the purchasers other than their name and that they were a Christian congregation. Later it developed that the members of Mount Sinai Congregation are Negroes and pressures have been put upon us to back out of the deal for no other reason than that the purchasers, though Christian, are also Negro. We regard such pressures as being violative of the principles of Americanism, of Judaism, of Christianity and of common decency.... Man has no dearer right than the privilege of worshipping God in his own way. To deprive any group of people of the right to meet and to worship merely because God chose to make them a part of the colored majority of mankind is repulsive to Americans who love their country and the great principles of democracy which distinguish our land from the totalitarian states wherein liberty and religion are destroyed.

In welcoming our colored brethren to our old synagogue of blessed memory, we are mindful of the quotation from Hebrew scripture, "Have we not all one Father; hath not One God created us?" We hope that they also will find God within its walls and that He will answer their prayers and ours that He teach us "to love one another." In the event you refuse to close the sale, we desire to be released from our listing agreement so that we may ourselves consummate the moral agreement we have entered into.

The synagogue was sold to the black congregation. The neighbors appealed to the City Council, but it refused to block the sale. In November, 1952, the Mount Sinai Church was dedicated. Tifereth Israel remained a small Eastside congregation for seventy-five years, gradually evolving from Orthodox to Traditional. In September, 1986, it merged with Shaarie Torah.

In the early days of Jewish South Portland, the synagogue, the Hebrew school, the *mikvah* and the preservation of Orthodox Jewish ways as the immigrants had known them in the old country were central to people's lives. Judaism also provided comfort and security in a confusing new world. Many South Portlanders, in fact, belonged to several synagogues and participated in a number of Jewish institutions. Frieda Gass Cohen speaks movingly of the bond that was created immediately between Jews who shared that unique, nearly intuitive, understanding of Orthodox life:

There is a difference when you enter a synagogue with a basic knowledge of He-brew, . . . when you go in and know the correct place in the prayer book. . . . It is like the old neighborhood, you have a comfortable feeling of belonging. I remember a few years back, a cousin's daughter was being married in Vancouver, B.C. Our traditionally close family, all of us, every cousin in this area, went to Vancouver to attend the wedding. The bride's and bridegroom's families were both from a Traditional synagogue in Vancouver. On Saturday morning we decided to attend services there. I remember sitting down near the groom's mother—the women and the men sat separately. I listened for a moment; the groom's mother was watching me as I picked up the siddur. Their chazzan was wonderful; I could understand every word he sang. As I flicked open the siddur and found the right place, tears came to the mother's eyes. She told me later that she didn't know any of the girl's family . . . but, when she saw us walk in, and saw us pick up the siddur, she knew that we belonged in a synagogue and that everything was going to be all right.

As the years passed, it became increasingly difficult to maintain the old, Orthodox forms: walking to synagogue, not working on the Sabbath, separate seating for men and women, the laws of *kashrut*. Both the Reform and the Conservative movements grew in America and in Portland, retaining cherished traditions while modifying ritual aspects of orthodoxy which are difficult to maintain in modern, secular life.

The Reform branch of Judaism, represented by Temple Beth Israel, has remained the largest branch of Judaism in Oregon. The Conservative movement is represented in Portland today by the large congregation of Neveh Shalom, which includes the former Ahavai Sholom and Neveh Zedek. Shaarie Torah has also modified its strict Orthodox customs of the past and become Modern Orthodox or Traditional, while the small Orthodox congregations, Kesser Israel and Ahavath Achim, also remain active.

13

Education in South Portland

The Importance of Education

The immigrant Jews craved education. In Eastern Europe, the educated man had always been held in the highest esteem. When the *shadchan*, or matchmaker, approached with an offer of marriage, he or she always began by citing the scholars, teachers and rabbis that were part of the pedigree of the family she was representing. In the reckoning of *yihus*, or status, the Talmudic scholar, the educated person, came first; virtue and moral rectitude, second; good works, third. But in America, where social and economic mobility was largely determined by wealth, the Eastern European Jew found a fortuitous conjunction of old and new values. Education was the fulfillment of Old World prescriptions for the most honored person, while it was also one of the only ways for poor immigrants to achieve higher status.

The Jewish family did everything in its power to provide for the education of its children. The parents saved and sacrificed; one child who had made it through would help the next. "For the majority of Jews education was the paramount concern. Dropping out of school rarely occurred," observes historian Kimbark MacColl. Another scholar asserts that Jewish parents brought their children to the first day of school, "as if it were an act of consecration." Their standards were high, and the goal was to become as educated as possible, to go as far as one could. The fabled introduction, "my son, the doctor," and today's "my daughter,

the lawyer," were high motivators for both parents and children. The professions were often seen as the highest attainment possible: honored and steeped in education, powerful enough to help the community, source of a dependable income as well as the independence and self-determination that offered some insulation from the age-old experience of anti-Semitism.

While Jewish children of South Portland played games and participated in sports with high spirits, there was always an undertone of serious intent. Rabbi Fain's daughter, Rachel, recalls that her father would "have a fit" when she wanted to play ball with the rest of the kids. "'You don't do that. You don't waste your time,' he said. 'You've got to come in; you've got to learn.'" Frieda Gass Cohen recalls her mother

had a hyphenated word for a ball player. It was either "a-ball-player-a-bum" or "a-bum-a-ball-player." ... My mother did not know what the right end of a bat was and if she did, she would have put it into her wood stove to burn it because she thought baseball was ridiculous. My father to the day he died didn't know what a strike was. Football was altogether a terrible thing because "es war geshlugen und gehackt" [there was hitting and hacking].... We did play outside; we were healthy; we swam; we did all these things, but only as secondary activities.

And Manly Labby remembers:

All the children in our family went to the Failing Grade School. During that time, my brother Bob and I also sold newspapers downtown, after school. We didn't engage in sports; we didn't engage in extracurricular activities—there wasn't the time. We went downtown right after school, sold papers and then came home with whatever few dimes we made there. We used to bring the money home and deposit it to the family exchequer. This truly helped out in a considerable way.

The Public Schools

Most Jewish children in old South Portland attended the Failing School, located between Hooker and Porter streets just east of Front Avenue. As many as half of the children at Failing School were Jewish during the first years of the century, and approximately 20 percent were Italian. Many who grew up in old South Portland speak reverently of Miss Fannie Porter, the principal of Failing School, and their teachers, including Miss Porter's sister, Kate. According to Besse Harris:

We were very attached to our teachers at Failing School. Miss Porter, our principal, was just like a second mother to all of us. Life was very close and very sincere, and teachers and students were very devoted to each other.

"Miss Porter was a large woman," recalls Maurice Sussman, "in some ways she reminded you of Mrs. Roosevelt." Sussman went on to extol Miss Porter and her sister, Kate, for their dedication to educating their students. To reach the school, they had to come from Oregon City on the inter-urban streetcar and then transfer to the South Portland streetcar; in bad weather they would take a taxi the entire distance at great expense. Sussman recalls Miss Porter standing in the rain under her umbrella, never missing a game when Failing played Shattuck or

About 1912, children play at Failing School as the principal, Miss Fannie Porter (right foreground), looks on. Half the children at Failing School were Jewish. Courtesy, JHSO.

Holman or Ladd, no matter what the sport. She was strict with students and demanded their best, but they loved her because they sensed that she cared deeply about them.

Jacob Weinstein, later to become a nationally recognized rabbi in Chicago, paid this tribute to Fannie Porter in 1920:

The Failing School baseball team in 1924 with Miss Porter, who is said to have never missed a game. Courtesy, JHSO.

The 1923 graduating class at Failing School with their principal. Graduation meant so much to both parents and students. Courtesy, JHSO.

Those of us of foreign birth who came under the guidance of Miss Porter must feel particularly grateful to her. She did not make the mistake of many American teachers who conceive Americanism as a completely formulated doctrine which is to be hammered into the minds of their students to the exclusion of all else. Miss Porter early recognized that the best Americanism is the most harmonious combination of the foreign elements of which it is composed. She knew that every foreign-born child possessed some trait that it would be to the best advantage of this country to maintain and develop.

There were also humorous stories told of Failing School. In 1915, one appeared on the front page of the *Portland News* involving Moe Levin whose mother, Dora, owned the fish market. It seems that Moe was delivering a ten-pound carp to Mrs. Buchwach's home when he heard the schoolbell ring. He decided to make the delivery to Mrs. Buchwach's son, who also went to Failing. Needless to say, he was hauled to Miss Porter's office and was in some trouble until he explained that it was her own "no tardy" rule that he was trying to live up to. She called the newspaper and the front page story resulted.

Graduation was an important event. Maurice Sussman recalls that all of the parents would be invited to the ceremony:

The class sat down and the parents were behind ... all immigrant parents; to them graduation from school meant so much. What Miss Porter did was have every child called and as they walked up, she would say something about that child, something good, what they did, what they could do, what she expected of them and she never lacked for words. She was just marvelous and it made the parents feel good. I've never seen it done; they never did it in high school, nor in college, but she did it for every child and I think it meant so much, and these things I remember to this day.

Shattuck School stages a play in the 1920s. About one-third of the children at Shattuck during this time were Jewish. Courtesy, JHSO.

Failing School recognized the immigrant nature of the district it served. It maintained a large, ungraded classroom where students of different ages, who had received some education in Russia, Italy or elsewhere but did not speak sufficient English could be taught until they reached their appropriate grade level. Sometimes they went directly into high school from the ungraded class. To encourage frugality, the school maintained a bank for the students. Cards would be punched to indicate the amount deposited, and Miss Porter would have a student take the collected funds down to the "real" bank where an account was kept. A night school was also established for adults which provided an eighth grade certificate and helped prepare the immigrants for citizenship exams.

A significant number of Jewish children also attended Shattuck School in the block bounded by Broadway and Park avenues and College and Jackson streets, a bit to the north and west of the immigrant district. When families became established and were doing better economically, they often moved six or eight blocks northwest in search of better housing and a sense of upward mobility. Some Jews of German background had long lived in the Park Blocks area, and the B'nai B'rith Building was nearby. By 1920, 35 percent of Shattuck School

children were Jewish.

Upon graduation from elementary school, most Jews went on to Lincoln High School, where many made their first real contact with the "outside" world. Jack Hecht recalls:

At Lincoln High School, I personally discovered that there was a whole other world. In those days, Lincoln High School was like a melting pot of Portland. You had the kids from South Portland, you had some very wealthy children from the Heights families, from Lake Oswego, from Dunthorpe.... I was invited to their homes. I saw how, so to speak, the other half lived.... You were accepted as an equal because you were all the same age.... Many of the friends I had in grammar school were still my friends in high school, but a lot of Jewish kids from upper South Portland, the Park Street crowd that went to Shattuck ... became friends of mine ... and I always did have a number of gentile friends.

Some Jews also went to the High School of Commerce at Sixth and Hall which primarily prepared students for office work. Eugene Nudelman, Sr., captures the tension for a young person trying to maintain the old ways and yet faced by new temptations at high school:

Grandma Rosencrantz lived in a duplex on College Street, between Sixth and Broadway. That was about two blocks from Commerce High School. When I started high school, she told my mother that I must come there and eat lunch every day, for she didn't want me to eat goyish food. This was great, you know, for a while. Pretty soon I got so tired of gefilte fish, but her cooking was unbelievable. She used to make pickled watermelon which I dearly loved and I only wish I could get my hands on some today.... I would go there at least two or three times a week, and then I got a hankering for something goyish, a hot dog, a cream puff—one of those twisted things with meringue all through the middle—or a coke, but invariably when I didn't show up, she'd call home, and she'd tell my mother, "He is eating goyish food again."

Small numbers went to other high schools in the areas where they lived, primarily Benson Polytechnic, Washington, Jefferson and Grant. Figures do not exist showing how many Jews completed high school and went on to college and other opportunities in higher learning, but a large number did. Reed College was a particularly popular destination for South Portland's Jews; many also went to the University of Ore-

gon, and others scattered to universities throughout the country. By the time students reached college age, some families were able to provide funds for college, but most had to obtain scholarships as well as work to pay tuition and support themselves.

Hebrew School

It is not clear when the Portland Hebrew School first opened its doors, but a note appeared in the *Jewish Tribune* of March 1, 1907, saying, "Dr. J. Seidel is meeting with flattering success in the financial backing he is obtaining for the new Hebrew School in South Portland of which he is the able head." Max Levin, an early Russian immigrant, was holding Hebrew classes in 1910. By 1913, the Hebrew School was incorporated under President Jacob Asher and held classes in Liberty Hall at Second Avenue and Meade Street; the following year it moved to the old Failing School building.

In 1916, to provide stability and broader community appeal, the school was moved to Neighborhood House and a new board of directors was organized. Leadership passed to a well-respected, more established group that had been in Portland for several decades and was associated primarily with congregations Neveh Zedek and Ahavai Sholom. Israel Bromberg, who had arrived with the group from North Dakota in the 1880s, became chair of the board, and Abe Rosenstein, its president, a post he retained into the 1930s. Joseph Shemanski, the wealthy owner of the Eastern Outfitting Company, was the school's treasurer and chief benefactor. Ida Loewenberg, the longtime headworker at Neighborhood House, was its secretary. The first task of the new leadership was to find a principal who would be able to modernize teaching at the school in order to increase the school's appeal to South Portlanders, many of whom were resistant to Old World teaching methods. They wanted to retain Jewish tradition and culture, but within a revitalized, American context.

Students in the class of 1923-24 at the Portland Hebrew School at Neighborhood House. Courtesy, JHSO.

Hebrew School principal H. I. Chernichowsky (left) with Joseph Shemanski, school treasurer and chief benefactor, about 1948. Courtesy, JHSO.

amination conducted by members of the board and several rabbis from Portland synagogues, including Rabbis Fain, Sachs, Tonitzky and Sandrow. Typically, twelve to fifteen students graduated each year until well into the 1950s. Many of the graduates became Sunday schoolteachers at the synagogues, and several were hired by the Hebrew School itself. At least two graduates, Jacob Weinstein and Alvin Fine, became nationally renowned rabbis in other cities.

Funding for the Portland Hebrew School came from tuition, which was often waived for those unable to pay; dues from the more established synagogues; annual picnics and balls; and large loans and donations, primarily from Joseph Shemanski. In the early days, money was in short supply, but by the late 1920s the school was flourishing and continued to do so under its new principal, H. I. Chernichowsky. Formerly principal of the Seattle Talmud Torah, he served the Portland Hebrew School from 1931

Bert Treiger, a young man with strong ideas about "modern" Hebrew education, was hired in 1918. He immediately instituted the *Ivrith B'Ivrith*, or direct method of teaching, which replaced the old *heder* with its system of *davening*. Hebrew was the language of the school, and English was rarely spoken. Students were trained and tested on the Bible in its original language, Jewish history, Jewish law and custom and the Hebrew language. The fundamental purpose of the school, according to Mr. Treiger, was "the perpetuation of Judaism." In the powerful, secular environment of America, effective Jewish education was essential if Jewish culture, language and moral precepts were to be instilled in its youth.

The Portland Hebrew School grew rapidly from sixty-five students in 1918 to one hundred and sixty-five by 1921. The school's first graduation was in 1921, and a graduation was held each three years thereafter until 1928, when twelve students graduated in the first annual commencement. To graduate, students had to pass rigorous exams, including a public oral ex-

Joseph Shemanski gave *Rebecca at the Well* to the City of Portland in 1926. A successful and generous man, Shemanski owned the Eastern Outfitting Company which employed many Jewish immigrants. Photograph by Walter Boychuk. Courtesy, OHS.

One Dollar Per Year   Ten Cents Per Copy

The
NEIGHBORHOOD
Official Organ of the Neighborhood House

Bernard Brounstein   Minnie Singer

Hannah Feves   Edith Schnitzer

Abe Olshen   Fae Jackson

Sylvia Overbeck   Helen Mozes

Jack Rosenfeld   Mollie Schnitzer

Bernard Brounstein, Hannah Feves, Abe Olshen, Sylvia Overbeck, Jack Rosenfeld, Dorothy Olds, Minnie Singer, Edith Schnitzer, Fae Jackson, Helen Mozes, Mollie Schnitzer and Grace Rogoway on Wednesday evening, June 6, 1928 received diplomas for having completed the course of instruction outlined by the Portland Hebrew School. The Neighborhood congratulates this chosen dozen of nine girls and three boys, and hopes they will continue their consecrated work. May this nucleus of twelve be multiplied to thousands of Jewish youth who will consider their education incomplete without the right Hebrew background.

Dorothy Olds   Grace Rogoway

Portland, Oregon, July, 1928

VOLUME 10   **NUMBER 2**

The graduating class of the Hebrew School in 1928. Students had to pass rigorous exams given by the board and Portland rabbis. Courtesy, JHSO.

through the early 1950s. Although teachers were paid modest salaries (typically one to two hundred dollars per month based on education and experience), the school was able to recruit high quality, dedicated teachers, who often came from the East.

In 1916, two other Hebrew educational organizations were formed: Agudath Achiever, whose purpose was to promote use of the Hebrew language, and the Hebrew Literary Society, which conducted programs in Hebrew. In addition, an Eastside branch of the Hebrew

School was opened in 1928 with thirty-one children and was still functioning in the mid-1940s. Beginning in 1928, it also offered adult Hebrew classes and annually published its own journal, the *Hazofeh* (the Observer).

Children attended the Hebrew School after a full day at public school. Diane Nemer remembers:

Our day consisted of going to school, coming home, and taking a bite to eat and then going out to Hebrew School.... We went to Hebrew School every day of the week and on Friday we had our services and on Saturday morning we had other services.... Our life at that time was strictly learning, going to school, home, Hebrew School, and home again for a late dinner.

And Frieda Gass Cohen recalls:

We went to Hebrew School from the time we were six years old and entered the first grade until we finished the eighth grade. We used to go from Monday through Thursday, again on Sunday, but never on Fridays. On Friday evening and Saturday morning we attended Sabbath services at the Jewish Old Peoples Home which was, at that time, on Third and Lincoln.... Woe unto you if you did not show up for Sabbath services on Friday and Saturday because when you returned to Hebrew School on Sunday Mr. H. Israel Chernichowsky would slam his gold ring down on the table till your teeth would rattle. You had better show up next week.

In addition to impressing the South Portland children with the importance of Jewish education, the Portland Hebrew School generated a resurgence of interest in Jewish culture among all of Portland's Jews. But most significant, the school also served as a vehicle for the expansion of Eastern European Jewish influence within the broader Jewish community. As Eastern European young people with both Hebrew and secular education grew into maturity in the 1920s and 1930s, they increasingly exercised leadership and began to emerge as the principal voice of Portland Jewry.

The Portland Hebrew School has operated continuously to the present date. After 1934, it functioned under the auspices of the Jewish Education Association. In 1986, the Jewish Education Association merged with Hillel Academy, a Jewish day school begun in 1961, to form the Portland Jewish Academy.

South Portland's Library

Because learning was so important to South Portland's Jews, its neighborhood branch library was often deluged, especially with children. After a long day of work, adults too could often be seen at the library reading the Yiddish *Daily Forward* just arrived from New York or checking out a book in English to help themselves learn the language. The strongest desires for self-improvement motivated the immigrant Jews; they wanted to use every opportunity to the fullest.

The first library was located on the corner of First Avenue and Hooker Street, the former site of the old Failing School. It was built in 1913 for the sum of $968, but was quickly outgrown. Then, in 1921, the Carnegie Library Endowment provided funds for the construction of a new branch library at Second Avenue and Hooker Street. A beautiful little building was designed, with large arched windows and graceful columns flanking the front entrance. And on October 1, 1921, the children of the neighborhood each carried armfuls of books up Hooker Street. Their procession was headed by the American flag, a copy of the United States Constitution and a picture of George Washington.

To recall the South Portland branch library was to remember Zerlina Loewenberg, who was its revered librarian for most of its existence. Like her sister, Ida, who was the headworker at nearby Neighborhood House, Zerlina never married, dedicating her considerable energy and love instead to the library and the community it served.

In 1975, Besse Harris said:

I still remember the library where Miss Loewenberg was such an adorable darling and we used to go there from the time we were old enough to read and she was always so good about letting us take out more than two books at one time. It was quite a monument to our neighborhood. It is still standing there and every time I go back—it's right across the street from my grandmother's house—I look at it and I am really very thrilled because I can only see that personality of Miss Loewenberg, who was absolutely priceless.

Mary Friedman Rosenberg recalled:

Miss Loewenberg, the one who was at the library, was just a darling person. She would walk all the way down to my place when I lived at Fifth and Jackson to tell me that they were going to have a speaker at the library one afternoon and that they were going to have tea for her, and wouldn't I come.... "Oh," I said, "this is awful for you ..." but she

The South Portland branch library, built in 1921. It was often crowded, and everyone revered its librarian, Zerlina Loewenberg. Courtesy, JHSO.

said, *"I wanted you to come. How else was I going to reach you?" You see, that was the difference; there was the contact, the warmth and most of the people I grew up with feel the same way.*

The library flourished in South Portland until the immigrant community dispersed, and in the early 1950s the building was converted by the city's parks department to an art center, which it remains today.

VOLUME I.   PORTLAND, OREGON, FRIDAY, AUGUST 10, 1894.   NUMBER 27

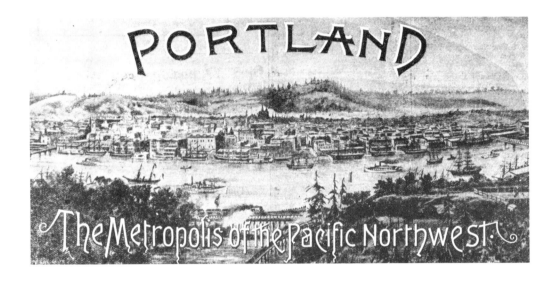

5654   **CALENDAR**   *1893-4*

New Year, 5654	Monday	September	11
Fast of Gedaliah	Wednesday	"	13
Day of Atonement	Wednesday	"	20
Tabernacles	Monday	"	25
Hoshana Raba	Sunday	October	1
Shemini Etseret	Monday	"	2
Simchas Torah	Tuesday	"	3
*New Moon, Hesevan	Wednesday	"	11
*New Moon, Kislev	Friday	November	10
Hanukkah, First Day	Monday	December	4
*New Moon, Tebeth	Sunday	"	10
Fast of Tebeth	Tuesday	"	19

5654   **CALENDAR**   *1894*

New Moon, Shebat	Monday	January	3
*New Moon, Adar Rashon	Wednesday	February	7
*New Moon, Adar Shenee	Friday	March	9
Fast of Esther	Wednesday	"	21
Purim	Thursday	"	22
New Moon, Nisan	Saturday	April	7
Passover, First Day	Saturday	"	21
*New Moon, Iyar	Monday	May	7
33d day of Omer	Thursday	"	24
New Moon, Sivan	Tuesday	June	5
Feast of Weeks	Sunday	"	10
*New Moon, Tamuz	Thursday	July	5
Fast of Tamuz	Sunday	"	22
New Moon, Ab	Friday	August	3
Fast of Ab	Sunday	"	12
*New Moon, Ellul	Sunday	September	2
New Year, 5655	Monday	October	1

*The day previous is at observed as New Moon.

The *American Hebrew News* (1893-1900) was the first Jewish newspaper published in Portland. Courtesy, OHS.

The *Jewish Tribune* was published and edited from 1902 to 1918 by the Reverend Dr. Nehemiah Mosessohn (also rabbi of Congregation Neveh Zedek) and his sons, David and Mose. The family moved the paper—which they saw as national in scope—to New York City in 1918. From the *Jewish Tribune*, March 25, 1904. Courtesy, Portland Public Library.

Jewish Newspapers

Newspapers served the Jewish community not only in South Portland, but city wide. Nearly continuously from 1893 there has been a Jewish newspaper in Portland reporting on issues of local importance to the Jewish community and informing readers of social, cultural and religious events. The local Jewish newspaper has also kept its readership in touch with national and international events of special importance to Jews, information often otherwise unavailable, and almost always carried an editorial, sometimes informative, sometimes fiery.

Before a Jewish newspaper existed in the Pacific Northwest, the *Weekly Gleaner*, published in San Francisco, attempted to serve the entire West Coast, but with limited success. In 1893, the *American Hebrew News* began weekly publication in Portland under its publisher, Isaac Stern, and its editor, L. Rosenthal. The

newspaper cost two dollars per year and reported news across the spectrum of the Jewish community. It is unclear why it ceased publication in 1900.

By 1902, the *Jewish Tribune* had begun publication in Portland. This newspaper had a more serious intent than its predecessor and featured correspondents in cities throughout the Northwest and as far away as Salt Lake City and Vancouver, B.C. It was published and edited by a remarkable triumvirate: the Reverend Dr. Nehemiah Mosessohn and his sons, David and Mose. Dr. Mosessohn had emigrated from Odessa in the early 1880s, where he was an Orthodox rabbi and lawyer. He was somewhat of a rebel from orthodoxy in Russia and decided to leave for America. He first obtained a pulpit in Dallas, then in Oakland, and finally at Neveh Zedek in Portland. David Mosessohn's son, Boris Dayyan, states that both his grandfather and father went to the University of Oregon Law School after arrival in Oregon. They graduated in the same class, his grandfather the oldest student, and his father the youngest.

David was the publisher and managing editor of the *Jewish Tribune*; his brother Mose was the news editor; and their father was the editor, meaning that he wrote the editorials. A strong editorial policy, restated often in its pages, governed the *Tribune*. The paper would "fight anti-Semitism wherever it is found and protect the interests of Jews." It would also "proclaim only one Judaism" and recognize no "factions or classes" but only "the beautiful monotheistic creed handed down to us by our ancestors." The Mosessohn's and their paper were dedicated to the cause of Zionism. The *Tribune* was published weekly on Fridays for a cost of two dollars per year.

Both Mose and David were involved with the Portland Chamber of Commerce; Mose was assistant secretary, and David produced its Bulletin. The *Jewish Tribune* was published in the Chamber Building. David also practiced law, and at one time was a deputy district attorney. In 1918, Mose moved to New York to become the director of the Associated Dress Industries of America (the dress manufacturers' organization). After the death of David's daughter, the entire family decided to move to New York City and publish the *Jewish Tribune* there, since they conceived of the paper as national in scope. Dr. Nehemiah Mosessohn remained its editor until his death in 1926, and David remained its publisher until his premature death from heart attack in 1930 at the age of forty-eight. The paper was sold two years later for three thousand dollars to the *American Hebrew News* of New York.

In Portland, David Cohen (no relation to David Solis-Cohen), the former business manager of the *Jewish Tribune*, purchased all assets of the paper except its name from the Mosessohn family after its last number appeared in June, 1919. Three months later, the *Scribe: A Record of Jewish Life and Thought* began publication. Jonah Wise, the rabbi of Beth Israel, who followed Stephen Wise but was not related to him, was the newspaper's editor; Max Merritt, associate editor; and David Cohen, its manager. It continued to be published on Fridays at the Chamber of Commerce Building until 1926, when Rabbi Wise left Portland to assume the pulpit of the Central Synagogue in New York. From then until 1951, when it ceased publication, the *Scribe* was edited and published by David Cohen with assistance in later years from his wife, Miriam. In 1926, it also moved its offices to the Railway Exchange Building. For many years, Abraham Rickles served as associate editor, and Rabbi Louis I. Newman, the father of present Oregon appeals court judge Jonathan Newman, served as contributing editor, writing a weekly column from San Francisco and New York where he held his pulpits. While the *Scribe* retained much of the serious content of the *Jewish Tribune*, it also dedicated considerable space to reporting the social events of Portland's Jewish elite.

Portland's current Jewish newspaper, the *Portland Jewish Review*, began publication in January, 1959, under the auspices of the Jewish Welfare Federation (the successor to Federated Jewish Societies). It is still published today, although in 1985 its longtime editor, LaNita Anderson, left the paper, and it is now under the direction of an enlarged editorial board.

David and Miriam Cohen were publishers of the *Scribe* from 1919 to 1951. Rabbi Jonah Wise of Beth Israel was an early editor of the paper. Courtesy, JHSO.

14

Making a Living

Up From Poverty

Eastern European Jewish immigrants either came to America as a family or followed the head of their household within a year or two after he had found work and was settled. Most men were either craftsmen or had held semi-skilled jobs in Europe. Unlike German Jewish immigrants a generation earlier, they did not have the support in America of established businesses maintained by relatives. But they often had either relatives or friends from the town or *shtetl* they had left in Europe who would assist them with housing and work.

Russian and Polish immigrants who had come to Portland in the 1880s and 1890s had opened secondhand stores and were able to employ these new immigrants to peddle their merchandise. Perhaps the largest employer of Eastern European Jews was Joseph Shemanski, whose Eastern Outfitting Company sold quantities of cut-rate clothing through such peddlers. Most Eastern European immigrants began as peddlers, junk dealers or clerks in secondhand stores. Many immigrant Jews, in fact, started by collecting whatever they could find of any value and reselling it wherever possible. David Finkelstein recalls:

In those days money was scarce.... One way to earn money was to go out and peddle. The children would go out and help their families by selling newspapers. The older people had a hard time making a living.

Many went out peddling, but it wasn't like it is today. Today we waste stuff. In those days, everything was saved. They peddled rags. They would bring a tire in, a sack or two of rags that they used to get from families, and the junk shops used to buy this stuff.

The Jews were poor when they came, often penniless, but they had dignity and pride. They never begged, and they avoided certain occupations because they were considered undignified. Few Jews ever worked for others as maids, butlers, cooks, coachmen or menial laborers. Although they had no money, they did possess an inner strength and resourcefulness as well as

Mr. Stein peddling from his horse and wagon, about 1910. Many immigrants from Eastern Europe began as peddlers. Courtesy, JHSO.

FRUIT & VEGETABLE PEDDLER – $30.00
2ND ✧ **1** ✧ **HALF**
LICENSE – 1924

Courtesy, JHSO.

an intense desire to use their newfound freedom to make good in America.

The oral histories of two immigrants—Louis Albert and Sam Schnitzer—both of whom were born in Russia and arrived in Portland shortly after the turn of the century, recapture for us in marvelous detail their breathtaking rise from poverty.

The Story of Louis Albert

I've lived in Portland since 1911.* I was born in Kiev, Russia, on March 15, 1891. My father brought his family to live in Fall River, Massachusetts, in April of 1906. I had a cousin in Portland by the name of Victor Krichevsky; he changed his name to Kaye. In 1907, I decided to come to Portland and stayed with him. I got a job at N & S Weinstein's clothing store waiting on customers. In 1908, I went back to Fall River and married Becky Freeman, a second cousin of mine. I came back to Portland in 1911, and have been here ever since.

When I came back to Portland, I had only $6.75 in my pocket and my wife was still back East. I walked on Third and Madison Street and saw that a fellow had a sign there which said, "Wagon for Sale." His name was

---

*Jewish Oral History and Archives Project, December 7, 1973 (Marianne Feldman compilation).

Kaufman; he was a German fellow. I asked him, "Mr. Kaufman, I understand you have a wagon for sale?" He said, "Ya, ich hab." I said, "How much do you want for it?" He said, "What are you going to do with it?" I answered, "I don't know." He showed me the wagon, and I said, "Alright, I'll buy it. I'll give you $1 down and $1 a week. Where can I get a horse?" He said, "On Front and Montgomery Street you can get a horse." I went over there and I asked a fellow there if he had a horse for rent or for sale. He showed me a horse which sold for $15. I said, "I'll give you $1 down and $1 a week." He said, "What are you going to do with this horse?" I answered, "I don't know." Anyway, I made the deal. I gave him the dollar and he gave me a receipt. He gave me the horse, a harness and a bag of oats. I led the horse to my wagon and hitched him up.

I met a fellow who was in the cleaning and pressing business and asked him, "If I solicit cleaning and pressing for you, will you do the work?" He said, "Sure." I didn't know any people, so I just walked up to a house on Fifth and Hall Street and rang the bell. A lady by the name of Mrs. Rosenstein came to the door. I told her my story and that I had a wife and thirteen kids, and asked her if she would give me some cleaning and pressing. She brought me down a bundle and she called her sister, Mrs. Hochfeld, next door. Mrs. Hochfeld gave me a bundle too. Anyway, that first week I made $40. I got acquainted with so many people, and they helped solicit business for me. I was young, curly haired, and I used to tell them stories. They took a liking to me. That's the way I started in business.

After a while, I thought to myself, "If cleaning and pressing is so good, why shouldn't I solicit laundry too?" I got a contract with a laundry and picked up laundry, too. In 1913, I had the first Ford truck on the streets. I started climbing to Portland Heights and, instead of getting laundry in South Portland for ten to fifteen cents a bundle, I used to get $4 or $5 a bundle. I was in the laundry business until 1917, and then I sold out to a laundry company for $5,000.

After I sold out my laundry business, I got into the jobbing business. I used to go out in the country and buy potatoes. In those days I would buy one hundred bags of potatoes for seventy-five cents a bag and sell them to restaurants for $1.25. I was very strong, and I used to deliver those potatoes ... and make myself $40 or $50 in one day.

One day in 1917, I drove to Tillamook. I had a big truck with solid tires. I stopped at a farmer's house and asked him, "Do you have anything for sale?" He answered, "I don't know." I said, "If you've got anything for sale, you ought to know!" He said, "Well, maybe. I've got nine calves." In those days there were no quotations in the papers and no radio, so we didn't know what things were worth. I had never bought a calf in my life. I said, "How much do you want for the calves? Give me an idea of how much they are worth." He said,

Starting with $6.75 in 1911, Louis Albert became known as the "Soda Pop King." Seen here about 1941, he invented and manufactured popular drinks in Portland. Courtesy, Mildred Saks.

"How about $30 for the nine calves?" I didn't know if they were worth $30 or worth $200, so when he said, "$30," I said, "I'll give you $25." "Oh," he said, "You look like a nice fellow. Give me $25." So I gave him the money and put the calves on the truck. I was afraid that, maybe, I might lose my $25. This was on a Thursday. Friday morning I took the calves over to Max Brill, the butcher, and I sold them for $95. That is how I started buying calves, cows and bulls. Then I found out from the slaughterhouses how to weigh cattle by looking at them. If the quotation was five cents a pound and the cow looked like she had one thousand pounds or eight hundred pounds, you would take a gamble and pay accordingly, so I learned to buy cattle.

I remember one time I drove back from Salem and I stopped in Woodburn, Oregon. The same thing, I said to a farmer, "Have you got anything for sale?" This was in September, and he said, "I have a load of apples and you can have them for a couple of dollars." So I took the apples and put them on the truck. Then I said, "Do you have anything else?" He said, "There are some sheepskins, wool from my sheep." There was a big bundle. I didn't know what it was worth. He said, "Give me $5 for it." I figured, what can I lose? I can only lose $5. I gave him the $5. I took the wool to Kahn Brothers—they used to be on Front Avenue—and they gave me $85 for the wool. As time goes by, you can learn a lot about buying and selling. I learned by doing.

In 1929, for $5,000 I bought out a fellow who had a soda-water business.... I started out with five trucks and, when I quit the business, I had thirty trucks and forty people working. Eventually, I bought $50,000 worth of machinery. I used to invent my own drinks. "Royal Flush Beverages" was my trade name, and I also had "Ace High," which was like "Seven-Up." I was the only one in Portland who had fruit drinks. I believed in giving the people a fruit drink. I used to buy orange juice in fifty-gallon barrels from Anaheim, California, to make orange soda pop. I used to make my own colors and I cooked my own *ginger ale with ginger I brought from Jamaica. I came up with a new syrup that was out of this world—a hot-cake syrup called "Morning Dew." You got up in the morning and "do" it for breakfast.*

Louis Albert became known as the "Soda Pop King," inventing and manufacturing the popular Portland Punch, made from raspberries and loganberries, (it can still be purchased today), as well as numerous other original drinks. By 1947, he was doing over a million dollars of business each year.

The Story of Sam Schnitzer

I was born in Russia on July 12, 1880.* My father and my three brothers all live in Portland. I came to the United States when I was twenty-four years old. I was drafted into the Russian army in 1903, when I was twenty-

---

*As told to Fred Lockley and published in the *Oregon Journal*, January 17, 1935.

The Schnitzer family in 1936. From left: Mollie, Morris, Rose, Gilbert, Edith (Manuel's wife), Manuel, Harold, Edith, Sam and Leonard. Sam started as a peddler and built a fortune in manufacturing and shipping. Courtesy, JHSO.

three years old. Right then Russia was preparing to fight Japan, but I didn't feel that I wanted to kill any Japanese or have any Japanese people kill me, so I watched my chance and without consulting the captain of my company I resigned one night and escaped into Austria. I had no money. I tried very hard to get a job at $1 a week, but nobody seemed to need my services. So I wrote to my uncle, who had gone to the United States, to send $110 to pay for my ticket to New York City. He sent me the money, but the letter was addressed wrong, and it was returned to the dead-letter office and finally sent back to him. He wrote me again, enclosing the money, but this was four months after I had deserted from the Russian army, and most of that time I went on very short rations.

When I got to New York I got a job at $4 a week. Four other young men and myself rented a room at $7.50 a month. That meant it cost me $1.50 a month for a place to sleep. No, we didn't have beds; we slept on the floor. I allowed myself five cents for breakfast and ten cents for dinner. Out of my salary of $208 for the year, I managed to save $85. I bought a second-class ticket to Portland, arriving here in 1905.

I found there were lots of junkmen in Portland, so I went to work for Sam Nudelman, working in his tobacco store at $6 a week, working sixteen hours a day. When I had saved $45, I went down to Astoria and started in business for myself. I had no money to buy a horse or wagon, so I started in the junk business and was my own horse and wagon. I bought old sacks, brass and copper, old iron and bottles, and carried them on my back till I got as much as I could carry. Then I would take them to a yard where I stored them. If I bought an old kitchen range or some heavy article, I would wait till I had bought enough to make a load, and then would hire an express wagon to go around with me and collect them and haul them to the dock. I shipped them to Portland.

After three years I came to Portland and started in the junk business here. One day I went to the basement of the Hotel Portland to bid on some junk. There I met another junkman named Henry Wolf. We talked the matter over and decided to go into business. We took in a third man, each of us agreeing to put up $1,000. When it came time to put up the money, Henry said he had a large horse and a wagon, which he would put in at $250. He had some old junk in his basement, which he would put in at $300. I had a lot of pipes that I had bought from the Union Oil Company after its big fire. I put these in at $500. When it came to putting up the cash, Henry and my partner and I found that all of us had figured on the others putting up the cash, as we were all short of cash. After a few months Henry Wolf and I bought out our partner, and Wolf and I went in together, agreeing to put the cash into the partnership when we had made it out of the business.

We had decided to call our firm the Alaska Junk Company. We started in a little building with twenty-five-foot frontage at 227 Front Avenue. The man we had bought out prospered, and eight years later came to us and wanted to buy back his third interest in the firm. He offered us $20,000 for a third interest, but Henry and I decided not to take any partners.

I was married in the fall of 1906 to Rosa Finkelstein. Like myself, my wife was born in Russia. We have seven children—five boys and two girls. . . .

We live at 1011 Vista Avenue. No, I don't carry old iron and junk on my back any more. Nowadays we ship it in carload or trainload lots. We paid $160,000 for the G. M. Standifer Construction Company's shipyard at Vancouver. We paid $226,000 cash for the Skinner & Eddy shipyard. We buy complete sawmills and logging camps and ship machinery to the Philippines, the Hawaiian Islands, to Alaska and pretty well all over the world. Right now we are selling a great deal of iron and metal to Japan.

Here in this folder I have two of my most cherished papers. They are my marriage license and my citizenship papers.

Sam Schnitzer, as most know, was the founder of a large Portland family. Four of Sam and Rose Schnitzer's sons—Manuel, Morris, Gilbert and Leonard—have been partners in the family's shipping, steel, cold storage and real estate interests on the West Coast and Guam. Harold, their other son, left the family company in 1950 to form Harsh Investment Corporation, which has real estate holdings throughout the country. In 1986, the Schnitzers were one of only two Oregon families to make the *Forbes* magazine list of the four hundred richest citizens and families in the United States.

Needless to say, while most Eastern European Jewish immigrants were not as successful as Sam Schnitzer or Louis Albert, nearly all managed to pull themselves up from initial poverty to live relatively comfortable lives. By the 1920s, many had become shopkeepers in South Portland and downtown, tailors and other artisans or wholesalers and small manufacturers. And a number of these enterprises have become household names in Portland, such as Zidell Explorations, Zell Brothers Jewelry, Mrs. Neusihin's Pickles, Tonkin automobile agencies, Calbag Metals, etc. In addition to commercial and entrepreneurial ventures, many Eastern European Jews entered the professions and a broad range of other occupations.

Sarah Neusihin (center) in her basement at 420 SW College Street with son, Irv (second from right), and three assistants. Rabbi Fain's sister, Sarah, started her famous pickle company in her house in South Portland and it always remained a home-based operation. Courtesy, Irv Neusihin.

The Newsboys

While immigrant adults in South Portland were earning a living as best they could, they encouraged their children to do well in school so that they might surpass their parents and make good in America. But before that day, many young boys were expected to help their struggling families, and many did by selling newspapers after school. Scotty Cohen remembers:

When I first came to Portland in 1911 [at age nine], the first thing I did was I sold newspapers at First and Alder Street. In them days, I got the papers at three for a nickel. When I sold them, I made a dime.... When I made a dime, I'd go to First and Madison where there was a cook; he used to sell a big sack of brown mashed potatoes for a nickel. The other nickel I took home to mother.... We had very hard times in them days, very, very, hard times. I really had to help the family and how!

Newsboys gather in 1912 on the steps of Portland High School to advertise a concert featuring David Bispham (center) for the benefit of the Portland Newsboys Association. Courtesy, JHSO.

In 1983, at the age of eighty-nine, Boris Geller recalled:

We were all immigrants at the turn of the century. My father worked for five dollars a week. There were three hundred to four hundred newsboys on the streets of Portland. For every quarter that came in, the boys could buy food for their parents. There were seven in our family and someone had to help. Ours wasn't the only family in that situation. Meat was ten cents a pound in those days. If you had fifty cents, you could feed a family of six.

Most of the newsboys were Jewish and Italian kids. They sold the four dailies published in Portland: the *Telegram*, the *Journal*, the *News* and the *Oregonian*. Competition was intense for key street corners in prime locations where a stream of people would converge on their way from work to the streetcar, because they read the paper traveling home. Lore grew around the "newsies." Ben Rosenbloom became famous for his ability to boom "Extra" at Broadway and Morrison, and Scotty Cohen was called the "King of the Newsies" because he sold three thousand copies the day the *Swan*, a pleasure boat, sank near Vancouver, Washington. The banner headlines that sold record numbers of papers are still remembered: "DEVASTATING EARTHQUAKE IN SAN FRANCISCO," "LUSITANIA SINKS," "AMERICA ENTERS WORLD WAR," "PRESIDENT WILSON DEAD." Being a newsboy was an important part of the lives of many boys. In fact, Nathan Schwartz credits his "success in life" to early experiences that he had as a newsboy:

At school I wasn't very studious, but I had colleagues in my newsboy days, such as Morris Rogoway, Nate Lakefish, Boris Geller and scores and scores of wonderful memories.... We used to sell the night edition; my corner was at the old Majestic Theater on Park and Washington Street, where I stayed until eleven o'clock, when I used to go down to the nightclub better known as The Quell at Sixth and Washington. I had a lot of custom-

Newsboy Hymie Schneiderman, age fourteen. "Newsies" fought for valuable downtown street corners to sell as many papers as possible to help support their families. Courtesy, JHSO.

ers coming out of this night club ... who were somewhat intoxicated, with girl friends, and whatever they gave me, although the paper was a nickel, we never gave them any change. The daily paper I used to sell on Fourth and Washington Street.... My experience as a newsboy was very, very valuable to me.... I met a lot of people who I know today and I cherish their friendship.

The newsboys were exploited by the circulators, who pressed more papers on them than they could sell and then refused to redeem unsold copies. Despite the intense competition among newsboys, however, they were able to agree on common actions to combat the circulators. Manly Labby, a newsboy who later became one of Portland's few Jewish labor leaders, describes this early struggle:

It was as a newsboy, in August, 1914, that I first learned how group action could be used to achieve economic betterment, that strength lay in union for a common cause.... We discussed the problem [with the circula-

The Newsboys Club gathers at Neighborhood House in 1914. Front row (on floor) from left: Sam Weinstein, Phil Unkeles, unidentified, Hy Solko, Morris Pomerantz, Henry Rosen, Frank Director, Sidney Weider.

Second row: Max Himmelfarb, Sam Weinstein, Reuben Glickman, Ben Enkelis, Arnold Fishel, Moe Scotty Cohen, Ben Dorfman, Hymie Weinstein, Sam Greenstein, Sol Greenstein, Abe Unkeles, Kenny Nichols, George Winan, unidentified, unidentified, Mike DePinto, Simon Scotty Cohen, Abe Vidgoff, Abe Brown, Max Pearlman, Sam Fendel, Hymie Tessler, Billy Smardin, Irving Weider, Abe Weider, Harry Vidgoff.

Third row: Ellie Gurian, Kivi Cantor, Jack Himmelfarb, Louis Yazzolino, Max Lewis, Abe "Hindu" Weinstein, Joe Weinstein, Sam Sherman, Harry Lewis, Sam Tessler, Maurice Solko.

Back row, standing: Abe Popick (in front of flag, upper), unidentified (lower), Jack Gurian, Morris Rogoway (president, with gavel), Meyer Dubinsky, Abe "Mt. Scott" Weinstein, Jacob Weinstein, Sam Gordon, Max Gordon, Moe Mesher, Isaac Vidgoff.

Courtesy, JHSO.

tors] openly, on the streets, in school, in classes, wherever we saw each other. We chose from our group three or four of the toughest boys who formed a committee which went to the circulators and asked them to take back the surplus papers.

They didn't get anywhere. Though the circulators were sympathetic to our problem, they were bound by the mandates of their bosses. We didn't get very far with them because we were talking to the wrong group. The circulators didn't have the authority to say, "Yes, we'll take back any papers you can't sell," and they refused to go to their bosses to ask for that authority. We realized then that other steps would have to be taken.

We decided that, on a certain day, we

would all meet in front of the Oregonian building. We were going to take our stand with one newspaper at a time and started with the Oregonian. We took a strike vote and every one of us agreed that we were not going to let a newspaper out of the building, whether it was by mail—many of the papers were mailed to subscribers—whether by truck or by street circulation. We wouldn't let the trucks back up; the trucks brought the papers out to various areas away from downtown, where the circulators distributed them to the route boys. When newspapers came out of the basement in bundles, we immediately shredded them to pieces and scattered them all over the street. The police came but there wasn't very much they could do about it. They had, at

that time, what was called a "Black Maria,"
an old top-heavy patrol wagon. As soon as it
drove up, a large group of us rushed to the
wagon and rocked it until it fell over on its
side. That took care of the patrol wagon.
There were some fights and a lot of confusion.
The chief of police came down to see what
was going on. Somebody dropped a bag of
water on his head and that took care of him
for a while.

The strike lasted for two days. No papers
were going into circulation and people were
clamoring for the news. That was the only
way they could get the news in those days be-
cause there were few radios and no television.
Finally the employers at the four papers
agreed to meet with us. It was decided that the
circulators would take back any newspapers
that were unsold by 6 p.m., and would give us
back the money we had paid for those papers.
We had won our case.

This gave us some food for thought. We
had achieved our objective because we joined
together and showed strength. Why couldn't
we organize ourselves and maintain that
strength? That was the birth of the Portland
Newsboys Association. A gentleman by the
name of Dore Keesey owned an old building
which was right across the street from the
Shaarie Torah Synagogue. He decided to re-
furbish it and give it to the newsboys. Here is
where we met; it was like a clubhouse. The
Newsboys Association had regular meetings
there once a week but the house was also open
at other times for recreational purposes. We
used this place for many, many years.

In order to retire the mortgage on the
Newsboys' Clubhouse, a major election was
held annually for boy mayor and city commissioners. Candidates would buy votes for a penny each. A headline in the June 12, 1912, *Oregonian* reported, "[Mayor] Rushlight Ousted; Boy
Mayor on Job. New City Head Says Special Privi-
leges to All, Equal Rights to None." Max
Swerdlik won the boy mayor's race that year
with 31,120 votes out of a total of 126,000 cast.
The boy mayor and council served in city hall

Courtesy, the Leshgold family.

for one week. The newspapers reported that
$1,360 had been raised for the clubhouse. Jew-
ish newsboys won a number of the boy mayor
elections.

The Ex-Newsboys Association still exists
today. Through the years, it has held annual
banquets with handsome souvenir programs
prepared each year. The fiftieth annual banquet, held in 1970, listed over five hundred lifetime members of the Association.

The Role of Women

The role of Jewish women in the work force and
as a key to success in the upward mobility of
immigrant families has not been generally recognized nor sufficiently appreciated. But William Toll, in his book on Portland Jewry, has
provided groundbreaking research on the role
of women.* While men were the primary wage
earners and had most direct contact with the
broader society, Toll asserts that "the lives of
women and their roles in organizing the new
community underwent more dramatic change
over several generations than did the lives of
men." Men tended to reconstruct the work
roles that they had known in the old country.

---

*William Toll, *The Making of an Ethnic Middle Class:
Portland Jewry Over Four Generations*; Albany, State
University of New York Press, 1982.

Women, on the other hand, were not only at the center of family life and the changes it was undergoing, but often entered this new American world of work themselves, particularly before marriage. This was in addition to the significant voluntary contributions they made to civic affairs in the Jewish community.

Jewish couples in Eastern Europe were often married in their teens in unions that were arranged by their families, and women almost immediately began bearing children. Families were large, and in the life of the *shtetl* the woman was legally subordinate to her husband. But since poverty was endemic, women often had to help earn money for the family, and this led slowly to the decline of the more rigid forms of patriarchy in late nineteenth century Eastern Europe. So even before coming to America, Jewish women had gained a measure of equality in family and community that provided some preparation for their immigrant experience.

Once here, patterns changed rapidly: family size diminished, marriage partners were chosen rather than arranged, the age of brides increased, and women began to be employed before marriage. Thus the old patriarchy eroded rapidly in America. Most young women from South Portland worked at first either in the family business or as seamstresses. But later, many joined German Jewish women who were working in large department stores, particularly Meier & Frank and Lipman, Wolfe & Co. The earnings of these young Eastern European women were critical in helping their families following their arrival in Portland. After marriage, however, most women did not work outside the home. But their previous employment often led them to an active role in the community, where they helped build the myriad social, supportive institutions that made old South Portland the warm, caring place that it was.

Labor Unions

Oregon never developed a Jewish industrial working class because its economy was based primarily on farming, natural resources and commerce. In New York, and in most other American cities where large numbers of Eastern European immigrants became industrial workers, a strong, intensely ideological Jewish labor movement emerged. But while a modest union movement existed in Oregon, it did not exhibit the militancy and power that it did elsewhere, where the union hall virtually became the secular equivalent of the synagogue.

By the 1920s, however, there was a small but growing garment industry in Portland that had sprung from smaller Jewish-run tailor shops. In 1924, Hyman Kirshner and Ben Vogel founded the Modish Suit & Coat Company which became, with the Beaver Coat & Suit Company run by Louis Olds, the largest manufacturers of ladies wear in Portland. Kirshner, who himself had been a cutter in a local factory, employed skilled workers who sewed complete garments. Olds hired less-skilled workers who sewed the same piece repetitively along an assembly line.

In 1928, Manly Labby, a young garment worker who worked for both Beaver and Modish, decided with other workers to organize a union in Portland's garment industry. It is rare to hear the same historical events described by those who fought on opposing sides of a conflict. But the Jewish Oral History and Archive Project run by Shirley Tanzer and many colleagues in the mid-1970s affords us that opportunity. Owner Hyman Kirshner and organizer Manly Labby, both born in Russia, both Orthodox Jews living in South Portland, report each side the way they saw it:

Hyman Kirshner, Owner
Modish Suit & Coat Company

I was the first ladies coat and suit manufacturer in the city of Portland that was forced to join a union, and that was in the year 1931. I had a manager running my business, also foremen, and key help while I was out on the road selling. One day I came home and my manager said to me, "We have received a letter from the committee of the International

Ladies Garment Workers Union and they want to talk to you personally." I answered, "O.K. That's fine." My manager told me, "The best thing to do is not to meet with them. We have no union and there is nothing to worry about." I thought that he knew the help, so I believed him. We received three letters like that and, on the advice of my manager, I ignored them.

One morning we came to the factory and all the workers were outside the building, on strike. That was the beginning. We phoned the International Ladies Garment Workers Union, met with them at the Labor Temple, and signed a contract. The contract they forced me to sign did not allow me to be competitive with the other coat and suit manufacturers.

In 1931, the union organizing activities were limited to the Portland area so, at the end of that year, we moved our entire plant, with four key people, to Vancouver, Washington. There we started operations again, without the union. We had no problem getting help because this was during the height of the Depression.

We were in Vancouver for several years, and had a pretty good-size plant going there. When Franklin D. Roosevelt became president, the Wagner Labor Act [The National Labor Relations Act of 1935] was enacted, and it seemed to me that an employer was not even allowed to talk to his own help. During that time the International Ladies Garment Workers Union, out of New York, unionized the ladies coat and suit industry throughout the entire country. Our factory had to join too, so we moved back to Portland and opened another plant under the ILGWU. It wasn't easy.

Despite contracts which stated that there were not to be any strikes, we had some wildcat strikes and work stoppages. There was a certain amount of harassment when a few people would walk out and cause work to stop. The union did little to rectify this situation; in other words, they had no control of their people in this area.

The one thing the union cared about was to get more money for their members. My employees always made more money than those who worked for other suit and coat manufacturers in Portland. In spite of this, when contracts came up for renewal, the union never just raised my competitors to the standard of wages I was paying; they would raise my workers too. As far as I could see, the union never did anything to improve the market situation or to help any manufacturer in this town. Before we were unionized they promised us everything; afterwards they actually gave the manufacturers nothing.

Eventually, the union decided to make Los Angeles their Pacific Coast headquarters. I believe that they decided to centralize the ladies coat and suit industry in Los Angeles so that they could police it better, and that they were actually out to drive the other manufacturers on the Coast out of business. . . . Every

Hyman Kirshner, owner of the Modish Suit & Coat Company, at one time the largest manufacturer of ladies garments in the West. Kirshner, once a "cutter" himself, employed skilled laborers. A number of them stayed with his firm for many years. Courtesy, Gussie Reinhardt.

time a union contract expired and a new one was being negotiated, they would always want more money. Every time they received a substantial raise, they knocked us out of certain price ranges. . . . I always tried to get the right deals so that we would stay in business. That's why I'm the only ladies coat and suit manufacturer left in the Portland area.

Manly Labby, Labor Organizer
Modish Suit & Coat Company

I am a union man. I am heart and soul in favor of unionization. I saw what could be done for people who were completely helpless as individuals, how the unions were able to better the circumstances of workers, not only economically, but physically, socially, intellectually and in every conceivable way. I, myself, have worked in the ladies garment industry in Portland unlimited hours at very low wages. I have worked from early in the morning until late at night at a steam press

Manly Labby, one of Portland's few Jewish labor leaders, in 1937. Courtesy, Carolina Labby.

Edward Mermelstein, a cutter working at the Modish Suit & Coat Company. Men did the cutting and pressing; women, the sewing. Courtesy, Gussie Reinhardt.

where you could not even see who I was because the steam shot into my face and covered my body from my waist up.

I learned that I was able to extract myself from conditions like that because the worker next to me was helping and the guy behind him was helping; we were all banded together. We could go to an employer as a group and say, "Mr., we think that we are entitled to this. You made a fair profit, how about sharing some of it with us?" If you go to an employer as an individual and say that, he'll kick you out so fast it won't even be funny, but if you go in representing the other workers who stand behind you, the boss has to think twice. No employer wants a union in his plant if he can possibly help it. . . .

We decided that we would organize one factory at a time. To take on the whole group of fourteen shops at once was a little too much for us, because we had our jobs and union activity was just a sideline. We started with Hyman Kirshner's Modish Suit & Coat Company. We began by distributing leaflets in front of the plant when workers got through work or in the morning when they arrived. These flyers told the people what could be accomplished if they decided to become collectively strong instead of individually weak. The workers in Modish became very interested in the union, and we had help from New York to bring this about. Finally we organized the workers, but Kirshner wouldn't talk to us so we called a strike. It lasted only a short time before he settled with us.

Later in the year, Kirshner retaliated by moving Modish across the Columbia River to Vancouver, Washington. That proved to be the undoing of our union. The ladies coat and suit workers were afraid they would lose their jobs. We were concerned that, when the rest of the manufacturers saw the success of the Modish transfer to Vancouver, the other factories would follow suit. This caused further union activities in our Portland industry to collapse.

In 1932, Local 70 decided once again to go after Modish Suit & Coat Company in Vancouver. . . . When Kirshner saw that we had all his workers back in the union again, he called for negotiations because he didn't want a strike. After we wrote the contract with Modish, such as it was, we started in on the other shops. They showed some resistance to us, but it was only a token resistance and they signed up, one at a time. Eventually the Portland ladies coat and suit industry was 100 percent organized.

It is true that there were many factories and small shops in and near Los Angeles that were making ladies coats and suits at less production cost than Portland manufacturers. The reason was that they were non-union; they were sub-standard shops which did not have to pay union wages, and many of them used Spanish labor very, very cheaply.

We couldn't organize the whole world; we could only do our best for the people who

Women attaching buttons and ornaments to garments before a final inspection at Modish. Courtesy, Gussie Reinhardt.

were organized. Los Angeles got no advantage over Portland insofar as the union contracts were concerned. We even gave the Portland manufacturers a few percent lower differential. . . . Los Angeles contracts were always negotiated first, and then the Portland contracts were patterned after them. . . .

I can see that it was well worthwhile to have dedicated my life to the betterment of the workers in our industry. I might add, as a final point, that no local coat and suit manufacturer had to suffer bankruptcy as a result of having his plant unionized and employing union labor. The owners all achieved a very, very fine degree of financial security and left considerable estates.

The ladies garment industry in Portland did not last beyond the immigrant generation. Jews were not attracted to factory work once they obtained education and, as wages rose, the owners were not able to compete with larger, more automated factories in the East and California. Hyman Kirshner's Modish Suit & Coat Company did, however, outlast the other manufacturers; it was still producing in the 1970s, with Kirshner at the helm, "more as a hobby than a business."

15

Neighborhood House

The most important social institution in South Portland was Neighborhood House. The center of a myriad activities, clubs, classes, health services and athletic events, as well as the Hebrew School, it touched the life of virtually every Jewish immigrant in South Portland. It was the social anchor of the neighborhood, and it sought to meet every need that was not being addressed elsewhere.

The Sewing School at Neighborhood House was the first school founded by the Portland Chapter of the National Council of Jewish Women. Begun in 1897, the school was directed by Mrs. Ben Selling from 1900 to 1932. Courtesy, JHSO.

Neighborhood House was founded by the Portland Chapter of the National Council of Jewish Women (Council). From 1912, when she assumed the directorship as headworker, until her retirement in 1945, its guiding spirit was Ida Loewenberg. The founding of the Portland Chapter of Council and the early life of Ida Loewenberg have been discussed earlier; let us turn now to Neighborhood House itself.

The first major settlement house activity undertaken by the Council was the founding of a Sewing School in February, 1897. Within several months, the school had over seventy pupils under the guidance of Mrs. S. J. Mayer and several assistants. In 1900, Mrs. Ben Selling assumed responsibility for the Sewing School, a role which she continued to fulfill for the next thirty-two years. The girls, typically between the ages of ten and sixteen, were taught hand stitching and other sewing techniques. Gertrude Bachman, reminiscing about Neighborhood House, described these sewing classes:

> *On Mondays they would have sewing and the women, they called them the German women of the Northwest [section of Portland], like Miss Hirsch, were my teachers in sewing. Mrs. Ben Selling taught me to make my first knot and it was really something.... We started with small running stitches and we made little articles ... and finally a beautiful silk bag which I gave to my daughter-in-law. They gave us a thimble, darner and a scissors for graduation.*

The first person to graduate from Sewing School was Grace Duncan, a young black girl. Programs sponsored by Council, while catering primarily to the Jewish community, were open to all.

After the Sewing School, further philanthropic innovations initiated by Council followed in rapid succession. Bible classes were begun; students paid ten cents a month to help support them. A kitchen garden or Household School was established which taught children through songs and games how to perform basic household functions. In 1900, a Manual School was opened to teach technical skills; Mr. William Standley was hired by Council to conduct five classes a week on Wednesdays. A free reading room was set up one night a week with a modest stock of books and periodicals.

With the exception of the Manual Training School, most activities were carried out by volunteers. Classes were held initially in the Newcastle Building at Third Avenue and Harrison Street, but were moved a short time after to a larger space in Mrs. Lichtenstein's building at First and Hall. It was difficult to retain qualified teachers for most of the schools because funding was a persistent problem, despite sporadic donations and continual fundraising activities. In 1898, for instance, a "Mother Goose Entertainment" was put on in which the children from the schools participated. It netted $950, a handsome sum for a single program, and was thought by Ida Loewenberg to be "the most notable Jewish occasion since the 1880s, when the pageant of Queen Esther with Lily Fleischner in the title role was a stupendous event."

Before the first Neighborhood House was built in 1905, the German Jewish women of Council were doing their best to help the immigrants who were arriving in ever-increasing numbers. Help meant doing what they thought was most useful for the newcomers: providing basic instruction, skills and religious education and introducing American ways primarily to the children. They hoped that this assistance would lead to the "Americanization" of the immigrants, thus making them more acceptable to the assimilated German Jewish community.

But by the turn of the century, with local experience and knowledge of the growing national settlement house movement, Council began to move away from older concepts of charity toward settlement ideals. These included relieving poverty through education and social services provided by professionally trained teachers and social workers, and through political and economic reform. Rabbi Stephen Wise helped immeasurably in introducing those ideals to Portland and implementing them with Council in specific programs which led to the formal establishment of Neighborhood House. But while the Council women had a strong desire to help and a new philosophy was evolving, there was little social interaction between them and the new immigrants. The gap was simply too wide.

In 1902, Neighborhood House formed its own board of directors. It was composed of five Council members, two members of the Beth Israel Altar Guild (the Temple's philanthropic arm), Rabbi Wise and Mr. Standley. The board was responsible for policy and fiscal decisions and functioned relatively independently from Council activity. Programming increased rapidly, and by 1903 a small gym had been added as well as cooking classes, a boys club (later called the Boys Endeavor Society), and the Junior Zion League. With that growth, however, space again became insufficient.

Under the leadership of Council president Blanche Blumauer, the board decided it was time to build a suitable structure for a settlement house. In 1904, they bought a lot on First Avenue between Lincoln and Hall across the street from Shaarie Torah for two thousand dollars. Subscriptions to the building fund were kicked off by significant donations from Jeanette Meier, Ben Selling, Mrs. Solomon Hirsch and others. Edgar Lazarus was engaged as architect, and the new building was constructed at a cost of approximately ten thousand dollars. At the same time, a constitution was drawn up, and the name "Neighborhood House" was formally adopted (technically "The Neighborhood Guild House of the Council of Jewish Women").

Important activities at Neighborhood House. Courtesy, JHSO.

Kindergarten

Cooking Class, 1914

Citizenship Class, around 1920

Well Baby Clinic

The new building opened on January 1, 1905, and was considered a model for settlement houses. It contained club rooms, an office and a gym with showers. The first event, held on January 8, was Rabbi Stephen Wise's Peoples Forum, which featured regular lectures and discussion groups. The next day, the first kindergarten was begun with Sarah Harris as its teacher. (Neighborhood House maintained a kindergarten until 1917, when that responsibility was assumed by the public schools, although it reopened its kindergarten in 1925 for several additional years.) Americanization classes which taught English and prepared immigrants for citizenship were also launched. A program

of cooperation with the juvenile court was started to curb vandalism and other delinquency. Existing programs including the various schools and the library were expanded.

As immigration to South Portland increased, the number of people using Neighborhood House grew dramatically. English classes mushroomed from eleven pupils and a single teacher in 1906, to three hundred pupils and fourteen teachers by 1909. Approximately half of the students were not Jewish. Even with the large new facility, Neighborhood House could not accommodate the numerous requests for meeting space, and, within five years of its construction, the building had already been outgrown. Yet another subscription drive was launched, headed by Ben Selling and Rabbi Jonah Wise of Beth Israel. Two lots were purchased from Joseph Simon and his law partner, C. A. Dolph, at Second and Wood for $3,750. A loan was secured to supplement subscriptions, and a new building constructed from designs by renowned Portland architect A. E. Doyle.

The new Neighborhood House, which still stands—with the addition in the late 1920s of a swimming pool, handball courts, stage, boxing, wrestling and weightlifting rooms—finally proved adequate to house the multiple social and athletic activities of the growing neighborhood. Blanche Blumauer, chair of the Neighborhood House board from 1905 to 1935, hired the first resident worker in 1911, Miss Sadie Bloch, a social worker from Baltimore. She remained until June of the following year, when Ida Loewenberg was hired as headworker, a post she held for the next thirty-three years. Her dedication to her work and her dynamic, energetic personality influenced every aspect of Neighborhood House life. Almost all those who grew up in South Portland remember her with respect and fondness.

The years following the hiring of Ida Loewenberg were ones of steady expansion. Athletic clubs multiplied for both boys and girls; social, music and literary clubs were launched; an orchestra and theater group were established; a free clinic and dispensary were opened (later replaced by the Well Baby Clinic run by the Visiting Nurses Association); and a high-quality newspaper with Ida Loewenberg as editor-in-chief was begun. An early, regular contributor to the newspaper, the *Neighborhood*, was Marcus Rothkowitz, who was raised in South Portland and later became famous as the painter Mark Rothko.

Adults were now becoming as involved as young people had been. The years of the First World War saw the Hebrew School move into rooms on the top floor free of charge, and the establishment of a dental clinic and a "Penny Bank," where over a hundred children had savings accounts. War support activities were also undertaken, such as the sale of war stamps and the housing of Red Cross units for sewing clothes and first-aid training. But sufficient funds to operate Neighborhood House were always a problem. Annual subscriptions, teas, sacrifice boxes, cookbook sales and scrambling at the end of each year made ends meet until 1920, when Neighborhood House became a member of the new Federated Jewish Societies and received an annual allotment.

One of the most important and still influential activities launched at Neighborhood House in these years was the South Parkway Club, founded by ex-newsboys in 1916. It was called "South Parkway" because the boys came from "South" Portland near Lair Hill "Park." The South Parkway Club, which was begun by young men aged sixteen to twenty-one, was unusual in the range of activities it undertook and the loyalty of its members over the years. In 1923, their wives formed the South Parkway Sisterhood with Mary Rosenberg as its first president because, as Sadie Horenstein put it, "We refused to stay home alone every Tuesday night." The Sisterhood held parties and other social events and raised funds for charity, in later years primarily for the Robison Jewish Home.

Neighborhood House, owned by the Council of Jewish Women and designed by Portland architect A. E. Doyle, was built at Second Avenue and Wood Street in 1910 to provide for the myriad activities of the mushrooming immigrant community of South Portland. Courtesy, JHSO.

The South Parkway Club in 1925. The "little club with a big heart" was founded by ex-newsboys at Neighborhood House in 1916. Courtesy, JHSO.

The club began as an athletic and social organization which fielded excellent basketball and baseball teams. In fact, in an article written in the Sunday *Oregonian* of February 18, 1951, Harry Glickman, current president of Portland's professional basketball team, the Trailblazers, indicated that, "Modern sports fans had probably not heard of Myer Dubin, Harry Hafter, Morris Rogoway, Harry Arback, Abe Popick, Max Lewis or Abe Cantor." But they all had played for South Parkway basketball teams and,

What teams they turned out! A former University of Oregon star, who used to watch them perform in hawk-eyed amazement, ... observed, "As a kid I watched those guys play by the hour. I've had the privilege of playing on some great teams, but South Parkway had the greatest of them all. They might not beat the giants of modern basketball, but for ball-handling, dribbling, passing and all-round cleverness those were the greatest basketball teams ever produced in Oregon."

The South Parkway Club was also dedicated to community service. Nate Schwartz, a charter member, recalls charitable work done by the club:

I would like to say a few words, in fact a lot of words, about a project that is closest to my heart and that is the South Parkway Club of which I have been a member for fifty-six years. The members consist of humanitarians and we call our club "the little club with a big heart." Neighborhood House had trouble with underprivileged children from broken families unable to take vacations. I instigated, with the help of the rest of the membership, the Parkway Club, which sent underprivileged children to camp, both day camp and out-of-town camp. We didn't care whether they were black, yellow, pink or what religion. Later we helped visually handicapped children as well. We have given thousands and thousands of dollars to charity and maintain scholarships for children and I am very proud of what we have done.

The social and entertainment functions of Neighborhood House and the South Parkway Club were important to an immigrant community that daily faced the hardships of making their way in a strange city. Dances were held on Sunday nights. Harry Mesher met his wife at a South Parkway dance; Frances Stein Slifman met her husband there; and many others also met their spouses at a South Parkway function.

Many remember Mel Blanc, who later went to Hollywood and became the voice behind Bugs Bunny and Porky Pig. He was also with the Jack Benny Show. Blanc received his start in an early South Parkway Club minstrel show. Edith Schnitzer Goodman remembers Mel living across the street from her and even as a kid making all kinds of "funny sounds that later became his way of life." Nate Cohen, known as "Uncle Nate," was another entertainer from South Portland who produced and was emcee of "Stars of Tomorrow," heard every Saturday morning on KEX and later on KPTV, until Cohen's death in 1964. The show began in 1926 and broadcast from the window of its sponsor, the Star Furniture Company. It helped launch a number of talented youngsters, including Jane Powell, who was born Suzanne Burce, and Johnny Ray. Nate's wife told the *Oregonian* in 1972 that his mother had always told Nate, "'Only bums go into show business.' So he went at it a different way. He spent his life giving children a chance to perform."

The South Parkway Club and its Sisterhood, and even the daughters of South Parkway members who formed the South Parkway Junior Sisterhood in 1933, met together for many years and retained the close friendships they had formed in their early immigrant days. The club finally disbanded in 1983, when eighty-four-year-old Nate Schwartz was the only remaining charter member and eighty-nine-year-old Boris Geller was the oldest living member. It had simply become too difficult for many of the club members to continue the activities they had maintained for sixty-seven years.

During the 1920s, as the public schools took on more and more of the early educational functions of Neighborhood House, the focus began to shift from an immigrant settlement house to a community center. Stable funding from Federated Jewish Societies and greater prosperity in the postwar years, together with the fact that by the 1920s many of the Jewish children were American-born and spoke English as their native language, placed different demands on Neighborhood House. Athletic

Mel Blanc, Hollywood's voice behind "Bugs Bunny" and "Porky Pig," had his start at a South Parkway minstrel show. Here he clowns with day campers in front of Neighborhood House in the early 1950s. Courtesy, South Parkway Club.

Nate Cohen, "Uncle Nate," a South Portlander, with Johnny Ray, one of the many stars he helped launch on his program "Stars of Tomorrow," which he broadcast for thirty-eight years. Courtesy, JHSO.

and social programs received greater emphasis for people of all ages, and Neighborhood House athletes competed with teams from the Multnomah Athletic Club and from small cities nearby. Health was also emphasized. Clinics were set up to provide prenatal care and serve preschool children, and a general health center was established which provided education on proper nutrition. An excellent staff served Neighborhood House in each of its departments of recreation, education, social activities and health.

While Neighborhood House was clearly the major undertaking of the Council of Jewish Women, it was not the only one. As Council became involved in settlement work at the onset of the progressive era early in the century, it also became concerned with other social and economic issues. At first cautiously, since it was treading new ground and at the forefront of the Jewish community, Council began to take stands on local and national issues. In December, 1899, it affiliated with the State Federation of Womens' Clubs and was recognized thereafter as an important Jewish voice on issues of civic welfare.

Thus the Council became involved in local issues affecting women and children. With the Portland Women's Club, it joined efforts to expand public education, to combat prostitution and venereal disease, and to enhance the rights and salaries of women. They were joined in pressing for these reforms by some Jewish men, particularly Rabbi Stephen Wise, David Solis-Cohen and Joseph Teal, Jr., a wealthy lawyer who gave funds to support Council work.

Mrs. Isaac Leeser Cohen, a Council leader, served on a committee appointed by the city juvenile court in 1906, stimulating much debate in Council meetings on issues affecting young people. She also fought for legislation to protect the newsboys as well as for other child welfare bills at the state legislature.

After long consideration, Council did not endorse women's suffrage in the state election of 1912, due to a concern that the organization would lose its primary philanthropic role by becoming too political. It did, however, become involved after passage and helped to assure its rapid implementation. In 1916, Council put up its own candidate for the city school board, Blanche Blumauer, who was a leader of Council and chair of the Neighborhood House board. She was not successful, however, as the school board remained the exclusive preserve of men in those years.

A fundraiser for the Council of Jewish Women, about 1920. From left: Flora Lippitt, Henrietta Friedman, Eva Langerman, Emma Steinhart, Rose Goodman, Helen Wise and Zerlina Loewenberg. Courtesy, JHSO.

A May Fete celebration held under the auspices of the Council of Jewish Women in Lair Hill Park, about 1925. Entertainment and community events were important in South Portland where immigrant life was often difficult. Courtesy, JHSO.

The Council of Jewish Women also took a leadership role in lobbying the city government on behalf of its clients at Neighborhood House and for South Portlanders generally. Julia Swett, a leading figure in Council, pressed the school board for the establishment of public kindergartens. As early as 1911, Council and residents of South Portland had petitioned the city for a park in the area, but to no avail. Cities did not readily respond to relatively powerless, immigrant districts, and Portland was no exception. The Council continued to agitate, however, and in 1916, the concept of filling Marquam Gulch to create a park was accepted. But the acquisition process was mishandled by the city, and filling the Gulch—which had in the meantime become an informal garbage dump that created seriously unhealthy conditions—took until 1932, when, at last, Duniway Park came into being, twenty-one years after it was first proposed.

Through the 1920s, Council continued to lobby for causes ranging from local concerns such as pensions for widows, increased welfare programs and improved working conditions for women to international issues concerning world peace and Council's desire to see the United States join the World Court. In 1920, when it was determined that a Jewish hospital would be too expensive for the community to build and support, the Council endowed hospital beds at St. Vincent and Emanuel hospitals to provide care for indigent Jewish women. Scholarship and loan funds were also made available, primarily to needy Jewish women, from the sale of Council's cookbook.

The Council of Jewish Women was a truly remarkable organization. Women who began with little training or experience outside the home built an organization that not only founded and operated the major settlement house in Portland, with its numerous and invaluable programs, but became a major force for progressive social reform. From its inception in 1896 through at least the 1920s, Council was the most effective and respected organization in the Jewish community addressing the major social and economic issues of the day.

16

A Tradition of Helping

The Many Organizations

The tradition of giving has deep roots in Judaism. While the Torah prescribed that providing charity was the way that one could "walk after the Lord your God" (Deuteronomy 13:5), it was the rabbis of the Talmud who adopted the word *tsedakah*, literally "righteousness" or "justice," to mean charity. The choice of this word reveals a great deal; charity is not a favor for the recipient, but a privilege for the giver, a *mitzvah*. The rabbis carefully defined how charity was to be dispensed, and it was most important that nothing be done to shame the recipient.

This was the teaching instilled in the Jews who came to America. While the early German Jewish pioneers developed a comprehensive network of charitable organizations, theirs was a relatively modest effort when compared to the intricate multitude of helping organizations, institutions, clubs and societies developed by Jewish immigrants after the turn of the century. Henry Feingold, a Jewish historian, states that, after 1900, the Jewish community "possessed the most elaborate organizational structure of any hyphenate group in America, and ... the most conscientious one." Carrying that assertion even further, the thesis of Max Dimont's *The Jews in America* is that—after the era of the Sadducees (2000-0 B.C.E.) and the era of the rabbis, dominated by the Talmud and synagogue (0-2000 C.E.)—we have now entered the era of multiple Jewish organizations centered on mutual help and social togetherness rather than congregational worship. Dimont believes that this uniquely American development allows Jewish culture to adapt to new conditions and, as has been its genius through the ages, to preserve itself. Whether such a sweeping theory proves itself over time or not, it can accurately be said that all over Jewish America, and certainly in Portland, a profusion of helping organizations blossomed after 1900 and have been nurtured by Jewish Americans ever since.

Michele Glazer and Jennifer Lenway, researchers for the Jewish Historical Society in the late 1970s, who examined every issue of the Jewish press between 1893 and 1940, uncovered the existence of over one thousand locally active Jewish organizations. And this occurred in a Jewish population that never numbered many more than ten thousand people. The sheer quantity of organizations indicates the importance they played in Jewish life and the need that existed to impress a certain order and communality on the chaotic situation in which many immigrants found themselves after their arrival in Portland.

Neighborhood House was the umbrella for a large number of organizations. In addition, there were fraternal organizations, their branches and auxiliaries; synagogues and their affiliated auxiliaries; religious schools; cemeteries; and social and educational clubs. The B'nai B'rith Building (which will be discussed in more detail later) came into existence in 1914 and, contemporaneously with Neighborhood House, operated as a social, recreational and cultural center.

There were also Zionist organizations, local affiliates of national Jewish organizations, such as United Jewish Appeal, and the myriad, short-lived clubs, classes and organizations set up to meet specific needs. While many of these organizations provided for some form of charity, there were also purely charitable institutions, such as the Jewish Shelter Home, the Jewish Old Peoples Home, the Jewish Service Association and the free loan and benevolent societies. Just a partial list of benevolent societies gives a sense of the complexity of charitable enterprise in the decade before Federated Jewish Societies began in 1920:

First Hebrew Benevolent Society;

Jewish Women's Benevolent Society;

Sisters of Israel Benevolent Society;

Hebrew Sick Benefit Association;

Committee for the Relief of Jewish War Sufferers;

South Portland Benevolent Society;

Jewish Consumptives Relief Society;

One of the major money-gathering organizations was the Jewish Relief Society. Begun in 1908, it raised millions of dollars to assist destitute Jews in Portland and elsewhere, thanks to the unrelenting efforts of its longtime president, David Nemerovsky, and its chief fundraiser, Ben Selling. In 1918 and 1919, over $150,000 was raised in Oregon to assist Russian Jews. In a typical year, 1926, the Society provided clothing to 138 people, transportation to 34, fuel to 29, loans to 5, assistance to 317 transients, *matzohs* to 29 families and to Jewish inmates of the state hospital, and also secured employment for 55 persons. Funds were raised by solicitation and received primarily from Jews, but non-Jews also donated. For instance, on the annual Jewish Relief Day in 1916, contributions from non-Jews included over $500 given by Christian Science churches. Ben Selling donated $10,000 in 1923 to celebrate his birthday.

Nearly all of the Jewish clubs and lodges also did charitable work. Louis Albert describes the charitable activities of the Rose City Lodge, the local affiliate of the Order of B'nai Abraham:

When I first came here I joined some of the organizations like the Hebrew Benevolent Association and the Rose City Lodge. The Rose City Lodge was started in 1905, and I became its president when I was not quite twenty-one years old. The Lodge used to have three hundred or four hundred members at its banquet.... We used to enjoy picnics ... at Oaks Park, Crystal Lake Park and Council Crest. They sang all the old songs from Russia, in Hebrew, in Russian.... I loved the old fashioned way. It was warm, sweet.

I did a lot of work for the Rose City Lodge. If anybody notified me, while I was president, that a certain family didn't have any matzohs for Pesach, the next day they had matzohs on their back porch and they didn't know where it came from.

I'll tell you a story. One day a man came to me and said, "Mr. Albert, Mr. President, I want to talk to you." I asked, "What is the matter?" He started to cry. He said, "I was peddling junk. My horse broke a leg so now I haven't got a horse. What will I do?" I said "You want a horse? O.K., I'll get you a horse." He said, "I haven't got any money." I said, "You didn't ask me for any money; you asked me for a horse."

I knew a certain fellow who had a stable and he was dealing in horses, so I drove over there. His name was Hackman and his stable was near Neighborhood House. I said, "Mr. Hackman, can I buy a horse?" He said, "What do you want a horse for? You've got a truck." I answered, "It isn't for me. I've got to help out a man." Hackman brought a horse over to me and I asked him, "How much do you want for it?" He said, "$15." I said, "I haven't got $15." He answered, "This horse costs $15." I said, "I'm telling you, it isn't for me, it's for charity." I had $12 in my pocket and I gave him the $12. He said, "You are a bandit ... but go ahead and take it." I said, "God will help you." He gave me a bridle and some rope.

So I tied the horse to my truck and took it over to the peddler and said, "Here is your horse, forget about the money. It's already paid for." He took the horse and went back to *work. Today his children are very rich, but I got him the horse and he never knew who paid for it. The rules of the Rose City Lodge allowed me to spend $10. I had spent $2 of my own money.... I used to enjoy doing things for people who were in need.*

The Jewish Shelter Home

The Jewish Shelter Home was established in 1920 to provide a home and Jewish environment for children who were orphans or whose parents were unable to care for them. Located at 975 Corbett Street, the Shelter Home was a favored charity of Jeanette Meier, who provided initial support and then retired the entire remaining mortgage on her eighty-first birthday in 1924. Her son, the future governor of Oregon, Julius Meier, was its first president and remained so for many years. "We owe the children whom birth and circumstances have cheated not only care but an open mind, vigilance and understanding so that insofar as we are able we can make amends to them," he said at the annual meeting in 1930.

The home had a capacity of fourteen, ten in the main house and four in a detached isolation

The Jewish Shelter Home was founded in 1920 for orphans and children whose parents were unable to care for them. Courtesy, JHSO.

hospital. The home was conceived as a temporary shelter and, as explained by its first resident director, Martha Thal:

Whenever possible the family home should be rehabilitated or maintained. If this cannot be done, an effort should be made to place children in a proper boarding home or foster home under supervision of the Shelter Home. All placeable children should be placed for adoption.

Typically, children were admitted to the Shelter Home because parents were separated, had recently died, or they were too ill or poor to continue to take care of them and no relatives were available locally. But cases varied widely. In one, the father was a shell-shocked veteran who was emotionally unstable which, in turn, also undermined his wife's health. In another, a single young mother had a mental breakdown, and her children were placed in the Shelter Home until she could recover.

The Shelter Home was essential because there was little public assistance, and help would come, if at all, from relatives or the Jewish community. Children were placed out whenever possible after Julia Swett or Mrs. Toba Narod, representing the board, made inquiries and adjudged the time and placement appropriate. Julia Swett, as a trained social worker, also served as liaison between the Shelter Home and the juvenile court, which often had custody of the children.

Federated Jewish Societies provided most of the operating funds for the home; in 1933, for example, it contributed $4,074 of the home's total $5,111 budget, with the remainder paid by relatives of the children. Jewish merchants and neighbors contributed supplies to the home and would sometimes take children out to movies or neighborhood events. Hanukkah parties, Passover *seders* and open houses were often held at the Shelter Home to give the children as much of a sense of warmth and caring from the community as possible.

The Jewish Shelter Home was merged with the Jewish Service Association (itself a 1927

At the Jewish Shelter Home, early in the 1920s. Courtesy, JHSO.

Children at play

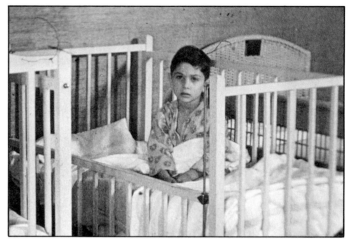

Ready for bed

amalgamation of the Jewish Women's Benevolent Association and the Sisters of Israel Benevolent Association) in 1947 to form the present day Portland Jewish Family and Child Service. This modern agency provides a broad range of services, including counseling for families, children, adolescents and the aged; homemaker services; family life education groups; immigrant resettlement assistance and emergency financial aid. The Jewish Family and Child Service is primarily funded by the Jewish Federation of Portland (the successor to Federated Jewish Societies) and the United Way.

The Jewish Old Peoples Home

In 1916, the Jewish Womens Endeavor Society remodeled its building at 647 SW Fifth Avenue and made it available to elderly persons needing shelter; Mrs. Levin, a widow, was in charge of the home. This early effort to care for the elderly merged with efforts by a group of men who formed the Old Men's Hebrew Fraternal Organization at the home of Leib Shank on Second Avenue in January, 1920. The organization, whose first president was Mr. Shank and whose vice-president was Joseph Nudelman, purchased a large lot and a sixteen-room house at

Third Avenue and College Street that became known as the Jewish Old Peoples Home. The home provided individual, pleasant rooms for each elderly resident, served kosher food at a large dining room table, and maintained a chapel for worship. A Sisterhood was organized at the outset of the home in 1920, with Tillie

The Jewish Old Peoples Home, also founded in 1920, provided a warm Jewish atmosphere for its elderly residents. Courtesy, JHSO.

At the Jewish Old Peoples Home in 1939. Courtesy, JHSO.

Kosher cuisine

Cheerful bedrooms

Maronek as its first president. It was reorganized in 1928 under the leadership of Rose Nudelman, who remained its president until 1935. The Sisterhood has raised large amounts of money and provided innumerable services to the home, which has been a major and significant charitable effort of the Jewish community since its inception.

In 1945, its name was changed to the Jewish Home for the Aged. Then, in 1953, it was renamed the Robison Home for the Aged in honor of Mrs. Hannah Robison. Encouraged by their attorney, Hy Samuels, her two sons, Charles and Edward, gave a substantial sum to complete the drive for a new building. Mrs. Robison (formerly Robinson) had run the Robison Dry Goods Store on First Avenue in South Portland with her husband Lazarus. She had lived at the home for a short while in 1947. In 1955, at the age of ninety-two, and shortly before the laying of the cornerstone for the new Robison Home, she explained to the *Oregon Journal* why she was so proud that she and her sons were able to return some of what they had received from this country:

I'm grateful to America. I say "God Bless America." I came from Europe with three little children and people were so nice to me and my children. I wasn't stylish and I couldn't talk very well—I still can't—but they paid me respect. They helped educate my children.

The Robison Jewish Home (its current name) is located at 6140 Boundary Road in the southwest suburbs of Portland. The home has continued to be remodeled and expanded with funds raised largely under the leadership of Eugene Nudelman, Sr., Joseph's grandson. The Robison Home Sisterhood is very active and numbers over twelve hundred members. Today, the Robison Jewish Home is a sophisticated, long-term care facility consisting of a medical infirmary with eighty-four residents, a semi-independent Home for the Aged with thirty-six residents, and twenty May Apartments for retirees. Abe "English" Rosenberg, who served for many years on the Robison Home board, told interviewer Michele Glazer in 1977:

There's an old adage about Jewish people. One of the commandments is "Honor thy father and mother" and that's been inculcated in us for years and years. Taking care of the elderly has always been something that children in the community take care of. It has always had a special appeal no other charity has, evidenced by the number of bequests and donations we received throughout the years.

Federated Jewish Societies

A significant move toward the coordination of Jewish charitable activity took place in 1920 with the establishment of Federated Jewish Societies. The purpose of the Federation was "to centralize the work of collection and supervise distribution with a view to added efficiency, greater effectiveness and more satisfactory progress." As early as 1908, an editorial appeared in the *Jewish Tribune* decrying the lack of coordinated Jewish charity in Portland:

> *There are over a hundred Jewish men out of work in Portland at present. The majority of them are family men. They do not know where their next meal will come from. They and their wives and children are starving.*
>
> *Is anything going to be done for them?*
>
> *Charity, such as it is, is being doled out to them, but those having our charities in charge confess to being incapable of meeting the emergency.*
>
> *Their impotence is due, they claim, to the fact that Portland's Jewish charitable organizations are divided. No united effort is made to help the poor. The result is that the charity that is given is often misplaced—one person gets all and the others nothing.*
>
> *The only remedy is united charity.*

While Neighborhood House and other Jewish helping agencies made valiant efforts, they were unable to meet the need, and there was, at times, intense competition for available donations. The need for a professionally coordinated, community-wide approach was clear.

That effort was led by B'nai B'rith. The Federation was organized by the Committee for Relief of War Sufferers, chaired by Nathan Strauss, the president of Fleischner, Mayer & Co., while Roscoe Nelson, Sr., a well-known Jewish lawyer, drafted its constitution and by-laws. In January, 1920, the initial list of Federated Societies included: Neighborhood House; the B'nai B'rith Building; Committee on Jewish Orphans, which was organizing and purchasing the Jewish Shelter Home; First Hebrew Benevolent Society; Jewish Relief Society; Portland Hebrew Free School; South Portland Benevolent Society; Jewish Consumptives Relief Society; and the National Jewish Hospital for Consumptives in Denver.

The list changed over the years, although major providers such as Neighborhood House and the B'nai B'rith Building remained members. Each constituent organization had one vote on the board to determine policy matters and elect officers. The role of the Federation was to raise monies which would be distributed to constituent societies according to their need. The individual societies remained autonomous. The first fundraising campaign, although smaller in scope, looked surprisingly like the "Super Sunday" campaigns of the Federation in the 1980s. Two hundred young Jewish men and women were divided into thirty-five teams to carry out an intensive three-day solicitation of twenty-five hundred prospective donors. The goal was fifty thousand dollars. The constituent organizations each received an allocation of funds. For the first time, they had defined the scope of their work in the Jewish community and could count on stable, annual funding.

Mrs. Hannah Robison (seated center) celebrates her birthday in 1940. The Robison Jewish Home, which is named for Mrs. Robison, provides comprehensive care for the elderly. Courtesy, Felice Lauterstein Driesen.

17

Zionism

Organized Zionism began in Oregon in 1901, with the founding of the Zionist Society of Portland. Rabbi Stephen Wise, who was already honorary secretary to the National Federation of American Zionists and a close friend of Theodor Herzl, was the prime mover. Judge Otto Kraemer was its first president, Julius

The Heller family gathers in 1896 in Copenhagen before emigrating to Portland. Paula Heller Lauterstein, the founder of Hadassah in Portland, is sitting directly in front of her mother. Henry Nathan Heller, her father (standing) served as rabbi of Neveh Zedek for seven years. Courtesy, Felice Lauterstein Driesen.

Meier its first vice-president, and its board was composed primarily of members of Beth Israel. The major role played by Beth Israel in Portland's Zionist Society can only be attributed to the charismatic personality of its rabbi. Reform Jews elsewhere in the country were generally hostile to Jewish nationalism and its dream of a homeland, due primarily to fear that it would subject them to the charge of dual loyalty and undermine their hard-won status in America.

The Zionist Society grew rapidly to more than three hundred members. Stephen Wise, David Solis-Cohen and Otto Kraemer gave many speeches to both Jewish and non-Jewish audiences. National Zionist speakers were also brought to Oregon and paid from dues collected from Society members. Both the *Jewish Tribune* and the *Scribe* editorialized consistently in favor of Zionism and reported the activities of the Society. In 1918, the Society joined the Zionist Organization of America, which regularly sponsored national speaking tours that included Portland in return for dues paid to the national organization.

The Portland Hebrew School, which sought to revitalize Jewish culture and learning, was another strong proponent of Zionism. Located at Neighborhood House, it became a major vehicle for the expression of South Portland's passionate support for both a Jewish homeland and the Zionist spiritual and cultural regeneration proclaimed by Achad Ha'Am. But after its initial surge of support, the Zionist Society lost membership and influence in the 1920s and 30s. Rabbi Philip Kleinman of Congregation

The preparation of annual Thanksgiving plum puddings in 1930 to raise funds for Hadassah hospitals and clinics in Palestine. Paula Lauterstein is second from left. Courtesy, Felice Lauterstein Driesen.

Neveh Zedek, who was a president of the organization in that period, recalls that it functioned only informally with a membership of about fifty people. And in 1937, he was forced to call on Harry Mittleman, a respected community leader and wealthy real estate developer, to help him raise funds to keep the organization alive.

Debbie Goldberg, whose Reed College thesis on Zionism in Portland is the primary work on the subject, states: "As was the case on the national scene, the most consistently influential Zionist organization in Portland was Hadassah." Hadassah, or the Women's Zionist Organization of America, which was to become the largest Zionist organization in the world and one of America's largest women's organizations, is "a voluntary, non-profit organization dedicated to the ideals of Judaism, Zionism, American democracy, healing, teaching and medical research."

Paula Lauterstein was the chief organizer of Hadassah in Portland. She was born in Copenhagen where her father, Henry Nathan Heller, was a rabbi as he later was for seven years at Neveh Zedek. Paula's husband, Jacob Lauterstein, who owned a downtown clothing store, came from one of the colony of families that had emigrated from Russia in the 1880s and had

tried homesteading in North Dakota before coming to Portland. They were all fervent Zionists. Paula became Hadassah's first president in the early 1920s and remained throughout her life a leading figure in Portland Hadassah. She also served on the national board, attending two World Zionist Congresses in Basel, Switzerland, and traveling to Israel to help establish and maintain Hadassah Hospital. Miriam Rosenfeld played a key role in the second generation of Hadassah leadership. She was president from 1943 to 1945 and was instrumental in organizing the well-known Braille project for the blind at Temple Beth Israel.

The main role of Hadassah in Portland was raising funds for the network of hospitals, clinics and infant welfare stations that were maintained by Hadassah throughout Palestine. Portland Hadassah members raised money through the annual sale of homemade plum puddings during the Thanksgiving season. Periodically, Hadassah also held theater parties and maintained sewing groups which made children's clothes and hospital gowns for Palestine. In 1927, five thousand dollars was raised to endow in perpetuity a Louisson Bed (named for a local Zionist activist) at Hadassah Hospital in Jerusalem by holding a large "Gates of Jaffa" bazaar.

Hadassah was the most vital organization for many South Portlanders and included women as diverse as Dora Levine of the fish market and Rachel Fain Schneider, daughter of Orthodox Rabbi Fain. Gussie Reinhardt, who joined Hadassah in 1943, remembers it as "the primary affiliation for many. Members were indeed ideologically motivated." And Hilda Simons describes the fundamental reason so many were committed to organizations like Hadassah:

I always remember Hillel's often quoted words: "If I am for myself alone what am I?" This undoubtedly stems from my family background, where pennies were collected each week in a little blue box for Hadassah and other charities. I couldn't possibly live for myself alone when hunger and deprivation are part of world Jewry.

Numerous smaller Zionist organizations were also organized in Portland as they were throughout America. Among them, auxiliaries of Hadassah were numerous: Junior Hadassah, the Hadassah Sewing Circle, the Hadassah Study Group and the Sophomore Hadassah Study Group. The Portland Junior Zionists was established in 1903, shortly after the Zionist Society, to provide a Zionist organization for young people. Keren Hayesod (the Jewish National Fund) and Junior Keren Hayesod were

Hadassah's Blue Box, a familiar sight in the Jewish community, was used to collect coins for charitable work in Palestine. Courtesy, JHSO.

set up in Portland shortly after the national organization was founded in 1921. Its first local president was Joseph Shemanski, and it collected funds for immigration and education in Palestine. The Mizrachi Zionist Society was begun in Portland in 1916, with J. Rosencrantz as its president, to provide a more religious orientation within the Zionist movement. And there was also the Portland Zionist Roll Call, headed by Rabbi Herbert Parzen of Ahavai Sholom, whose purpose was to register public opinion in support of Jewish Palestine; the Zionist District of Portland; Lovers of Zion Society; the Kadimah Society for high school students; and, beginning in 1945, a Portland Zionist Council, organized to help coordinate the work of the many Zionist organizations in the city.

This listing gives a sense of the critical importance that most of Portland Jewry attached to the establishment of a Jewish homeland in Palestine. Zionism was an integral part of the consciousness of Jews who came from Eastern Europe. Organizations such as the South Portland Benevolent Association, which had nothing ostensibly to do with Zionism, contributed significant sums to Zionist groups in Palestine, such as Histadrut (the Jewish Labor Federation) and the Irgun and Haganah (Jewish Defense Forces in Palestine).

While ambivalence toward Zionism existed in the Reform Jewish community, particularly in the early years of the movement, and some Reform Jews did join the American Council for Judaism (an anti-Zionist organization founded nationally in 1942), a large number of well-established Jews at both Beth Israel and Ahavai Sholom were strong Zionists. Rabbi Edward Sandrow of Ahavai Sholom delivered sermons on Zionism and brought Golda Myerson, later Israeli Prime Minister Golda Meir, to speak at the synagogue on the Histadrut labor movement. B'nai B'rith often co-sponsored Zionist events in Portland, and presidents of the B'nai B'rith District, such as David Solis-Cohen, Isaac and Zachary Swett and David Mosessohn, were avid Zionists.

Portland was unusual in the broad and vital support Zionism received from the Jewish com-

A tree certificate from Keren Hayesod (the Jewish National Fund) signifying the planting of five trees in Palestine. Alex Miller was the owner of a Portland clothing store and president of Congregation Ahavai Sholom. He died in June, 1933. Courtesy, JHSO.

munity. The stature and charismatic personality of Portland's early Zionist leaders, Stephen Wise and David Solis-Cohen, were instrumental in involving the established Reform and Conservative communities in the Zionist cause. Wise brought his personal contact with world Zionism and its leaders, particularly Herzl, to the Beth Israel pulpit and to numerous speeches he gave throughout Portland. Solis-Cohen, building on the views of America's best-known Zionist, Supreme Court Justice Louis Brandeis, eloquently lectured on the compatibility of American and Zionist ideals. In fact, nearly all of Portland's rabbis were Zionist sup-porters, and many played leadership roles in the movement.

Zionism appealed to both the frontier heritage and pioneer spirit of Oregonians, their closeness to the settling of a new land and their tradition of philanthropy, which had been led by Ben Selling and the Council of Jewish Women. Although the spirit of Zionism fit well into Oregon traditions, its preeminent appeal was the fundamental hope of Jews for the revitalization of their religion and culture after its continual degradation in Europe, a hope based on building a safe haven in the ancient Jewish homeland, Israel.

18

B'nai B'rith and Community Leadership

The Lodges

At the turn of the century, Oregon had four B'nai B'rith lodges: two older lodges formed by early Jewish pioneers, numbers 65 and 314, and two that had been organized in the 1890s, numbers 416 and 464.

Portland Lodge 416 was composed largely of German Jewish offspring of the early pioneers. Their relatives had organized the elite Concordia Club in the 1880s and they themselves, middle-aged by 1900, had inherited much of the Jewish business network from their fathers. The lodge's approximately ninety members were affluent, lived primarily in Northwest Portland, and maintained an aloofness—except for charitable enterprises on behalf of their less fortunate brethren—from the other lodges and the growing Jewish community.

Sabato Morais Lodge 464 had been formed in 1897 by early Eastern European settlers who had become modestly established by that time as secondhand merchants, tailors and small proprietors, with a few working as professionals; a number of these men lived near their stores in downtown Portland. Many of them—Isaac Swett, David Nemerovsky, Israel Dautoff, Ben Pallay and the Weinstein and Holzman brothers—were beginning to assume leadership roles in Jewish organizations.

The early pioneer lodges 65 and 314 had lost membership through the 1890s. In 1905, they joined with Lodge 464 to create a new Lodge 314 that was named for the recently de-

ceased leader of Zionism, Theodor Herzl. Lodge 416—the German Jewish group—remained aloof from this consolidation until 1919, when a strong movement to integrate all Jewish services in the community led to the establishment of Federated Jewish Societies and to B'nai B'rith's consolidation into a single lodge. Ben Selling, Joseph Shemanski and Nathan Strauss worked for unification, and seven hundred members were initially recruited, with Shemanski as president.

The newly formed consolidated lodge was numbered 65 in honor of the founding lodge in Oregon, and it grew to become the largest lodge on the West Coast, involving more than 35 percent of Portland's adult Jewish men in the years after its founding. Portland Lodge 65 and Daughters of the Covenant, its auxiliary, sponsored numerous social and cultural events in pursuit of its goals of providing sociability for its members and education and unity for the entire Jewish community. The leadership of reconstituted Lodge 65 was drawn from prominent figures in both the Eastern European and German communities. With this consolidation, B'nai B'rith became a unifying and democratizing force in the Jewish community.

In 1912, an independent lodge associated with the Order of B'nai Abraham was formed and called the Rose City Lodge. The lodge organized a Mutual Benefit Society in 1917 to provide health benefits and burial costs for its members, who numbered over four hundred in 1919. The membership of the lodge and benefit society were primarily Eastern European

B'nai B'rith installs officers at the District Grand Lodge convention in the Multnomah Hotel, Portland, 1921. Back row from left: Sam Kohs, Milton Margulis, Jacob Lauterstein, Nathan Weinstein, Joseph Shemanski, Ben Rubin, Anselm Boskowitz, Sol Bishoff, Sam Tonkin, Edward Weinbaum. Seated: Jess Rich, Alex Miller, Isaac Swett, Zeke Swett, Jonah Wise, David Solis-Cohen, Sam Mendelsohn, Alex Weinstein, Sigmund Lipman. Courtesy, JHSO.

immigrants who needed mutual insurance, as the B'nai B'rith lodges had terminated most insurance programs as their members became more affluent. The Rose City Mutual Benefit Society held its meetings at the B'nai B'rith Building and put on many social and cultural events for its members and the general public.

The B'nai B'rith Building

In July, 1910, David Solis-Cohen, Isaac Swett and Rabbi Jonah Wise filed articles of incorporation for the B'nai B'rith Building Association. Several months later, some sixty men met at Beth Israel to purchase shares in the Association, whose purpose was to build a Jewish community center in Portland. The Association was independent of lodges and had an initial capital stock of twenty-five thousand dollars, divided into twenty-five hundred shares costing ten dollars each.

Initially, leadership came from members of Beth Israel: Ben Selling, Sig Sichel, Dr. J.J. Rosenberg, Anselm Boskowitz and Rabbi Jonah Wise. But during the four-year process of fundraising and site selection, a new group of men assumed much of the responsibility, a group that would continue to lead the Jewish community toward consolidation and unity by the end of the decade. These men had come primarily from Eastern Europe in the nineteenth century, but they were by then established and closely associated with the increasingly prosperous Lodge 314 and with Congregation Ahavai Sholom. They included Isaac Swett, Joseph Shemanski, Alex Miller, David Mosessohn and Dr. Aaron Tilzer.

The site selected for the proposed Jewish community center was on Thirteenth Avenue between Mill and Market streets, where a lot was purchased for fourteen thousand dollars. The location was central for those association members and other prospective users who

The B'nai B'rith Building was completed in October, 1914, on Thirteenth between Mill and Market streets. The building housed numerous activities and served as Portland's Jewish community center for over half a century until the current center was built in 1971. Courtesy, JHSO.

mostly lived in Northwest Portland, the Park Blocks, the Shattuck School area and on the fringes of downtown. It was not expected that residents of South Portland would use the facility, since they already had Neighborhood House.

Jacob Dautoff was engaged as architect. The handsome, two-story brick structure with tall second-story windows and an ornamental entranceway was completed in October, 1914, at a cost of approximately fifty thousand dollars, and dedicated the following year. Inside there were expansive lodge and meeting halls, a gym,

showers, swimming pool, billiard room, handball court, clubroom and library.

The building provided meeting space for a range of community activities: the lodges, the Rose City Mutual Benefit Society, the Beth Israel Religious School, the Sephardic community's High Holiday services and numerous clubs and societies. The board saw its function as providing a center for all sectors of the Jewish community. For the most part, however, it primarily served an emerging Jewish middle class which sought recreation and entertainment as well as

The B'nai B'rith Orchestra, January, 1927. Cultural programs were important at the Center. Courtesy, JHSO.

intellectual and cultural events. Activities of importance to the immigrant community in South Portland, such as basic skills, citizenship preparation and health clinics, were left to Neighborhood House.

There was a sense in South Portland that the kids who attended B'nai B'rith were "ritzier." To Harry Mesher, "the B'nai B'rith, which was known as the Jewish Community Center, was for the rich kids. The poor kids, they went to the Neighborhood House." Seen from South Portland, the new middle class that used the B'nai B'rith Building seemed a world apart, but as years passed and South Portlanders grew increasingly prosperous, the two communities came closer together.

The physical education program at the community center developed into one of the finest in the city under the guidance of Millicent "Mickey" Hirschberg and later Harry "Polly" Policar. Mickey joined the staff in 1924 and developed a renowned hydrotherapy program for victims of polio. She remained the Jewish Community Center's aquatics director for forty-nine years. Polly, an alumnus of B'nai B'rith athletic teams, became full-time athletic director in 1933, building both the sports program and the B'nai B'rith summer camp. B'nai B'rith fielded fine basketball teams through the years, as well as teams in other sports, and formed its own Amateur Athletic Association in 1921.

An important social club, the Ramblers (Right, Ambition, Merit, Benevolence, Love, Energy, Religion, Service), was founded at the B'nai B'rith Center in 1921, with Tom Charack as its first president. Similar to the South Parkway Club at Neighborhood House, the Ramblers was started by young men between the ages of eighteen and twenty-three. It sponsored popular monthly dances at the B'nai B'rith Building and other locations, such as aboard the *Swan* on the Willamette River. Proceeds from dances and social events were often given to charity and a scholarship fund. The club organized its own orchestra, which later became part of a community center orchestra under Aaron Avshalomov. (Aaron's son, Jacob, followed his father's footsteps and has conducted the Portland

Youth Philharmonic since 1954). The club also fielded basketball and swimming teams that competed as far away as Seattle. Annual Rambler banquets were the major social occasion of

Millicent "Mickey" Hirschberg, aquatics director for many years, was honored for her work with polio victims. Courtesy, OHS.

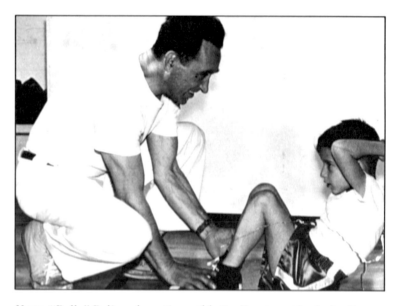

Harry "Polly" Policar, long-time athletic director at both the Center and summer camp. Courtesy, JHSO.

The Ramblers annual banquet in 1930 was held at the Multnomah Hotel. An important social club, it was founded by young men at the B'nai B'rith Center in 1921. Courtesy, A. E. "English" Rosenberg.

the year for members. A Ramblers Auxiliary was also quite active, as was the case for most all-male Jewish clubs.

Other major organizations at the center included the B'nai B'rith Youth Organization (BBYO), the local affiliate of the large national organization and Aleph Zadik Aleph (AZA). The Junior B'nai B'rith Lodge, an AZA branch of BBYO, was established in 1927 and grew out of a boys' group called the Sphinx Club and other informal junior lodges which had existed in the 1890s. The charter president of Portland's AZA chapter, the third oldest on the West Coast, was Maure Goldschmidt, who later was a professor at Reed College. Harry Kenin, who became executive director of the B'nai B'rith Center, was one of AZA's organizers and its first advisor. AZA sponsored active youth programs ranging from basketball and debating to annual father-son banquets, lectures on Jewish subjects, dances and parties. In 1949, Richard Brownstein of Portland was elected international president of AZA; twenty-seven years later, his son, Jeb, was the second Portlander to be honored by election to the same post.

A primary activity of the B'nai B'rith Center

from its early years has been a summer camp for boys and girls. The camp was begun in 1921 at Bass Lake in Stevenson, Washington; two years later, it was moved to Neskowin on the Oregon coast. In 1928, it was permanently located on a large acreage donated by Julius Meier on Devil's Lake at Neotsu, near Lincoln City, Oregon. Children between nine and sixteen were admitted to camp, with July reserved for boys and August for girls. A diverse program of camping, athletics and arts was provided within a Jewish atmosphere. The camp is still in operation and its programs have expanded to provide camping opportunities for families, couples, singles and seniors, as well as children.

The B'nai B'rith Building was renamed the B'nai B'rith Center in 1923 in recognition of its diverse activities and membership. In the 1930s, when many residents of South Portland moved to other parts of the city, they also began to join the Center. In 1938, with leadership from Center presidents Sam Weinstein (1937-1941) and Harry Mittleman (1941-1948), the facility was expanded and it was formally named the Jewish Community Center, reflecting its growing appeal to the entire community.

The Center remained at the B'nai B'rith Building until 1971, when a modern facility was built in the Southwest suburbs, where many in the Jewish community were then residing. Julius Zell served as chair of the building fund drive. The new Center was named in 1976 for Helen Mittleman, the wife of Harry Mittleman, who donated a large sum of money to retire the Center's mortgage. Today, the Mittleman Jewish Community Center employs a permanent staff of thirty-seven, plus sixteen early childhood teachers and assistants, who provide comprehensive programming for the Jewish and general communities.

Children swimming at B'nai B'rith camp at Neotsu, Oregon. Donated by Julius Meier in 1928, the camp still thrives today. Courtesy, JHSO.

Community Leadership

"The most important ... event of the years just before and after World War I was the emergence of a new middle class which gave direction to the community," William Toll writes in his study of Portland Jewry. This new pattern resulted from the shifting relationship between three generations of Jews in Portland. The first provided primary leadership prior to 1910, and was made up of the American-born children of German pioneers: Ben Selling, Anselm Boskowitz, Isaac Fleischner, Julius Meier and Rabbi Jonah Wise. While these men and their wives were often involved in philanthropy, they were also somewhat isolated from the broader Jewish community, since their social lives tended to be concentrated in the exclusive enclaves of the Concordia Club and, later, the Tualatin Country Club.

The second generation was composed of early settlers from Eastern Europe, primarily merchants and several lawyers: Zachary and Isaac Swett, Joseph Shemanski, David Nemerovsky, David Mosessohn and Israel Bromberg. They cooperated with sympathetic members of the German elite, forming the B'nai B'rith Building Association together, for instance, but they were dedicated to a more united and democratic Jewish community. They began to assume more leadership in the years before the First World War, and this led to greater unity within the Jewish community, as exemplified by the founding of the Federated Jewish

Rabbi Jonah Wise of Beth Israel (right) and Jacob Weinstein, later to become a well-known rabbi in Chicago, at Camp Wallula, the first B'nai B'rith summer camp in the early 1920s. Courtesy, JHSO.

Societies and the establishment of consolidated Portland Lodge 65. They were at the forefront of a growing middle class that coalesced around the B'nai B'rith Building and helped to develop a new ethnic ideology that stressed cultural pluralism within the Jewish community. This ideology would lead in time to the melding of all sectors of the community, one which would include the still separate German Jews of Beth Israel as well as the more Orthodox, immigrant Jews of South Portland.

By the 1920s, Ben Selling's generation had grown into old age, and many of the early Eastern European Jews of the second group had become immersed in business and other pursuits that limited their involvement. Thus, a new cadre of well-educated, American-born professionals, mostly of Eastern European background, began to emerge as leaders of the Jewish community: David Robinson, a lawyer and founder of the local Anti-Defamation League; Harry Kenin, director of the B'nai B'rith Center and a lawyer; Harry Herzog, an architect; Roscoe Nelson, a lawyer who had come from Virginia; Sam Weinstein, an attorney and Leo Ricen, a physician. In concert with others, these Jews brought a broad knowledge and concern for civic reform and national and international Jewish issues to the community.

In the two decades after 1910, the population of the Jewish community in Oregon more than doubled to approximately ten thousand. By the end of the 1920s, many of the immigrants were gaining a measure of prosperity and moving from old South Portland to the Shattuck School area and the city's growing Eastside. In the context of rapid population growth and residential dispersion, no individual or group could legitimately speak for the whole Jewish community. Hence the 1920s saw the emergence of a secular Jewish middle class as the major force within Portland Jewry, a class which has retained leadership to the present day.*

---

*Much of the material that is contained in this section was derived from William Toll's *The Making of an Ethnic Middle Class: Portland Jewry Over Four Generations*, pages 107-109.

German Jews and the Other Early Settlers

What had become of the German Jewish merchants who had done so well in the pioneer generation? In the years between the 1880s and the 1920s, their children had inherited their business networks, but German patriarchal tradition (whose exclusivity yielded few possible mates) led to smaller families. In fact, many German Jews never married: more than 20 percent of German women remained unmarried in 1900, as compared with less than 4 percent of women of Eastern European descent. Because these German Jews were able to move easily into positions in the business community established by their parents, they did not put as much emphasis on education as did immigrants from Eastern Europe. But by the 1920s, education, in addition to wealth, was becoming an important prerequisite for leadership in the Jewish community. Perhaps, though, the major reason that German Jewish leadership began to fade was its relative isolation from the main currents of the much more populous and increasingly prosperous Eastern European Jewish community.

Jonah Wise, rabbi at Beth Israel from 1907 to 1926, was well known in Portland as a leader in local B'nai B'rith lodges 416 and 65 and president of the B'nai B'rith Grand Lodge in San Francisco. Rabbi Wise, the son of Isaac Mayer Wise, the founder of Reform Judaism in America, delivered his thoughtful sermons to the still largely German membership of Beth Israel. He was well-educated, witty, somewhat cynical and a devotee of golf and fishing. In fact, Rabbi Wise, while visiting the Metropole Golf Club in New York, determined that Portland must itself have such a club and he became the major force behind the founding of the Tualatin Country Club in 1912. Only the fourth country club in Oregon, Tualatin was established as a golf and social club on seventy acres of the former Sweek Homestead near the town of Tualatin in Washington County. Its members were former members of the Concordia Club and for many years exclusively of German descent.

Many in the German community continued to experience business success. Meier & Frank, Lipman, Wolfe & Co., Fleischner, Mayer & Co., and other enterprises, such as Philip Feldman's Mt. Hood Soap Company (established in 1905), prospered during the first decades of the century and many for years after. German Jews made exceptional contributions, with Ben Selling and the Council of Jewish Women the most prominent examples. But the social exclusivity that was preserved in Beth Israel, Lodge 416 and the Tualatin Country Club meant some of the offspring of the German pioneers became ingrown. They became further isolated as they moved to the posh West Hills and Dunthorpe.

When the B'nai B'rith Building was constructed to provide a place for the new middle class to gather, many older German families refused to help or to associate with it. Consequently, they lost standing in the increasingly middle-class Jewish community. After Ben Selling and Julius Meier died in the 1930s, the surviving older German families seldom represented or spoke for the community. Sylvan Durkheimer, the son of a successful German

Drawing of the Tualatin Country Club, founded in 1912 by German Jews as an exclusive golf and social club located near the Tualatin River in Washington County. From *In the Beginning*, published by the Women of the Tualatin Country Club (1984).

merchant who was the mayor of Burns, Oregon, later described the situation that resulted: "The present generation of German Jews has apparently gone to seed, in part. They are not as aggressive or progressive or of the same standard as their fathers."

The congregation of Ahavai Sholom took a

Confirmation at Temple Beth Israel in 1918. Rabbi Jonah Wise is the tallest male to the rear. Courtesy, JHSO.

quite different path from that of Beth Israel. It was the synagogue chosen by many of the Eastern European immigrants who arrived before 1900. They established themselves as merchants and professionals by the teens, and provided leadership to the growing middle class. South Portland residents who began to rise in social status often turned to the Conservative Judaism of Ahavai Sholom or Neveh Zedek in the years before 1930. Ahavai Sholom, which moved its synagogue to Park Avenue and Clay Street in 1904, was led for many years by a number of cantors who also served as rabbi. Rabbi Robert Abrahamson had the longest tenure (serving at periodic intervals from 1880 to 1922), and several other rabbis of Ahavai Sholom became prominent locally and nationally, including Herbert Parzen (1928-1932) and Edward Sandrow (1933-1937).

Jewish life in Oregon outside of Portland diminished substantially in the decades after 1900. The German Jewish merchants who had become prominent in nearly every town and city in the state came to Portland or other larger cities toward the end of the nineteenth century. Since the railroads now supplied ready-made, low-cost goods from the East and Midwest, their isolation from Jewish communal life became unnecessary and burdensome. A Jewish community remained in some outlying towns, such as Baker, but that was unusual. In Eugene, the state's second largest city, a small Jewish community thrived, and a Jewish fraternity was established at the University of Oregon (Delta Epsilon, pledged as the local chapter of Sigma Alpha Mu, the national Hebrew fraternity).

Rabbis, primarily from Portland, would travel to Eugene and at times other towns in Oregon to celebrate major holidays. But Jewish immigrants from Eastern Europe seldom found their way to smaller communities as had the German merchants of the previous generation. It was not until the 1930s and 1940s that there was sufficient Jewish population to support a B'nai B'rith lodge (Willamette Valley Lodge 1181, founded in 1934 to serve the entire valley), or synagogues in Eugene (Temple Beth Israel, founded, 1934; current synagogue built, 1952) or in Salem (Temple Beth Shalom, founded 1947).

Confirmation at Congregation Ahavai Sholom in 1924 with Rabbi Naban Krueger sitting. Courtesy, JHSO.

19

The Rise of Eastern European Jews

In a single generation, Eastern European Jews came from immigrant poverty to share fully in the life of the city. They had arrived in Portland carrying battered Old World valises and speaking Yiddish, but they found success in business, the professions, the arts and a host of other occupations. They became active, vital citizens of Oregon and America. How was such a rapid transformation possible?

Eastern European men and women gloried in the American experience of freedom that they had yearned for in the Old World. Their long-suppressed energy flowered. The attributes traditionally nourished in Jewish life—family, education, motivation to achieve, thrift and moderation—were all useful in adapting to American life. The immigrants' recent experience of deprivation in Europe also provided them with a high threshold for discomfort and a resilience and ingenuity that proved invaluable in forging ahead in America's open economy.

Jewish women played a key role at the center of family life. The tradition of mutuality brought from Eastern Europe, with both men and women helping to provide support, proved unusually useful in a commercial center like Portland. Women provided emotional sustenance for men seeking to establish themselves in a strange city and for children caught between old and new ways. They also forged the intimate ties between extended families and within the neighborhood that made South Portland a cohesive, nurturing incubator for these nascent Americans.

The Eastern Europeans retained their vital sense of being Jews. Despite moving away from South Portland—by 1930, one-third had moved nearby to the Shattuck School area and 20 percent to the Eastside—they maintained strong loyalty to and involvement in the Jewish community. By sheer force of numbers and the energy they brought to everything they did, the Eastern Europeans reshaped Jewish life in Portland and gave it direction and leadership.

PART III

BUILDING
A UNIFIED JEWISH COMMUNITY

1920-1950

20

Anti-Semitism

Introduction

As World War I came to a close, the Jewish community of Portland was taking its first significant steps toward unification. The B'nai B'rith Building had been constructed to bring diverse segments of the community together and it succeeded in providing a center for the growing middle class. The consolidation of B'nai B'rith lodges and the creation of Federated Jewish Societies involved a broader cross section of the community in important fraternal, social and philanthropic initiatives. It was at this time that the World War ended, Prohibition began, and the xenophobic twenties arrived.

The First World War had basically stopped the flow of immigration to America, and national legislative restrictions in the 1920s froze the Jewish population at approximately its prewar numbers. While many Jewish immigrants were beginning to experience upward mobility, strong nativist, nearly paranoid forces were growing throughout the country. In Oregon, they expressed themselves primarily through the growth of the Ku Klux Klan, raising the spectre of anti-Semitism which had driven so many Jews from Europe. The Jewish community pulled together nationally and in Oregon to fight anti-Semitism, particularly when its most virulent form, Nazism, menaced the world in the 1930s and 1940s.

Early Instances of Anti-Semitism

Jews blended easily into frontier society. While they did well economically and politically in Oregon, and only rarely confronted hostility toward Jews, they did face isolated oubursts of anti-Semitism—as in the diatribes of Thomas Dryer, owner of the *Oregonian* in the 1850s, and Judge Waldo in the 1880s. Jews also experienced institutionalized anti-Semitism in other areas, for instance, credit rating and exclusion from the elite gentile clubs. Nineteenth-century German Jews worked around these constraints, developing their own exclusive club and credit networks. But the experience of Jews after 1900, and particularly between the World Wars, was quite different.

As large numbers of Eastern European Jews came to South Portland after 1900, they found their surroundings at first strange and unfamiliar. However, according to over one hundred interviews with former residents by the Jewish Oral History and Archive Project in the mid-1970s, for the most part they lived harmoniously with Italians and other neighbors and confronted little organized anti-Semitism in their new neighborhood. Several report that they were called names such as "Christ-killer" or "sheenie" by other children. But the most common experience seems to have been that of Nettie Olman who, with some nostalgia, recalls:

Everybody was warm. We never heard anything against being Jewish.... There were Italians that lived in the neighborhood and we had a few black neighbors. We never thought of color or race. You were all one. When we went to Failing School it was the same way. You skipped, hopped and carried your little pail or your lunches and if you had an apple you would divide it. If you had an orange you would divide it. You never thought well, you're Italian, you're black and I'm Jewish.... We were all alike and everybody spoke with an accent, so it was all one big family.

Eastern European Jews who worked or lived outside of South Portland seemed to have a more difficult time, perhaps because they lacked the cultural buffer that the immigrant district and Failing School provided. Leon Feldstein, whose family moved from South Portland to Union Avenue near Burnside, describes the following occurrence at the Hawthorne School:

I was going to grammar school, a school called Hawthorne School, which is no longer in existence. One day I came home singing "Merry, merry, merry Christmas bells." When my father heard this he practically hit the ceiling. He believed that no Jew should sing Christmas carols, so he called the principal of the school and told him, "This is a free country. No Jew is required to observe gentile holidays. Please tell the teacher not to make my son sing Christmas carols." The principal was apparently not a very nice fellow and told my father, "This is not the way we do things. Too bad if you don't like it."

At that time there was a very fine Jewish man in Portland named Ben Selling—a man of great importance and greatly respected in the city. Father called Ben Selling and Ben Selling spoke to the principal of the school. As a result of this conversation, the principal told my teacher that I didn't have to sing Christmas carols at school, and from then on, I didn't.

Both the Council of Jewish Women and B'nai B'rith took action against derogatory or demeaning references to Jews in the juvenile court, the local theater and the press. Mrs. Isaac Leeser Cohen, who served on a committee at the juvenile court, reported to Council in 1907 that the juvenile court, contrary to the purpose for which it was formed, would often denigrate the cleanliness and appearance of Jewish children. Council passed a resolution criticizing the court, and apparently the practice stopped.

Another problem was the particularly troublesome habit of the local press and some magazines of referring to the ethnic origin of those alleged to have committed crimes only if they were Jewish or of another minority background. Council passed another resolution on March 6, 1907:

Resolved: the Portland Section of the Council of Jewish Women in meeting assembled does most earnestly protest against the uncalled for designation of the word "Jew" or "Jewish" coupled with the name of any individual whenever it becomes necessary for the newspapers to report the arrest or conviction of any person of Jewish faith. Unless newspapers all adopt the same system against all others and designate them as Presbyterian, Episcopalian, Catholic, Unitarian or otherwise as the case may be.

A Council delegation followed up the resolution with a visit to Portland newspapers, where they secured agreements to change this practice. B'nai B'rith's Herzl Lodge 314 formed a "Caricature Committee" in 1908 chaired by Anselm Boskowitz that was charged with rooting out discriminatory references to Jews. Boskowitz told the *Oregonian* in 1966:

I worked hard to correct derogatory references to Jews in vaudeville, magazines and newspapers. In the local paper, when a Jew did something objectionable they identified him as a Jew. That was wrong. We campaigned to eliminate that—and we did.

The Anti-Defamation League

While Boskowitz, a salesman for Fleischner, Mayer & Co., was effective locally, he believed that a national organization was necessary to combat anti-Semitism. One day, while browsing through childrens' books at the Lipman, Wolfe Department Store, he noticed a Mother Goose story with the rhyme, "He sold his shoe to a rogue of a Jew." Boskowitz wrote to the Supreme Lodge of B'nai B'rith in Chicago, urging that a protest be made to the publisher. His letter and the offending poem were published in the national monthly *B'nai B'rith News*. In 1913, within six months of his second letter pressing for national action, the Anti-Defamation League of B'nai B'rith (ADL) was established nationally with two Oregonians—Sig Sichel, an attorney, and Dr. Nehemiah Mosessohn, editor of the *Jewish Tribune*—as signatories to the original

documents. Its purpose was to promote brotherhood and protect Jews from slander and discrimination. Sigmund Livingston headed the organization from its inception until his death in 1946.

In 1915, the lynching of Leo Frank, the Jewish manager of an Atlanta pencil factory, shocked Jews across the country and gave impetus to the founding of local chapters of the Anti-Defamation League. In Portland, an ADL committee was formed in 1916, chaired by Boskowitz for nine years.

In 1925, David Robinson, a lawyer who had been Oregon's first public defender, became the local director and western representative of the League. Robinson devoted the next thirty years to making it an effective and respected organization. The approach of ADL was to work closely with non-Jewish organizations to combat discrimination in all forms. Hence Robinson assumed important civil rights leadership roles in the city and state: first chair of the Mayor's Commission on Human Rights, president of the local Urban League and the City Club of Portland, and chair of the Civil Rights Division of the Oregon Labor Bureau. Robinson often described in his speeches the stained glass "friendship window" donated by Christians to Temple Beth Israel with the words inscribed below clasped hands symbolizing friendship: "Have we not all one Father? Hath not one God created us?"

The Anti-Defamation League continued to fight anti-Jewish stereotypes. In 1931, for example, Robinson reported to the Portland lodge that he had obtained agreement from a local actor to stop using derogatory language about Jews in his performance. During the 1930s and '40s, the League played a major role with its parent B'nai B'rith in mobilizing the Jewish community in Portland to help combat Nazism in Europe. David Robinson became assistant national director of ADL in 1955. He died in 1963 at the age of seventy-three. Since the mid-1950s, a Portland branch of the American Jewish Committee has worked closely with ADL in combatting anti-Semitism and promoting understanding among different religious and racial groups.

Anselm Boskowitz (sitting) in 1938, a key figure in establishing the Anti-Defamation League of B'nai B'rith, both nationally and locally. He is joined by his nephew, Edward Aiken (left), and a customer at the wholesale belt business he operated after Fleischner, Mayer & Co. closed in 1930. Courtesy, Edward Aiken.

David Robinson was director of the Anti-Defamation League in Oregon for thirty years. He made it a respected organization, effective in combatting anti-Semitism. Courtesy, Janet Robinson Stevens.

The Ku Klux Klan

While American entry into World War I inspired intense patriotism, the immediate postwar years produced even greater excesses of nationalistic and xenophobic fervor. In 1920, Henry Ford began publishing his viciously anti-Semitic *Dearborn Independent*, while in Portland, Mayor George Baker (1917-1933) whipped up local hysteria against "aliens" and "reds." Oregon was fertile ground for Ku Klux Klan organizing, and in 1921, Klan headquarters in Atlanta, where the birth of the second Klan had occurred in 1915, sent organizers to Medford and Portland.

Oregon's largest city became the center of Klan activity west of the Rockies. The Klan mushroomed in size, gaining over ten thousand members in Portland, fifteen thousand in the state, and over two million nationally within a few years. While nationally the Klan was blatant-

ly anti-Semitic as well as anti-black and anti-Catholic, in Oregon its primary venom was focused on Roman Catholics. Its activities forced passage of a compulsory school bill in 1923 that was designed to destroy parochial education. Although Jews did not receive the brunt of the Klan attack in Oregon, anti-Semitism here rose to an unprecedented level.

A leading Klan spokeman, Reverend Reuben Sawyer, the minister of an Eastside Christian Church, told a gathering of Klansmen in 1922:

> ***The Jews are a race apart from the white Christian people. [They] are either Bolsheviks undermining our government or Shylocks in finance or commerce who control and command Christians as borrowers or employees.***

The Klan as a whole though, was ambivalent in its approach to Jews. The Royal Riders of the Red Robe admitted Jews who were "loyal Americans" to Klan activities, and the *Oregon Voter*, an independent weekly magazine devoted to public policy issues, stated that Fred Gifford, the exalted cyclops, and therefore the highest official of the Klan in Portland, did not approve of Sawyer's anti-Semitism because there were "so many Jews in Portland who are . . . widely known as this state's finest citizens."

The Klan attempted to mount a boycott of Meier & Frank Department Store to express its anger at the nomination of Julius Meier to serve on a 1925 state exposition committee, but after the *Oregon Voter* condemned the Klan for attacking Meier because of his religion, the boycott fizzled. However, a *100% Directory* was published listing white, Protestant-run businesses and discouraging patronage of Jewish, Catholic and other minority establishments.

In Vancouver, Washington, David Finkelstein bought a grocery store which had a Klan office upstairs. He recalls that a Klan member came into the store and threatened to boycott him. Finkelstein threw him out saying, "When the time comes that I need the Ku Klux Klan to help me make a living, I'll quit." The Klan did boycott his store, but local Catholics rallied to

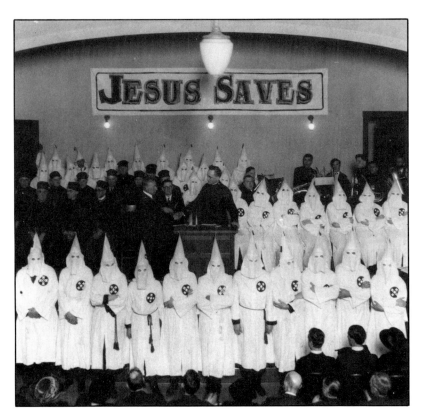

A Ku Klux Klan gathering in Portland in 1923. The Klan was powerful in Oregon for a few years in the early 1920s. While anti-Semitic, they directed most of their venom against Catholics. Courtesy, OHS.

and obtain citizenship. Some members of Portland's B'nai B'rith lodge expressed concern about the speaking of Yiddish and felt that South Portland was too conspicuously Jewish. But while assimilationist pressure increased, Jews also took steps to protect themselves from external attack. The Anti-Defamation League was strengthened when David Robinson assumed the directorship, and Rabbi Wise was a leading figure in an ecumenical group that counterattacked the Klan.

In South Portland, the Jewish community, and particularly the board of Neighborhood House, was confronted with the difficult problem of a proselytizing Methodist mission. The Portland Settlement Center (also known as the Manley Center), located near Failing School, apparently attempted to convert Jewish children through provision of a kindergarten and other school activities. Concern was serious enough that Neighborhood House, in response, reopened its own kindergarten to provide early ed-

his side, becoming customers of the store, and "it all worked out." In 1923, both Beth Israel and Ahavai Sholom were victimized by arsonists who were never apprehended. Ahavai Sholom repaired its building, and Beth Israel used the insurance money and additional contributions to build its beautiful domed temple in Northwest Portland.

In 1925, the United States Supreme Court unanimously declared the Klan-sponsored Oregon Compulsory School Measure unconstitutional before it ever took effect, concluding a long legal battle that had been led by Father Edwin Vincent O'Hara and Rabbi Jonah Wise of Beth Israel. The Klan in Oregon lapsed into internal bickering and declined rapidly, vanishing into obscurity within a short period.

The xenophobic tensions in the 1920s led the Jewish community, as they did most Americans, to seek security in cultural conformity. There was greater urgency to "Americanize"

The Portland Settlement Center, a Methodist mission, was located near Failing School and attempted to convert Jewish children. The Jewish community reacted strongly and the mission's influence diminished. Courtesy, JHSO.

ucation within a Jewish framework. Proselytizing continued, however, for several years. The threat from the Methodist mission finally diminished after a meeting in 1929 of rabbis and leaders of the Council of Jewish Women condemned the center and warned the Jewish community through sermons and letters.

Exclusionary Practices

While the Klan had disappeared as a political force by the 1930s, considerable anti-Semitism remained. At times, posters containing anti-Semitic slogans were found in downtown and other parts of the city. Frohman Wax, who ran a clothing store at Burnside and Third Avenue for over sixty years, reported that there were instances when a customer would

come in the store and would say, "This is a Jew store and I won't buy in a Jew store" and that kind of stuff. I had a lot of that you know. Troublemakers.

Like Nazis or something like that. You don't get that anymore. People don't realize how bad it used to be years ago. It was a lot worse than it is today [1978]. Of course, there are a few people yet that are prejudiced, but there is very little of that going on anymore.

With the rise of Hitler and Nazism in Germany, it became less fashionable to be overtly anti-Semitic in the United States. But troublesome though more subtle forms of discrimination persisted. As a result, Jews were excluded from certain schools, social clubs, fraternities and sororities, high levels in business and partnerships in the professions.

At one point, the Council of Jewish Women investigated exclusion of Jews from high school fraternities in Portland. Jews were also excluded for many years from fraternities and sororities at Oregon universities. As had typically occurred in the past, the response was to create parallel Jewish fraternities and sororities.

Anti-Semitic devices were also used to lim-

it the number of Jews entering colleges and universities throughout the country: geographical and ethnic quotas, alumni screening committees and character tests. Such mechanisms were in wide use until after the Second World War, when talent was increasingly seen as important, and non-discriminatory legislation was passed and enforced.

As the twentieth century progressed, their exclusion from the major social clubs upset many Jews in business and the professions. While non-Jewish colleagues and competitors socialized and made important business decisions at these clubs, Jews were excluded solely on the basis of religion. Harold Hirsch remembers that his father, Max, a nephew of Jeanette Meier and a business leader in Portland, resented exclusion from the Arlington and University clubs. When meetings were scheduled at these clubs, Hirsch refused to go because, "The club didn't take Jews. The meetings were changed to a spot less embarrassing."

Gus Solomon, who grew up in South Portland and served as a federal district judge from 1949 to 1987, consistently spoke out against exclusion of Jews from social clubs. He was not so much concerned with the social aspects of club membership, but realized that it would be difficult for Jews to obtain jobs in major corporations or law firms if they were unable to socialize in the elite clubs. Solomon advised both violinist Isaac Stern and Vice-President Hubert Humphrey not to speak at the University Club because of its exclusionary practices. Neither did, which resulted in considerable publicity on the issue. Judge Solomon never joined Portland clubs that once excluded Jews, although his agitation and the work of Moe Tonkon and others in the 1960s finally opened the clubs to Jewish membership.

While exclusion from social clubs was unfortunate, the inability to obtain employment in major corporations or law firms was particularly serious. Judge Solomon was instrumental in opening major law firms to capable Jewish applicants. Shortly before his death in 1987, he provided an extensive oral history to the Oregon Historical Society, which describes how the first Jew was hired by Portland's largest law firm, now known as Stoel, Rives, Boley, Jones and Grey:

I recall that I called Lloyd Davies. He was a hiring partner in Hart, Spencer, McCulloch, Rockwood and Davies, the largest office in the city. I said to him, "Lloyd, I would like to talk to you about your hiring policy." He said, "What's wrong with our hiring policy?" I said, "Nothing is wrong with it, except that you don't hire any Jews." So he said, "You don't think that I am anti-Semitic." And I said "Hell, no. If I thought that I wouldn't be talking to you." Davies is a nice person and a good friend. He said, "You know how careful we are in our selection." And I said, "I know that, but I have sent you students from Harvard, Yale, Columbia, Pennsylvania and Chicago. They had all the amenities and social graces. They wore hats and vests. They were well educated." And he said, "Maybe they just don't fit." I said "Lloyd, how old is your office?" He said, "About seventy-five years old." And I said, "Are you telling me that in seventy-five years you have never found a Jewish lawyer that fit?" He looked at me and said, "Send me the next man."

A few days later, a young man [Leon Gabinet] who was working in the litigation department of the Oregon Tax Commission came to see me. He had excellent credentials. He graduated from the University of Chicago Law School and had clerked for a justice of the Oregon Supreme Court. He told me that he would like to leave his present position and get a job with a private law office. He asked me if I knew where he could get a job. I said, "Go and see Lloyd Davies in the Hart office." He looked at me and said, "They don't hire Jews." I told him to apply, and then I said, "How well do you know Justice Lusk?" That was the judge for whom he clerked. He said, "I know him very well. He is very friendly." I said, "Ask him to call Lloyd Davies and say he is sending you down to see him." He said, "Should I tell Justice Lusk to tell him that I'm Jewish?" And I said, "Don't tell Justice Lusk

what to say. He knows what to do."

About three days later, the young man returned to my office, and he was all smiles. I said, "You got the job, didn't you?" And he said, "Yes. Justice Lusk did more than I asked him to do. When I told him what I wanted him to do, he said 'I'm going with you.'" So Justice Lusk drove him to Portland and brought him up to see Davies. That was the begining of a whole new era when Jews were able to get jobs in that office. Now the office has about 110 to 120 lawyers, and at least 20 are Jewish.

Today, there are many Jewish partners in Stoel, Rives, Boley, Jones and Grey and most other major firms in the state. Over the years, Judge Solomon also helped women and blacks to obtain positions.

While anti-Semitism was a serious problem in Oregon, it is essential to keep its overall importance in perspective. Many Jews who gave oral histories attest that they confronted little anti-Semitism during their lives in Oregon. Richard Neuberger, a state legislator and United States senator, asserts in his book, *Adventures in Politics*, that he faced virtually no anti-Semitism during his political career. Most Jews feel, despite the existence of some anti-Semitism, as Nate Lakefish did when he said:

[Oregon] is a wonderful, wonderful state for the Jewish people to live in because there isn't the hostility against Jews here that there might be in other places.

And Adelaide Selling, the wife of Ben Selling's son, Laurence, when asked whether she was happy here, said:

I loved Oregon. I loved the life it afforded, the simplicity, the mellowness of the relationships between men and women, the kindnesses. I found that wherever I looked. There wasn't the specter of insecurity. You had opportunity here.... You could simply enjoy what you had and I always enjoyed that.... I am glad that my lot was placed here.

21

Jewish Concern for Civil Liberties

The Contribution of Jewish Lawyers

During the 1920s and 1930s, tumultuous years of Klan and other xenophobic activity, a new cadre of young Jewish leaders emerged. Although prominent rabbis—Wise and Berkowitz at Beth Israel, Parzen, Sandrow and Sydney at Ahavai Sholom, Kleinman at Neveh Zedek and Fain at Shaarie Torah—were key figures in the community, a highly educated group of young lawyers was also becoming active.

This was the first time in Oregon that merchants did not assume primary leadership in the Jewish community. These lawyers, together with several other professionals—medical doctors Leo Ricen and Laurence Selling and architect Harry Herzog were involved in the local, national and international issues of the day. They sought to educate the Jewish community and to bring to it the commitment and professional standards with which to address contemporary problems.

Already the Council of Jewish Women had pioneered Jewish action in social reform, and it continued to take positions on issues and to lobby for a range of humanitarian causes. The civil rights activism that emerged in response to anti-Semitism became a central aspect of Jewish concern. Community service and the defense of civil liberties became core modern components in fulfilling the traditional requirement of Jewish heritage, the injunction to act righteously. Jewish lawyers led the way.

As early as 1907, Louis Brandeis, a young Jewish lawyer from Boston, argued a case before the Supreme Court of the United States defending one of Oregon's early social reform laws, the 1903 statute limiting to ten the number of hours women could work in factories and laundries. The owner of a laundry had required women to work beyond the maximum, and after conviction he appealed all the way to the highest court. Brandeis gathered extensive data to demonstrate that the law was reasonable and protected women from the harm of long hours of labor. The case was won by unanimous decision and the remarkable legal brief, which for the first time relied heavily on sociological and economic data, became widely known as the "Brandeis Brief."

Both Brandeis and Felix Frankfurter (another Jewish lawyer from the East, who, like Brandeis, would one day become a justice of the United States Supreme Court) assisted the Oregon Attorney General with the defense of several progressive Oregon statutes before the Supreme Court. These prominent national Jewish lawyers helped to inspire similar commitment in Oregon's small cadre of Jewish lawyers.

Roscoe Nelson, Sr., was born in Virginia in 1879, moved to Oregon in 1911, and became a widely respected lawyer within both the Jewish and general communities. He was one of the first Jewish lawyers to become a partner in a major firm (Dey, Hampson and Nelson), was chair of the Board of Bar Examiners for a decade, and, in the judgment of Judge Gus Solomon, "was probably the most distinguished Jewish lawyer of his day in Portland."

Nelson championed social responsiblity within the Jewish community, perhaps nowhere more eloquently than in his eulogy before an immense crowd at Ben Selling's funeral in 1931. He was a superb orator and delivered what may have been his finest address to the convention of the Union of American Hebrew Congregations in February, 1929, in San Francisco. Speaking to members of Reform congregations, which included numerous individuals of wealth, Nelson proclaimed:

Justice, not charity, is the end of religion.... If we thought of charity, therefore, as the culmination of religion, it would mean that we contemplate with equanimity that throughout all eternity there must be boundless luxury for some, while others suffer for the barest necessities; ... that some shall be bred in palaces, and others exist in slums; that one group shall be pampered, and another continue so undernourished as to invite the ravages of disease and death.

In addition to Roscoe Nelson and David Robinson of the Anti-Defamation League, another member of the core group of progressive

Roscoe Nelson, Sr., pictured here in 1932, with his wife Rebecca. Nelson was a superb orator and one of the most distinguished lawyers of his day. Courtesy, Roscoe Nelson, Sr. (son).

Harry Kenin with his family at Long Beach, Washington, in 1918. Behind his parents, Anna and Samuel, are from left: Frank, Herman, Harry, Ida and Fannie. Courtesy, Fannie Kenin Friedman.

attorneys in the 1920s was Harry Kenin. Kenin was born in 1898 in Philadelphia of parents who had emigrated from rural Latvia; his father worked for many years in Samuel Gompers' cigar makers union. The family moved to Oregon when Harry was ten years old. Harry, the eldest of five children, went to Reed College, as did his siblings, and then to the University of Chicago for graduate work. He returned home when his father became ill and began his career as the salaried director of the B'nai B'rith Center while studying for his law degree at night at the Northwestern College of Law.

Harry's law practice was devoted nearly entirely to public service. He served on the Portland School Board from 1932 to 1942; as a state senator from 1938 to 1942; on the Oregon Welfare Commission, the Oregon Industrial Accident Commission and the Port of Portland Commission; and beginning in 1942, as legal advisor to the Bonneville Power Administration. As a state senator, Kenin fought for legislation to improve wages, hours and working conditions. He was the first to introduce strong civil rights legislation in Oregon. On the occasion of Harry Kenin's sudden death in 1954 at the age of fifty-six, Rabbi Julius Nodel of Beth Israel delivered a eulogy praising Kenin's devotion to social justice as "in keeping with the highest tradition of his Jewish faith and heritage."

This commitment to civil rights was shared by two of his siblings. His younger brother, Herman, a musician and lawyer, became the international president of the 300,000-member American Federation of Musicians. His sister, Fannie Kenin Friedman, was a trained social worker who fought for the rights of Japanese internees. She was head social worker at the internment camp at Tule Lake, Oregon, and later director of the War Relocation Authority responsible for resettling Japanese in Oregon after the war.

There were other influential Jewish lawyers involved in the protection of civil liberties —Hy Samuels; Leo Levinson; Sam Weinstein; Gilbert Sussman, who worked in the Roosevelt administration and later returned to Portland to become senior partner in a major firm; and the young Richard Neuberger, a newspaperman and lawyer before becoming a legislator and United States senator. But there were two whose contributions to civil liberties were truly exceptional: Gus Solomon and Irvin Goodman.

Richard and Maurine Neuberger in Salem in the early 1950s. They were the first husband and wife team to serve in the Oregon Legislature. Richard Neuberger was a newspaperman and lawyer who fought for civil rights as a state legislator and for six years as a United States senator. Maurine, who was not Jewish, ran for the Senate upon her husband's death in 1960 and served for one term. Courtesy, OHS.

Judge Gus Solomon

Gus Solomon, the youngest of five children, was born in 1906 on First Avenue between Lincoln and College streets in South Portland. His father, who had come from Rumania, and his mother, who came from the Ukraine, met and married in Portland shortly after her arrival in 1895. Gus' father, Jacob Solomon, had several stores that sold men's clothes, and he later built

the well-known Caruthers or "Solomon" Apartments at First and Caruthers.

Gus attended a number of schools en route to becoming a lawyer: Shattuck Grade School, Lincoln and Jefferson high schools, the University of Washington, Reed College and the University of Chicago, where he obtained his undergraduate degree. He went on to Columbia and Stanford universities for his law degree.

In 1929, at the beginning of the Great Depression, I began to practice law in Portland. It was hard to get a job, particularly for a Jew. My academic record had been fairly good. Other young men who were not Jews and who had fewer qualifications got jobs, but I didn't. I tried to get a job for fifty dollars a month and couldn't get one. Then I tried for twenty-five dollars a month, and finally I tried to get a job without pay if I could just get office space. Even that did not work out. When I was looking for a job, I was treated miserably by the lawyers to whom I applied. I resolved that, if I ever got on my feet, I would treat job applicants a lot differently from the way I had been treated. I opened my own office in the old Panama Building. Twenty years later, I got my first job—President Harry Truman appointed me a United States district court judge.

Gus Solomon's family, about 1911. Standing, from left: his mother Rose, Sam, Eugene; sitting: his father Jacob, Gus, Delphine and Claire. Courtesy, Bernice Rosencrantz.

Gus Solomon's principal contribution to the protection of civil liberties lay in the organizational work that he undertook to establish legal aid for the poor and to set up a branch of the American Civil Liberties Union (ACLU) in Oregon. While his assistance in obtaining jobs for Jews and others hampered by discrimination and his effective protests against exclusion from clubs were extremely important in breaking down barriers, his work building legal aid and the ACLU helped to institutionalize the ideals of social justice.

During the Depression, in 1935, Gus Solomon felt that Portland should have a legal aid office. With help from David Robinson, with whom Solomon had worked for a summer while in school, and Tom Stoel, senior partner in the present firm of Stoel, Rives, Boley, Jones and Grey, Solomon approached the Works Progress Administration. It offered to provide several lawyers, support staff and rent, if money were available for furniture and supplies, and if the local bar association was willing to officially sponsor the office.

Solomon recalls that when he appeared before the Multnomah Bar Association to seek sponsorship, he was accused of being "a communist, a socialist and an anarchist" and attacked for "wanting to take bread out of the mouth of lawyers." He prevailed, however, by approaching the newly organized Oregon State Bar at a meeting in Baker and obtaining its sponsorship. After the small office was established, however, its board of directors refused to allow it to handle certain types of cases. Solomon and others took those cases without fee.

As a student at Columbia Law School, Gus Solomon attended a gathering called by the ACLU in the mid-1920s at which Roger Baldwin, its national director, and other leading lawyers spoke in opposition to the pending execution of Nicola Sacco and Bartolomeo Vanzetti for the alleged murder of a payroll clerk in South Braintree, Massachusetts. Solomon later said:

This ACLU meeting opened up new horizons for me and had a great impact on my life. In late August, 1927, I went to Seaside,

Oregon. On the night that Sacco and Vanzetti were executed, I recall that I walked up and down the beach during the time they were scheduled for execution. I was deeply affected by the fact that they were executed, and I thought they were being unfairly executed.

In 1929, when Solomon finished his education and returned to Portland, he attempted to establish a local ACLU office. Despite the fact that two national board members lived in Portland and, in Solomon's judgment, civil liberties were being abused by the police and vigilantes here, he could not generate sufficient enthusiasm. Irv Goodman tried to assist by writing to the national director of the ACLU in December, 1933, recommending Solomon to be the ACLU attorney in Portland.

Finally, in 1935, a local chapter was begun when several individuals became interested, particularly two elderly sisters, Emily Nunn and Lucy Trevitt, and Ruth Catlin of Catlin Gabel School. Initially, the chapter passed resolutions and wrote letters to the editor, but when Irv Goodman, who shared offices with Solomon, did not appeal his client, Dirk DeJonge's, conviction to the United States Supreme Court, Solomon brought the case to the fledgling ACLU.

DeJonge had been convicted under Oregon's criminal syndicalism law for having merely participated in a meeting held under the auspices of the Communist party. Solomon believed that DeJonge was being used by the Communist party, which preferred him to be a jailed martyr. Wanting to vindicate the court system and democratic process, Solomon was able to obtain help from Roger Baldwin of the national ACLU and Osmund Fraenkel, a well-known civil liberties lawyer in New York. Solomon wrote the brief in support of jurisdiction and prepared the transcript, while Fraenkel drafted the main brief and argued the case.

DeJonge v. Oregon, one of the most famous cases ever to arise in the state, was unanimously reversed. Chief Justice Charles Evans Hughes wrote the opinion, which declared Oregon's criminal syndicalism law unconstitutional as applied to DeJonge. The case upheld

Judge Gus Solomon served as federal district court judge from his appointment in 1949 by President Truman to his death in 1987. His tenure was longer than any other federal judge in Oregon's history. Courtesy, Libby Solomon.

the right to hold a public meeting regardless of the unpopularity of the cause espoused. In 1937, after substantial efforts by Richard Neuberger, then a law student at the University of Oregon, the ACLU led the successful effort to repeal the state's criminal syndicalism law. Solomon recalls that after *DeJonge* was decided his income dropped to as low as $1,800 a year. He later learned that the "Red Squad" of the Portland Police was telling his clients that he was a communist and that the ACLU was a communist organization.

While practicing law for a number of small business clients, Solomon helped to organize public utility districts and rural electric cooperatives. He handled *In Re Tillamook People's Utility District*, which established the constitutionality of the Oregon Peoples Utility District Law. He also took the first cases under the state's minimum wage laws for women and the Fair

Labor Standards Act of 1938. Solomon was "outraged" at the internment of the Japanese during World War II and he chaired the committee which worked to return homes and farms to them following the war.

Gus Solomon was often vilified and threatened for his defense of civil liberties; even his own mother once inquired, "Why can't you represent nice people?" But Solomon believed in social justice, and this led him to represent people and causes that were not always popular. As he put it in 1976:

I believe that government exists for all the people and that we must be alert to ensure that government protects those who are least able to help themselves. I believe that everyone, regardless of his color or religion, has rights that cannot be taken away from him, and that everyone, regardless of wealth, is entitled to a lawyer in both criminal and civil cases. I also believe that this country's great natural resources should be used for the benefit of all the people. From the time that I left law school, I tried to put these beliefs into practice.

In 1949, President Harry Truman nominated Gus Solomon to be a federal district court judge. Solomon recalls:

My opponents sent a former Portland city official [former Mayor Joe Carson] to Washington, D.C., to tell the president that the people of Oregon didn't want a Jew for a federal judge. Fortunately, President Truman was not impressed.

They regarded the federal judiciary as a stronghold of the propertied classes. They did not want a Jew, particularly a Jew who was a liberal. Only two Jewish men had ever held judgeships in Oregon. They were minor judicial positions and they held them for short periods [Otto Kraemer as justice of the peace and Julius Cohn as Multnomah County district judge]. My appointment and confirmation as United States Judge of the District Court of Oregon opened the whole field.

There have now been two Oregon Supreme Court justices, Hans Linde (1977-) and Jacob Tanzer (1980-1982); the first chief judge of the Oregon Court of Appeals, Herbert Schwab (1969-1981); the United States Attorney for Oregon, Sidney Lezak (1961-1982); and numerous other judges at various levels in the judicial system.

Despite an attack labeling Solomon a "communist" at his confirmation hearings, a number of well-respected public officials and attorneys from Oregon testified on his behalf, and, after a unanimous subcommittee report in his favor, he was confirmed as federal district judge by the United States Senate. Judge Solomon died in February, 1987, having had the longest tenure of any federal judge in Oregon history.

Irvin Goodman, Defender of the Underdog

"My only crime was that I wanted a roof for every family, bread for every mouth, education for every heart, the light for every intellect."

It was Bartolomeo Vanzetti who spoke those words. Together with Nicola Sacco he had been sentenced to die.... On August 22, 1927, in Charlestown Prison, Boston, the two Italian immigrants, one a fish peddler, the other a shoemaker, were put to death in the electric chair. Throughout the world, millions of people from all walks of life, who believed the defendants were innocent ... were profoundly moved by the execution.

So begins the unpublished manuscript of *They Were Called Reds*, written by Irvin Goodman. As Gus Solomon had paced the Seaside beach that night, so for Goodman was the trial and execution of Sacco and Vanzetti a crucial motivating force in his life and law practice. Even earlier, as a boy growing up in Chehalis, Washington, Goodman had witnessed the local police beating several prisoners, and he re-

Irvin Goodman (left) in 1946 with defendant Nicolai Redin. Goodman, known as "the lawyer who never gave up," was a champion of the underdog. Courtesy, Ora Goodman.

solved that he would be a lawyer and that his "practice would involve only cases of social injustice." His family moved to Portland at the end of his high school years, after which he worked his way through Reed College and Northwestern College of Law by clerking at Meier & Frank.

He began practice in the late 1920s, and shared offices in the Yeon Building with Gus Solomon and Leo Levinson for several years in the early 1930s. Goodman was often approached to handle civil cases, but he only wanted to do civil rights work. He and his associates had agreed that he would refer the civil cases to them and that they in turn would assist with some of his civil rights cases. They stopped their office-sharing arrangement when Solo-

mon became uncomfortable with Goodman's determination to defend politically unpopular clients, sometimes on behalf of the International Labor Defense, which was thought to be associated with the Communist party.

Ben Boloff was an illiterate sewer digger who had been born in Russia and had come to Portland at age eighteen. For nineteen years he was a laborer. Then, on November 1, 1930, he was arrested on a street in Portland on a charge of "vagrancy" that was later changed to "criminal syndicalism" when he admitted to police that he was a member of the Communist party. At the trial, members of the "Red Squad" of the Portland Police Department testified as experts on "communism" and described why it was a menace to the nation. Irv Goodman called several witnesses, and then Boloff briefly testified in his own defense. There was not much to say; his words were halting, his accent heavy:

Q: *What is your name?*

A: *Ben Boloff....*

Q: *Have you ever been convicted of a crime?...*

A: *Never.*

Q: *I will ask you to state if you did sewer work in Portland?*

A: *That is what I do in Portland all the time... well, sometimes I dig the ditch; sometimes I lay the pipe, sewer pipe....*

Q: *Will you explain, if you can, why you are not a citizen?*

A: *Well, I figure it is pretty hard to get citizenship papers, so I can't read, can't write, can't speak English, so I don't think I could get it and I never tried to get it....*

Q: *Just explain ... why you joined the Communist party. Speak up loud so the jury can hear you.*

A: *Well, the Communist party is the working-class organization, that they try to get better conditions and so I tried to go with them as a worker and it was for that purpose.*

לשנה טובה תכתבו

Portland Lodge No. 65 -- B'NAI B'RITH
FIRST MEETING OF 1939-1940 SEASON
TUESDAY, SEPT. 12 in place of Wednesday
Jewish Community Center, 8:15 p. m.

By popular request, we again present a

SYMPOSIUM

~ FEATURING ~
Irvin Goodman and
Richard Neuberger

ON

"CAN WE STAY OUT OF WAR?"

(AS CITIZENS?)
(AS JEWS?)

Discussion and questions by the membership

AN INTERESTING EVENING WHICH SHOULD BE
ATTENDED BY EVERY BEN B'RITH. COME EARLY.

Louis Schnitzer   David H. Greenberg
President   *Secretary*

Come to the **MEETING** at **YWCA**
CORNER BROADWAY & TAYLOR STS.
TUES., JANUARY 10, 1950
AT 8 P. M.

Help Us End JIM CROW in Portland

SPEAKERS . . .

DR. DENORVAL UNTHANK
Prominent Portland Physician

MRS. MARY M. DUNCAN
Editor, The Enterprise

ROBERT W. FRITSCH
Pres. Holladay School Parent-Teacher Association

IRVIN GOODMAN
Attorney for Citizens Committee for Civil Rights and
Author of Ordinance to End Jim Crow, submitted
to City Council on Jan. 27, 1949.

ALSO AN EXCELLENT MUSICAL PROGRAM   **ADMISSION FREE**

Irvin Goodman spoke widely, defending civil liberties and the causes he
believed in. Courtesy, Ora Goodman.

"Red" hysteria was rampant. Hearings had been conducted in Portland and in other cities in 1930 by a congressional committee, headed by Hamilton Fish of New York, for the purpose of exposing the danger of communism. Newspaper headlines of the day read, "Revolution Cited as Aim of Reds," "Robbing of Banks Planned by Reds," and "Reds in Schools."

Ben Boloff was the first to be tried under Oregon's criminal syndicalism law, which had been passed eleven years earlier. He was found guilty. The jury recommended leniency, but on March 2, 1931, the judge sentenced him to the maximum, ten years in the penitentiary. Goodman appealed to the Oregon Supreme Court, which affirmed the decision, four to three.

Many considered Boloff's conviction a travesty of justice. The *Oregonian* and the *Oregon Journal*, which had often abetted the hysteria, now ran editorials headlined "Putting Ideas in Jail," "Set Boloff Free," and "Ben Boloff Victim." After eighteen months in jail, Boloff's sentence was suspended, but, accustomed to the open air, he had become quite ill in his small, poorly ventilated cell. After release, he was admitted to the tuberculosis hospital at the county poor farm and died shortly thereafter.

Irv Goodman defended the downtrodden whomever they might be. In the 1930s, they included communists like Ben Boloff, Dirk De-Jonge and Kyle Pugh, a news vendor given five years in prison for distributing leftist literature he had received in the mail. Goodman fought for the rights of labor throughout the West, defending, for example, striking mine workers in Juneau. He won their acquittal, but only after he had slept for nights with a pistol under his pillow and met with witnesses at the foot of a glacier to ensure privacy. When his steamer left at midnight, four hundred miners and their families were there in the deep snow to bid him goodbye.

Irv Goodman also defended black people against the sometimes virulent prejudice of the day. As counsel to the Portland NAACP, Goodman was asked to help Wardell Henderson, a young black soldier convicted of killing a white man at Vanport in 1945. The trial was widely seen to have been unfair, and when appeals failed, Goodman helped organize a campaign for executive clemency. Hundreds of attorneys wrote to the governor, as did numerous organizations, including the Portland Federation of Women's Groups and the Council of Churches. The *Oregonian* editorialized in support of Henderson, but Governor John Hall refused to commute the sentence and Henderson was executed in the gas chamber on January 24, 1948. He gave Irv Goodman a letter written shortly before he was executed, which was later printed verbatim in the *Oregonian*:

> *First of all I want to thank you, Mr. Goodman, and everyone who tried to save my life. I told the [warden] I had no hate in my heart for anyone.*
>
> *I have lived in America for twenty-five years, not as an American but as a Negro. Just between you and I, you see, Negroes are not called Americans.*
>
> *I was looking at that woman called Justice. . . . I'll be darned if she didn't tell the difference between a Negro and a white man.*
>
> *I knew all the time that the jury was prejudiced. . . . They didn't look at the case after they saw that I was a Negro. They just convicted me because of my race.*
>
> *I want to thank you and Mrs. Argow and many others for their desperate attempts to save my life. The Negro race shall never forget the gross injustice that has been done to me. A lot of people are wondering how I can hold up after such injustice. Well I'll tell you why. It is because I am innocent.*

A year later, in 1949, after a young black woman and her child were forced to sit in the segregated balcony of the Egyptian Theater on Portland's Union Avenue, Goodman drafted a statute to end "Jim Crow" in Portland and helped lead the fight to get it enacted before the city council. On February 22, 1950, by unanimous vote, Portland became only the second city in the United States to ban racial discrimination in places of public accommodation.

Only five feet, five inches tall, and always

Wardell Henderson painted this scene in prison as a gift for Irvin Goodman. All appeals failed and Henderson, a twenty-seven year old black man, was executed in 1948. The *Oregonian*, January 19, 1948.

carrying an overstuffed briefcase, Irv Goodman became known as "the lawyer who never gave up." Like Clarence Darrow, who was his friend and whose signed photograph hung in his office, Goodman remained true to his ideals: he only took cases of social injustice and always championed the underdog. Albert Gunns, in his recent book on civil liberties in the Northwest, says that Goodman was in the "forefront of Portland's civil liberties lawyers" and the "person most instrumental in the creation and maintenance of a civil liberties movement in Portland."* Irvin Goodman died on July 1, 1958, at the age of sixty-one and was buried in the cemetery of Kesser Israel. He was truly an unsung hero, who fulfilled the finest traditions of his religion by protecting the least fortunate, and doing so with little financial or public reward.

---

*Albert F. Gunns, *Civil Liberties in Crisis: The Pacific Northwest 1917-1940*; New York and London, Garland Publishing, Inc., 1983.

22

Julius Meier, Governor of Oregon

Julius Meier (left) and Aaron Frank in July, 1930, planning an addition to Meier & Frank. Unknown to Meier then, events would propel him into the governorship three months later. Courtesy, OHS.

The tumultuous 1920s and 1930s, with their undercurrent of anti-Semitism, did not prevent Julius Meier, a well-known Jew and the youngest son of Aaron Meier, the founder of Meier & Frank, from becoming governor of Oregon. The story of how the affable lawyer and department store president with no previous political experience was catapulted into the governorship is both incredible and fascinating.

It all began with the writing of a will in 1913. Henry Wemme, a German, non-Jewish pioneer and eccentric, had once owned the Willamette Tent & Awning Company, which he sold to Max Hirsch and Harry Weis, and which later grew into White Stag. Wemme wished to leave one half of his considerable estate to six Christian Science churches in Portland for the construction and maintenance of a home for "wayward" girls. As he had neither wife nor children, the remainder of his estate was left to relatives in Germany and to several older employees.

The lawyer who drew up the will was George Joseph, who had spent his childhood in Lake County, Oregon. After completing law school, he joined Julius Meier (who had previously practiced with Dolph, Mallory and Simon) in law practice in 1895. The Meier-Joseph law partnership lasted until Julius Meier became general manager of Meier & Frank after the death of Sigmund Frank in 1910. But they remained close friends through the years, and George Joseph later became legal advisor to Meier & Frank.

The ill-fated Wemme will launched a decade of bitter struggle, with quite far-reaching consequences for the political future of the state of Oregon. After Wemme's death, the White Shield Home was built in Northwest Portland according to the terms of the will, but was then sold to the Salvation Army. The German heirs sued for the entire estate, claiming the will was too vague and the churches should not have sold the home. As the heirs began fighting with each other, the complex case was pursued through the courts, reaching the Oregon Supreme Court twice. Both times Justice (later Chief Justice) John Rand played a key role.

When it was shown that Rand shared business dealings with the lawyers representing several of the German heirs, Joseph criticized Rand publicly and vigorously opposed his re-election to the Supreme Court. Rand won, nonetheless, and Joseph, brought before the court on charges of misconduct "for undermining confidence in the Supreme Court," was disbarred for life.

Joseph was devastated. He decided that the best way to vindicate his name and continue to fight for the causes he believed in was to seek the governorship, which would give him the power to appoint Supreme Court justices. His platform for governor in 1930 proclaimed freedom of speech and justice, as well as progressive stands on public power and the abolition of preferences for private utilities. His campaign was managed by Henry Marion Hanzen, a lawyer and political editor of the *Portland Telegram* from 1917 to 1930, whose unpublished manuscript fully describes the events recounted here.*

While the theme of public power dominated the campaign, Joseph's integrity and good name were very much at stake. When he won the Republican primary, it was widely viewed as public vindication for him. The general election campaign began with every indication that Joseph would prevail. Tragically, on June 16, 1930, while reviewing maneuvers of the Oregon National Guard at Camp Clatsop, George Joseph

State Senator George Joseph was Julius Meier's law partner and close friend. When Joseph died after battling the Oregon Supreme Court and winning the Republican nomination for governor in 1930, Meier agreed to pick up the torch and, running as an independent candidate, won overwhelmingly. Courtesy, OHS.

suffered a heart attack and died within hours.

The Republican state central committee was to nominate Joseph's successor. Some, including Hanzen, began to mention Meier as a possible nominee, but Julius indicated that he definitely did not wish to seek the governorship, pleading that he had recently become president of Meier & Frank (when his elder brother, Abe, passed away); that he knew little

---

*See the unpublished, untitled manuscript by Henry Marion Hanzen in the Oregon Historical Society Manuscript Collection, No. 1019 (1945).

of politics; and that he feared that his wealth and religion would be damaging. But as it began to appear that the Republican central committee was leaning toward an old guard Republican, the chorus grew for Meier to carry the banner for his close friend. After testing the water and finding, to his surprise, substantial support, Meier tossed his hat into the ring. Nonetheless, the Republican central committee rejected him and the Joseph platform, nominating instead Phil Metschan, the Republican state chair.

In an unprecedented move, Meier was nominated as an Independent by convention on the night of August 7, 1930, pledged to support Joseph's platform. In his acceptance speech, he declared:

I stand foursquare on the platform of the late Senator Joseph, without equivocation, reservation or qualification. Oregon's water power resources, what part of them still belong to the people, will be kept for you and me.

Julius Meier was an effective governor. He stabilized the economy, established the respected state police and protected Oregon's environment. Courtesy, OHS.

The overwhelming issue of the campaign was public power and it produced major battles. Meier's campaign opened with a radio speech excoriating "the power monopoly and its subservient press:"

Our country is now in the clutches of the power octopus. Its tentacles radiate from Wall Street into every section of the nation....

It acquires these [power] sites for a pittance, capitalizes them for all the traffic will bear, and exacts exorbitant rates from the people to whom they originally belonged....

It controls legislatures and city councils. It subsidizes the press, civic organizations and public officials, reaching in instances even into the nation's schools, colleges and pulpits.

Which shall it be—private development for further enrichment of the coffers of the power trust or public development for the benefit of the State of Oregon and its people?

The continuance of private development means the surrender of our last and greatest natural resource to the power monopoly, means that the people will forever pay tribute to the monopoly in the way of high rates and retarded economic development. Public development means the preservation of our power sites—their development for the benefit of the people—power at cost for light, heat and industrial expansion.

Let us go forward for Oregon, its people, their welfare and prosperity.

Meier was attacked continually by the *Oregonian*; during the campaign he would pick up the paper and point to the Meier & Frank ad on the back page, noting that it was the only thing worth reading in the paper. But his campaign generated tremendous support, and an overflow crowd gathered at the Civic Auditorium for his closing rally. When the votes were counted, Julius Meier had more votes than both major party candidates combined (Meier, 135,608; Bailey, Democrat, 62,434; and Metschan, Republican, 46,840) and was the first Independent ever elected to a major office in Oregon.

The interior of Menucha, the Meier summer home, built along the famous Columbia River Highway. Julius Meier was known as the "father" of the scenic highway. Courtesy, OHS.

At Meier's inauguration as the twentieth chief executive of the state, Senator Brown intoned, "Hear ye, hear ye, Governor Julius Meier, a governor of the people, by the people and for the people." Meier refused to be sworn in by any justice of the Supreme Court, and in his inaugural speech delivered a moving tribute to George Joseph.

Julius Meier was a good governor. While the power companies were strong enough to prevent, to a large extent, the implementation of public power in Oregon, he was able to accomplish a number of valuable initiatives. The Depression demanded economy, and Meier retrenched where necessary, bringing the state's economy back to solvency. He established the highly regarded state police force and began a new system to provide for a non-political judiciary. He advocated conservation programs to reduce exploitation and pollution of forests, rivers and beaches. He continued his interest in

highway beauty. Years before he had become known as the "father" of the Lower Columbia River Highway for his leadership in financing the famous scenic route along which he built Menucha, his summer home.

Governor Meier was, like so many other Jewish lawyers of his day, deeply committed to humanist ideals. He fought for old age pensions, declaring, "the poorhouse should be abolished forever." He authorized free textbooks for school children, and he commuted all death sentences during his tenure.

Despite urging from both the Democratic and Republican parties to seek a second term, Meier declined. Poor health plagued him shortly after leaving office, forcing him into seclusion at Menucha, where he died at sixty-two on July 15, 1937. He is buried in the cemetery of Beth Israel, the congregation he had once served as president.

23

The 1930s: Depression Years

Hard Times

During the early years of the Depression, when Julius Meier was governor, many Jews faced difficult times. Gus Solomon's father, for instance, who had suffered earlier losses due to fire and market conditions, finally lost the Solomon Apartments and moved away from Portland in 1931. Jimmy Berg, whose family owned a movie theater, remembers that, despite "using country store methods of giving away bags of groceries and sets of dishes" to the lucky ticket holders, even five or ten cents a show was difficult for families to afford. His father lost all three theaters that he had worked for many years to acquire and he, too, moved away. Frieda Gass Cohen speaks for many when she remarks:

During the Depression, from 1929 on, things were rough for most everyone in our area [South Portland]. We didn't feel any different; we never considered ourselves poor; we just didn't have any money. My parents were very frugal, and again we never ate out but we didn't lack for anything. Things were difficult as far as money was concerned, but my friends did not have money to spend either . . . so we did not particularly feel the lack of money.

Small merchants were hit hard and most were losing money. Struggling to retain his clothing store at Third and Burnside, Frohman Wax remembers that he couldn't pay his bills:

There was no business. Nobody had any money. . . . We had a little money in the bank and we lost it. At that time Neustadter Brothers was the big jobbing house in Portland . . . and I owed them a considerable amount of money and I couldn't pay it, so they were very good to me. We made an assignment and I turned over everything I had to them and to the creditors and they trusted me and I didn't have to leave the store. They let me run it and buy it back on a percentage. So I got a fresh start. My wife and I worked in the store and it just happened that we had some very good friends, Julius Meier and Mrs. Selling. They heard about it and they came to our rescue and each one gave us a check for three thousand dollars to start us to buy back the stock. We paid them all back with interest . . . and we have been a success ever since.

The new generation of professionals managed to find work, although sometimes with difficulty. And many of the young people were able to continue their college educations through scholarships and part-time work. But it was not always easy for families to pay the mortgage on their homes, and several avoided losing them only through the great kindness of others. Harry Mesher and his wife had bought a "beautiful, little house" on the Eastside for $4,500 early in the Depression; his mother had helped with the down payment. Then several years later, when Mesher was unable to make payments, the former owner, a man named Goldberg who lived in Lebanon, Oregon, let them live there for over three years without paying anything. And Frieda Gass Cohen tells this moving story:

During the 1930s my father had difficulty in meeting the payments on the first and second mortgages which were on our house. He wished to refinance the house, but according to the regulations of the Homeowners Loan Corporation . . . you couldn't have a second mortgage on your house. . . . So my father went to a poor man in the community, a man who owned a little grocery store, Mr. Nathan "Nusky" Rosen, who had lent my father some money and had given him a second mortgage on our house. When my father explained to him that he could not refinance our home as long as there was a second mortgage on it, Mr. Nusky Rosen, out of the goodness of his own heart, tore up the second mortgage in front of my father, threw it in the wastebasket and said to him "Just between you and me, you know you owe me the money." This is the way people in our community really helped one another.

Often families worked out systems to assist each other. Eugene Nudelman, Sr., describes the approach of Joseph Nudelman:

Grandpa Nudelman had a great philosophy about keeping the family together, and he established what was known as the Nudelman Family Association. All the brothers and sisters and eventually their children joined this association, and paid five dollars a month dues. Whenever someone had a problem and needed some money, they could borrow it from the association and pay it back if and when they could. My dad was the treasurer and subsequently I became the treasurer. . . .

The fund became defunct, but it lasted for at least twenty years. In connection with this association we would meet every two weeks at a different home in the family. My grandfather really held the family together.

Residential Dispersion

Despite the hardships of the Depression, many South Portland Jews continued the patterns of the late 1920s, moving to new areas of the city and, whenever possible, purchasing a home. Because the economy remained unstable, they put available funds and savings into home ownership, so even during the Depression, many more young Jews owned homes than had their immigrant parents.

When young couples married or when families managed to increase their income and status, most moved to the Eastside. By the 1930s, there was a strong migration out of South Portland, primarily to the Irvington and Ladd's Addition neighborhoods, with smaller numbers settling in Laurelhurst, Alameda and other parts of the city. It was not always easy to leave the

Joseph Nudelman, who brought the Nudelman family to Portland, was also an important community leader. He helped to found Congregation Shaarie Torah and the Jewish Old Peoples Home. Courtesy, Eugene Nudelman, Sr.

This house in Irvington (2627 NE 17th Avenue) was typical of those to which young Jews were moving when they left South Portland. Dr. Harry Semler moved here in 1927. It was built by the respected Jewish builder, Max Shimshak. Courtesy, Larry Semler.

Kings Heights and Dunthorpe, while the less wealthy moved to the terraces above Northwest Portland, to Ladd's Addition and to a small area above Coe Circle near Northeast Glisan Street and 39th Avenue on the Eastside.

A different stratification was developing: the German families were finding new exclusive enclaves, the rapidly growing Jewish middle class was moving to the Eastside, while many of the older and less successful immigrants remained in or near South Portland. By 1947, a Jewish Welfare Board study showed that South Portland contained the largest percentage of Jews over fifty years old but only 15 percent of Jewish children. For the first time, elderly Jews were separated from their middle-aged children and grandchildren. Jack Hecht's parents, for example, refused to move away from South Portland:

Home is where the heart is. It's where they lived, where they shopped, where they raised their family. That was their world. They wanted no part of moving to a strange neighborhood. They didn't drive an automobile. My mother could never read or write English, and it was comfortable.... There was never a consideration of moving out of old South Portland until they began to tear it down and make room for a freeway.

These patterns of residential dispersion were similar to those in other American cities at the time. It would only be after the Second World War that many Portland Jews, like those in New York and elsewhere, would leave for the suburbs.

In the 1930s and 1940s, many Jews also left Portland. From a population of approximately ten thousand in the 1920s, the 1947 Jewish Welfare study showed just over seven thousand Jews living in Portland in 1946. Many young people, when they left the state for college or for other reasons, did not return. Oregon maintained a tone of "moderate conservatism," as it had historically, and many talented and ambitious children of Jewish families sought wider possibilities elsewhere.

neighborhood of their youth, where the *shuls* and the kosher stores remained and often their parents as well. But the second generation had a strong desire to improve their lot. They had grown up in America and shared its dream of building a new and better life. Diane Nemer, who moved from South Portland to Irvington when she was married, describes

the feeling of moving up from one area to the next ... always a step in the right direction.... Each one of us married and moved away from South Portland to where we felt the homes were better, to a better district. It was sort of something you were striving for.

Irvington, with its fine houses and tree-lined streets, and Ladd's Addition, laid out like a park in Southeast Portland, were lovely, growing neighborhoods, ideal for raising a young family and for taking that first step away from the old, immigrant neighborhood.

Jews who had moved to Northwest Portland some years before—mostly wealthier German and early Polish and Eastern European settlers—were also moving up. The wealthy German families moved to Portland Heights,

For the first time since the nineteenth century, a small number of Jews migrated from Portland and other cities to smaller communities in the state seeking new opportunities. The largest of these communities was Eugene. By the early twentieth century, few of the German Jews who had previously settled in Eugene remained. Among the first Eastern European Jews to arrive in Eugene was Esy Rubenstein, who came in 1912, followed shortly by several relatives. By 1920 there were approximately eight Jewish families in Eugene: the Rubensteins, Millers, Goldens, Fendrichs, Fines, Charlottes, Mitchells and the Gans children (both parents had died the same night in the influenza epidemic of 1917). Esy Rubenstein and his wife, Bella, had four sons and after initially trying hides and wool and the scrap metal business, he founded the furniture store which still bears his name.

These early families came together in each other's homes for Friday night and holiday services (with *minyans* often gathered from as far as Junction City, Cottage Grove, Albany and Roseburg). As the Jewish population increased, the need for a synagogue became apparent. Jack Brenner, who came to Eugene from Latvia in the early 1930s, was instrumental in organizing a congregation. After Hymen Rubenstein's death in 1933, his home at 231 West Eighth Street was remodeled and named Temple Beth Israel. It served Eugene's Jewish community until a new synagogue was built in 1952. Services were conducted by lay members of the congregation with Hyman Pressman becoming the regular cantor for Friday night services after his arrival in Eugene in 1930. After the 1952 synagogue was built at 2550 Portland Street, Marcus Simmons from England was engaged as the first rabbi by the congregation. The congregation's current rabbi, Myron Kinberg, came to Beth Israel in 1977.

In Salem, the Jewish community was considerably smaller. In the early 1930s, a Jewish Aid Society was organized which formally changed its name to the Salem Jewish Congregation on October 18, 1934. Twenty-two charter members were present at the congregation's inception. That same year, the Willamette Valley B'nai B'rith Lodge 1181 was established, and a chapter of Hadassah was organized by Jewish women in Salem in the early 1930s.

Services were conducted by lay members in private homes. In 1938, a committee was chaired by Mike Steinbock with Dr. Henry Brown, David Holtzman, Abram Volchok and S. Cline to begin to raise money for a synagogue. A formal building committee was put in place in 1942 with Max Schusterwitz as its chair. With the war intervening, it was not until November 30, 1947, that Temple Beth Shalom was dedicated. A number of Portland rabbis assisted at the dedication ceremonies of its synagogue at 1795 NE

Congregation Beth Israel in Eugene worshipped in this lovely Victorian house on Eighth Street from 1933 until their new synagogue was built in 1952. Courtesy, Congregation Beth Israel, Eugene.

Broadway and often returned to officiate at High Holiday services. In 1987, Bruce Diamond was engaged as the synagogue's first full-time rabbi.

A relative of Gus Solomon's, Kiva Sugarman, had opened a store in Klamath Falls in 1906 that was located in the middle of two warring sections of the city. He adopted the motto which became well-known in Southern Oregon: "I ain't mad at nobody." In 1936, Rabbi Berkowitz of Beth Israel was invited to Klamath Falls by Kiva Sugarman on behalf of its fifteen Jews and became the first rabbi to speak in the city. Harry Rubenstein, his young wife, Anne, and her brother-in-law, Jerry Kaplan, moved to Medford in 1927 and opened a secondhand furniture store and a hardware store. They tried to remain kosher, but meat shipped from Portland would not keep. When their son, Ted, was born in 1932, a *minyan* was formed with members of his well-known family from Eugene, and Rabbi Fain came to perform the first *bris* ever held in Medford. Rubenstein recalls:

We always closed the store for Jewish holidays. We would put up a sign which said,

The *bar mitzvah* of Merritt Linn in February, 1950, the first to be held in Beth Shalom's synagogue in Salem. In 1982, Merritt Linn published an acclaimed book on the Holocaust entitled *A Book of Songs*. Courtesy, Dina and Ted Linn.

Harry Rubenstein (center) in his secondhand store in Medford, about 1935. He always closed for Jewish holidays. Courtesy, Ted Rubenstein.

"Closed for Jewish holiday. We will be open after sunset." One holiday, which fell on a Saturday, I came to the store about 7 p.m. There was a line of about fifteen or twenty people waiting to get in. I did more business that evening than I did on a normal Saturday. There was one fellow ... his name was Applegate and he lived in the countryside there. He said to me, "We came into Medford about ten o'clock this morning and when I saw your sign I said to my wife, 'We are going to wait till they open up because if they respect their religion and give up their business for a day, we are going to wait,' so we did." Then he spent about three hundred dollars with me.

During the 1930s and 1940s, small populations of Jews returned to various towns in Oregon and in the years since their numbers have slowly continued to increase.

Jewish Community Structure

Although Jews dispersed to different neighborhoods in Portland, they retained a strong loyalty to their religion and a sense of unity fostered by their many social and service organizations. Neighborhood House and the Council of Jewish Women continued to provide essential services in South Portland for those who needed them and developed several unique responses to the hardships, such as the shortage of clothing, brought on by the Depression. In the fall of 1932, Junior League women organized a Sewing Unit at Neighborhood House, with cloth provided by the Red Cross from government surplus cotton. Four hundred women working two days a week were able to make over four thousand garments for their families. The project lasted two years, until 1935, when clothing became more plentiful.

Then, in 1934, the Council, together with the B'nai B'rith Women's Auxiliary, established the Opportunity Bake Shop to employ women needing work to assist their families. The shop was in an annex to the B'nai B'rith Building, but when expansion of the building was planned toward the end of the decade, it moved to the garage of the Jewish Shelter Home. As many as eighteen women were employed at the shop, earning modest amounts of money for two or three days' work each week to supplement family income.

The shop's major products were noodles and caramels, but seasonally it also prepared pickles, herring, chicken fat, bagels, strudel and cookies. Customers included Kienow's and Ideal Dairies. The shop took in over three thousand dollars in 1936 and more in later years, as it became better known. But by 1941, few women were requesting work because other, more remunerative opportunities had become available, and the shop closed its doors.

Another neighborhood effort that had existed for some years, but proved particularly useful during the Depression, was the Ladies Free Loan Society. Frieda Gass Cohen remembers it as

To help supplement family income during the Depression, women cut noodles at the Opportunity Bake Shop, located in an annex to the B'nai B'rith Building. Courtesy, JHSO.

a remarkable organization, one of the most remarkable I have ever known. Today [1975], perhaps it is not a necessity, but in those years it kept many a family going. These women, who had nothing, would get together once a month and each put in twenty-five cents and from these quarters they accumulated a treasury. When a family needed a loan of fifty or one hundred dollars, which was a tremendous amount of money then, they would go to the Free Loan Society and make their request. It was never known who came for money, only the officers who had charge of the fund knew. The money was given freely, no interest was charged and it was paid back at the rate of one, two, or five dollars at a time.... It was almost always paid back; I think they had practically no losses.... It functioned all during the Depression.

Federated Jewish Societies continued to raise and distribute funds during the Depression, as it always had since its inception in 1920. Its officers were well-known and often wealthy individuals from both the German and Eastern European Jewish communities. The division between German and Eastern European Jews, once so apparent, had all but disappeared by 1937. For instance, in 1937 its president was Max Hirsch, and its officers were Joseph Shemanski, Zachary Swett, Arthur Eppstein and Julia Swett. Julia, often the only woman on the board, had succeeded her husband, Isaac, as executive secretary to the Federation, a post which she held for many years. The largest sums that year were given to the B'nai B'rith Center, Neighborhood House and the Jewish Service Association; funds were also given to the Jewish Relief and Benevolent Society, the Jewish Education Association and the Jewish Shelter Home.

B'nai B'rith Portland Lodge 65, which had grown rapidly in the early 1920s to well over a thousand members, began to decline late in the decade. The Lodge and its predecessors had always been run by successful merchants. But by mid-decade, men with professional training had assumed leadership, and they were more

A national historic landmark which houses Oregon's largest Jewish congregation, Temple Beth Israel is a beautiful, domed synagogue built in the Byzantine style in Northwest Portland in 1927. Courtesy, OHS.

interested in civic activism and lectures of national or international interest than previous forms of socializing and entertainment. Many clerks and skilled workers felt out of place and left the Lodge, while those who were upwardly mobile tended to find its new direction to their liking. As William Toll points out in his keen analysis of B'nai B'rith membership, a natural tension existed between social mobility and cultural continuity. It was hard for the Lodge to fulfill its goal of providing a meeting ground for all sectors of the Jewish community in a period of rapid change, when newly trained professionals were changing the leadership and focus of the organization.

By the mid-1930s, however, the Lodge's fortunes had reversed themselves again; from fewer than three hundred members in 1933, the Lodge grew to more than six hundred and fifty members in the next six years. The growing menace of Hitler in Germany and anti-Semitism at home drew Jews together, and with the increase in home ownership, leaders of the Lodge—Harry Mittleman, Ben Medofsky, David Robinson, Sam Weinstein and others—were able to recruit new members to their ranks, particularly from the Eastside.

During the 1930s and 1940s, Portland's major synagogues achieved a measure of stable leadership from their rabbis, but experienced the turbulence of the times with respect to finances and membership. The extended tenure of rabbis at their synagogues was extraordinary during this period. Rabbi Henry Berkowitz officiated at Beth Israel from 1928 to 1949; Rabbi Charles Sydney at Ahavai Sholom from 1937 to 1951; Rabbi Philip Kleinman at Neveh Zedek from 1937 to 1956; and Rabbi Joseph Fain at Shaarie Torah from 1916 to 1946.

The membership of Beth Israel began to change in the 1920s, when families of Eastern European background were more readily accepted as members, although leadership was still provided by men of German descent. Many of these Eastern Europeans also retained membership in other synagogues; even leading members of Ahavai Sholom—including its president, Alex Miller, David Robinson, Harry

Kenin and Harry Mittleman—also joined Beth Israel, which they saw as the most "modern" synagogue addressing important issues of the day. The Sisterhood, begun in 1917 with Mrs. Alexander Bernstein as its first president, rapidly became an integral part of Beth Israel.

Beth Israel's membership grew in the years following the building of its new synagogue in 1927 and the installation of a popular new rabbi, Henry Berkowitz, in 1928. The beautiful domed synagogue in the Byzantine style was constructed on a full block in Northwest Portland only after a considerable internal debate in which the young Julius Meier and his supporters prevailed over older members such as Ben Selling and Joseph Simon, who wished to remain at the old downtown location.

Jonah Wise had left in 1926 to assume the pulpit of the Central Synagogue in New York. After two brief interim appointments, Henry Berkowitz, a warm, friendly man with a special love for children, became Beth Israel's rabbi. Felice Lauterstein Driesen, whose family was one of a considerable number moving from Orthodox roots to Conservative and Reform affiliation, fondly remembers him:

The only thing that really comes to my mind in my growing up years, as I am sure it will to all the rest of us who had the job of growing up in my era, was our wonderful relationship with our Temple due in great part to our beloved Rabbi Berkowitz. He was a character who was a very enormous part of our youth and maybe because mother [Paula Lauterstein] was so very close to Rabbi—we used to call him "Rab," everyone did—I think this kept our generation close to Temple.

During the Depression, however, many Beth Israel members were forced to resign because they could no longer pay the high dues. It also became difficult for the synagogue to meet mortgage payments on its new building. But in 1935, the will of Benjamin Blumauer provided $150,000 to Beth Israel and lesser amounts to a number of local and international Jewish institutions. The funds helped to revitalize the congregation: the Octagonal Club, a youth group, was formed; well-known national Jewish figures spoke at the Temple; the religious school expanded rapidly, becoming considerably larger than those at other synagogues and larger even than the Portland Hebrew School; and membership began to grow again. Tragically, Rabbi Berkowitz contracted a rare illness while serving as a military chaplain during World War II and died in 1949. In the postwar period, Beth Israel has continued to grow with its congregation today numbering over nine hundred families, the largest in the state.

Conservative synagogues Ahavai Sholom and Neveh Zedek also experienced difficulties with finances and membership through the Depression years. Ahavai Sholom was able to repair its building, which had been damaged by fire in 1923, and continued to pay its mortgage through fundraising efforts headed by Sam Swirsky, Nathan Weinstein, Abe Asher and the Sisterhood, as well as with a bequest from the will of Abraham Wildman. But the synagogue was barely able to make ends meet, and

The interior of Temple Beth Israel. Courtesy, BI.

Confirmation at Ahavai Sholom in 1933 with Rabbi Raphael Goldenstein. Courtesy, JHSO.

This fine wooden synagogue on the Park Blocks at Clay Street was used by the Ahavai Sholom congregation from 1904 to 1952. Courtesy, JHSO.

concern was often expressed about declining membership and limited attendance at the religious school. Merger discussions took place several times with Neveh Zedek with the objective of creating a center for Conservative Judaism, and once with Beth Israel, but none of these discussions came to fruition. Ahavai Sholom and Neveh Zedek maintained themselves during the Depression years by keeping expenses to a minimum. Slowly, as times became better, they instituted programs oriented toward increasing and diversifying membership.

Ahavai Sholom introduced junior membership for those under thirty-five. Rabbi Edward Sandrow also launched successful drives to increase membership in both the synagogue and the religious school. His successor, Rabbi Charles Sydney, continued these efforts. By the end of the 1930s, the synagogue had a membership of two hundred families and by

1951, when Rabbi Sydney completed his tenure at Ahavai Sholom, the membership had mushroomed to three hundred and fifty families. The Park Avenue Synagogue, which had served for nearly half a century, was no longer adequate. After considerable debate about location, the congregation purchased a half block at Thirteenth Avenue and Market Street—across from the Jewish Community Center—and built a handsome, brick edifice with a beautifully panelled pulpit which was dedicated in September, 1952. Ahavai Sholom's Park Avenue Synagogue was sold to the First Christian Church, which used it as a community center. It was later briefly used as a gymnasium by Portland State University and reused as a church for Sunday school classes. Finally—after an unsuccessful battle to save it—the venerable neo-colonial, wood-frame landmark was demolished in September, 1978.

Rabbi Philip Kleinman came to Neveh Zedek in 1937 after eleven years at Temple Beth El in Milwaukee, Wisconsin. He helped to revitalize the congregation with innovations oriented toward youth, such as junior services for young people, special programs for recently married couples and a Jewish Boy Scout troop. Neveh Zedek also continued to grow, and Rabbi Kleinman remained as spiritual leader for twenty years.

Again urban renewal devastated the Jewish community. Ahavai Sholom was informed that its new synagogue—less than a decade old—was in the path of freeway construction and would have to be torn down. This news spurred renewed consideration of merger between Ahavai Sholom and Neveh Zedek. In 1961, the merger was consummated, the new congregation being called Neveh Shalom. The decision was made to build in the Southwest suburbs, where most congregants now lived. In 1963, a large new building—with the ten commandments boldly inscribed high on its exterior stone—was dedicated at 2900 SW Peaceful Lane. Neveh Shalom has prospered. Today it is the spiritual home of over seven hundred families and hosts a wide variety of religious and community activities.

As the first generation of immigrants began to pass away, it was hard for the Orthodox synagogues to retain the allegiance of their children, who had been educated in American schools and sought ways to combine their desire to be Jewish with their newly won status in America. Alice Mandler points out how difficult it was to maintain strict orthodoxy:

We just don't have that many strict Orthodox people anymore. Youth is ... not that Orthodox anymore. An Orthodox Jew has a very hard life.... You cannot work after sundown on Friday or on Saturday.... A doctor is a doctor and he cannot say on Saturday, "Sorry, I'm not going to see you." We ... live in modern times. It is very hard to be an Orthodox Jew.

A wedding is celebrated at Neveh Zedek about 1930. Courtesy, JHSO.

As a result, many with Orthodox roots shifted to Conservative synagogues and to Beth Israel over the years. Shaarie Torah, the major strictly Orthodox synagogue through the first half of the twentieth century, has itself now become Modern Orthodox or Traditional. Conservative and Traditional Judaism retain many of the religious practices brought to America by Eastern European immigrants, but they provide an accommodation with secular needs by modifying many aspects of Orthodox ritual. Today, Kesser Israel, located where it has always been, at Second and Meade in old South Portland, and the Sephardic synagogue Ahavath Achim are the only strictly Orthodox synagogues that remain in Oregon.

By the 1940s, Oregon's Jews had become fully integrated into American society. They had done well. Nearly all had found their way to become stable, contributing members of the middle class. Many—well beyond their proportion in the general population—had entered the professions and other prestigious occupations. Most were homeowners and many sent their children to summer camp and spent the summer themselves at Gearhart, Long Beach or other resort towns along the coast.

In 1938, the B'nai B'rith Center officially became the Jewish Community Center, a name change which was required in order to obtain a significant grant from the Blumauer Fund to expand its facilities on Thirteenth Avenue. But the name reflected the reality; while social life had once centered in the synagogue, "the Community Center," in the view of Harold Schnitzer, "had become the focal point of the whole community." As South Portlanders moved to other neighborhoods and no longer needed the services of Neighborhood House, many also joined the Center. As stated in a later Center *Yearbook*, "while actively welcoming the entire community, the Center is a unique and vital institution for positive Jewish identification." And so it was and remains today. The old divisions within the Jewish community, so visible earlier in the century, became largely a thing of the past; German Jews and Eastern European Jews had both become American Jews.

Cantor and choir at Shaarie Torah in 1927. Courtesy, JHSO.

24

War Years and the Founding of Israel

The Nazi Menace

The rise of Hitler in Germany impelled the Jewish community in Oregon and elsewhere in America to draw together for mutual support and concerted response. The Portland Hebrew School and the synagogue Sunday schools had seen dramatic increases in attendance in the late 1930s as Jewish culture and religion gained renewed significance. B'nai B'rith and the Anti-Defamation League fought incidents of anti-Semitism. But with few exceptions, the Oregon Jewish community had been reticent to take political positions on international issues in the years after Stephen Wise left Portland. Rabbi Jonah Wise had cautioned against interference in American foreign policy. Now the dangers represented by Nazism served to mobilize and politicize the Jewish community. The B'nai B'rith Lodge became the focal point for discussion and action.

In May of 1933, shortly after Hitler seized power, the leaders of the Lodge—including Alex Miller, Harry Mittleman, Milton Tarlow, Nathan Weinstein, Harry Kenin, Harry Gevurtz, Anselm Boskowitz and Dr. H. I. Chernichowsky—put forward resolutions to boycott German goods, to support the work of the Joint Distribution Committee (the leading American organization trying to rescue Jews from Europe) and to urge President Roosevelt to condemn anti-Semitism in Germany. Major Jewish industrialists in Portland—the Schnitzers, Zidells and Rosenfelds—were in the forefront of those who boycotted German products. The Portland Lodge continually sponsored national speakers and tours by recent German Jewish émigrés to keep the community in touch with the latest developments. During the war, the Lodge sponsored major drives for the purchase of war bonds and helped to secure facilities for stationing troops. Meier & Frank's war bond drive was cited by the Treasury Department as "the most outstanding of any department store in the United States."

In August of 1936, the Oregon Émigré Committee was organized by Max Hirsch as part of a national effort to resettle as many Jewish refugees from Germany as possible. The Committee sought affidavits from persons who would pledge financial support for a refugee. The Blumauer Fund, the Federation and the Hebrew Benevolent Society assisted the committee with expenses. Sidney Teiser, a Portland lawyer who had come to Oregon from Virginia in 1911 with his close friend, Roscoe Nelson, traveled rural Oregon and Washington to seek placements for émigrés. Sometimes he was accompanied by one of those recent émigrés, Kurt Schlesinger, who was able to describe first-hand the plight of Jews in Germany. The Committee tried every means available to bring German Jews to Portland. Fannie Kenin Friedman, for instance, obtained Wayne Morse's assistance in bringing over the parents of a German "orphan" who had escaped and was living in her home. By March, 1939, the committee had placed sixty-six families.

It was an exceptional group of German

Portland's rabbis lead the community in prayer on November 19, 1938 to protest *Kristallnacht* (the night of broken glass). The Nazi pogrom had just occurred in Germany. Thousands of Jews were attacked; synagogues and Jewish shops were burned and looted.

From left: Rabbi Philip Kleinman (Neveh Zedek), Rabbi Joseph Fain (Shaarie Torah), Rabbi Henry Berkowitz (Beth Israel) and Rabbi Charles Sydney (Ahavai Sholom). Courtesy, JHSO.

Jews who escaped to America during those years, and they would exercise a profound intellectual influence in their new land. Albert Einstein, Hannah Arendt, Theodor Adorno, Bruno Bettelheim and Otto Preminger were but a few. While those who settled in Oregon were not as famous, they were for the most part professionals or high-level managers. They included Hans Linde, currently a justice of the Oregon Supreme Court, Frederick Littman, who became a well-known sculptor and Fred Rosenbaum, an insurance executive who chaired the Housing Authority of Portland for many years. The stories told by émigrés were heart-wrenching accounts of their harrowing escapes and the fate of those left behind.

John Miller, who arrived in Portland in 1941, was put in prison in Germany for six weeks in 1936 when a Nazi customer who did not wish to pay his bill accused him of "insulting the Fuehrer." Released virtually by chance,

All Jewish congregations in Portland gather at Temple Beth Israel on November 19, 1938 to pray and express their horror at *Kristallnacht*. Courtesy, BI.

he had to leave Germany without his wife and two children or be put in a concentration camp. When he arrived in the States, Miller tried desperately to get his family out of Germany, and after much difficulty he finally arranged a four-month American visa for them.

I got a sailing for her from Genoa, Italy, but Italy went to war. She had to stay in Germany and missed the ship. Three weeks later I had a sailing for her from Athens, Greece. Greece went to war with Italy. She had to stay, missed the ship, and her visa expired. It was only good for four months. The whole deal was sent to Stuttgart in triplicate another time. She was called in and got another visa. I arranged for a sailing in January from Lisbon, Portugal. Portugal did not allow any refugees to travel through the country and again she missed the ship.

It was 1941. We were running out of time. I was running around ... and couldn't do anything. In the meantime, tickets had gone up from four hundred to one thousand dollars. Do you know how much one thousand dollars was in 1941? I had gone to the people in Gainesville, [Florida, where he was temporarily living] and asked them to lend me the money. I told them, "I'll pay the money back. If it takes me years, I'll pay it back!" They gave me the money; they were nice.

In March, I got another sailing for her from Lisbon. At this time Portugal relaxed the restrictions and let everyone who had an American visa through. She came over on the Exeter *of the Wilson Line, one of the last ships to go.*

Kurt Schlesinger had been a prominent lawyer in Berlin. But by 1938, Nazi decrees and Gestapo pressure had stripped him of nearly all his clients. He recalls the morning before *Kristallnacht*, November 9 and 10, 1938, when a hundred thousand Jewish men were arrested in Berlin alone:

I got a call from a [Christian] friend of mine in one of the ministries, "Kurt, I under-

John Miller, who narrowly escaped from Nazi Germany, experienced great difficulty in getting his family out. He was later president of the Friendship Club founded in 1948 by German Jewish refugees. Courtesy, JHSO.

stand that you are going to Leipzig today." (Leipzig is a town, a few hundred kilometers from Berlin). At first I didn't understand, so I said, "I haven't any intention of going to Leipzig today." He said, "Well, that's what you told me the other day." Finally I understood and thanked the man. I went to Ulla, my wife, and told her that I would be gone for awhile and to tell anyone who asked for me that I was on a business trip to Leipzig.

I grabbed a hat and coat, climbed into a taxi, and told the driver to drive me to a far part of the city. I was crouched in the back seat. After the man had driven me around for awhile, I said to him, "If you don't want to drive any more, just tell me and I'll get out some place." He answered in his Berlin dialect, "As long as you pay me, I'll drive. It's nobody's damn business who I am driving and where I am driving. As long as you want to pay me, I don't care."

Along the way, I stopped several times at telephone booths and called some of my Christian friends to see if there was any possibility of getting help. I knew that I couldn't go back home because the Nazis were waiting there for me. I finally talked to the executive secretary of a client of mine, an industrialist. She understood my situation and told me to call her back an hour later. I did call back and she gave me an address in a suburb at the other end of Berlin, in Wilhelmshagen. I took the taxi out to the railroad station in that suburb and then got out and walked.

By this time it was evening. I found my way to a little house at the end of the road. I rang the door bell and the door opened. The first thing I saw was a coat rack in the hall and on it hung a Nazi uniform with the swastika arm band and the Nazi hat. You can imagine my feelings. I didn't understand. I knew that the lady who had sent me to this address was beyond any reproach but here I was faced with this uniform. Next I saw, in the doorway, a middle-aged woman and her husband who was blind. They welcomed me in. It turned out that the uniform belonged to their son who was a member of the S.A. [*Sturm Abteilung, Storm Troopers, the National Socialist militia*]. Millions of people, at that time, belonged to the Storm Troopers and would march through the streets to the "Horst Wessel" song. Some of the words to this song ran, "Everything goes doubly fast when the blood of the Jews spurts forth." The people asked me in and I found a family of warm understanding, with a desire to help, father, mother and son alike.

I want to stress that these people ran a terrible risk for me. If anybody had found out that they gave shelter to a fugitive Jew, it is hard to know what would have been done to them. They put me up in the basement of their modest home and I spent two weeks there. The dark basement was sparsely furnished but it did contain a shortwave radio and I listened to that radio. Every evening at nine o'clock the voices of Elmer Davis and Edward R. Murrow would come over the air from Schenecta-dy, New York. (I spoke very little English, but I knew enough to understand.) These broadcasts, for me, were the voices of reason, of sense, of human beings instead of robots. I just can't describe what it meant, in my desolation, to hear the voices of these men.

In the weeks that followed, Ulla arranged to come out to Wilhelmshagen where I hadn't seen the light of day for days on end. The son of my hosts went, in full Nazi uniform, to pick her up at the railroad station, so she came out three times, protected by an honest-to-goodness Storm Trooper.

After two weeks, I got the report that the police action was at an end and that it was safe for me to come out of hiding....

By the beginning of 1939 the Jewish situation in Germany became perfectly intolerable. At the end of 1938, all licenses held by Jews were revoked and I could no longer practice [*law*].

On March 8, 1939, my wife, my daughter Jane and I left Germany. A man with whom I had worked at the Reichsvertretung [*Federal Association of German Jews*] and who had emigrated to the United States a year earlier devoted a lot of time and energy trying to get an affidavit for me and my family. He buttonholed anybody who he thought could be helpful and when all that didn't work, he went to the Los Angeles telephone book—he had settled in Los Angeles—and tried to persuade all the Schlesingers in the directory. He finally found a man who was willing to give me an affidavit and thereupon I got a visa. This man has never accepted any thanks from me. When I was in Los Angeles, I called to make an appointment to see him and to express my gratitude in person, but he thought that there was no reason to do that. I will be forever grateful to this man who, without knowing anything about me, made it possible for me and my family to live here.

Nobody can describe the feelings of a man or a family who, coming out of slavery, and coming into New York harbor at six o'clock in the morning, sees the Statue of Liberty for the first time. Being one of the "hud-

dled masses," coming to these shores and see-
ing the symbol of liberty, of freedom, makes
your heart beat at an unbelievable pace.

The Émigré Committee provided apartments for newcomers, usually near Beth Israel.
The main difficulty was finding jobs. There was
still substantial unemployment in America, and
longtime residents resented jobs potentially being taken from them by émigré Jews. Their fear
was so strong, in fact, that the committee had to
help defeat a bill in the Oregon Legislature that
would have prevented any émigré from practicing law, medicine or dentistry. Nevertheless,
most émigrés were not able to continue the careers they had pursued in Germany.

Kurt Schlesinger describes the warm welcome afforded by the committee, as well as the
frustrating search for work that followed:

Kurt Schlesinger with his wife, Ulla, in 1926. A
prominent lawyer in Berlin, Schlesinger narrowly
escaped arrest during *Kristallnacht*. After emigration to Portland, Schlesinger worked for the Émigré
Committee, helping to find lodging and work for
German refugees. Courtesy, Jane Rosenbaum.

The Oregon Émigré Committee found us
an apartment within a few days. It was in the
Cecilia Apartments, modest but clean. The
committee showed great consideration in
furnishing the apartment, in stocking the
pantry with all that was needed and in hav-
ing a hospitality committee show us around.
The Council of Jewish Women held classes in
English for the foreign born and a number of
people did everything they could to make the
transition easier.

Finding a job was our main and overrid-
ing goal. It proved extremely difficult because
of circumstances. Nineteen thirty-nine was
the end of the Depression and there still was a
tremendous lot of unemployment in the
country. As a consequence, many people in
Portland, as I am sure in other cities, resented
the influx of newcomers. It didn't matter that
our number was small. In all the years of Ger-
man Jewish immigration, from 1933 to the
beginning of the war in 1941, the newcomers
numbered not more than two hundred fami-
lies in Oregon, and they were not all in Port-
land. Despite this, the feeling was widespread
that newcomers "take jobs away from old
timers." An often-expressed reaction was,
"Why should they have jobs when we have
none?" This feeling has been repeated
through every wave of immigration to this
country. It happened before we came and
since we came, when the Puerto Ricans came,
or the Cubans came, or the Koreans came. You
heard exactly the same arguments. Meier &
Frank had hired, amongst its two thousand
employees, only two German immigrants,
both of them very qualified, but rumor had it
that Meier & Frank had hired hundreds of
Jewish immigrants at the expense of Ameri-
can-born employees. That rumor persisted for
many years.

The hunt for a job began. Another Ger-
man Jewish family arrived in Portland on the
same day we did—the Peter Optons. They also
had an apartment in the building where we
lived. Every evening Peter and I would come
home, slap each other on the shoulder and
say, "Don't get discouraged. Everything will

turn out alright." That was the refrain that we heard as we walked the pavement, for endless hours, trying to find a job. Peter got his first job selling Fuller Brushes and he has been a successful salesman ever since. [Mr. Opton later became a respected insurance agent.]

Six endless weeks I looked for a job. During this time I began to think that I was just good for nothing, that there would never be anything coming my way.

Finally—I don't even remember how I got the job—I got a job in a filling station, pumping gas and taking care of the books. I have never been any good with my hands, so I'm afraid that I spilled a lot of gas.

After some months, Schlesinger was hired by the Oregon Émigré Committee as a field worker, and he later opened a grocery store which did not succeed. Finally, he found a niche with the Oregon Department of Revenue, where he remained for nineteen years although he still longed for the profession he had left in Germany. So Schlesinger studied law at night at Northwestern College of Law in Portland, earn-

Meier & Frank provides the latest war news. Courtesy, OHS.

ing his degree again at age sixty. He put it to work after retirement as legal advisor to students at Portland Community College and in a small law practice. Kurt Schlesinger's experience was typical of both the early struggles of the émigrés and their persistence and courage, which eventually led to stability in a new land.

In 1940, the émigrés organized themselves into discussion groups to share common problems and practice English together. After the war, with the arrival of additional refugees who had survived the Holocaust, the Friendship Club was founded in 1948. It offered a comfortable place for German émigrés and refugees, a unique cultural group which shared mutual needs and concerns, and helped its members find jobs. The club held meetings once a month, presenting programs, such as the successful performance of *Die Fliedermaus*, and sponsoring speakers. When Governor Holmes spoke to the group in 1956, its president, John Miller, pointed out that members—such as Max Lehmann (the Northwest Packing Company), Julian Shipley (Dennis Uniform Company) and Herman Lowen (Alice Love Jam)—were by then able to provide a large number of jobs for other members. In 1977, the club disbanded, since it had fulfilled the purposes for which it had been established.

Edward Weinbaum, after retirement from his many years with the Portland Chamber of Commerce, was made honorary consul to the Federal Republic of Germany in 1960. He was able to secure restitution from the German government for many Jews then residing in Oregon whose property had been confiscated by the Nazis.

During the war, many Oregon Jews served in the armed forces and many at home worked for the Red Cross and civil defense and in local war industries, the largest of which was the Kaiser shipyards. They weathered rationing and shortages better than most because, as Diane Nemer put it, "I had lived so many years as a youngster without, that it didn't affect me much." But it was often difficult for those with relatives in the armed services. Rachel Fain Schneider, Rabbi Fain's daughter, was pregnant when her husband, Leo, was called up in December, 1940. In September of the following year, he shipped out to the Pacific and she did not hear from him until:

On a Sunday, the doorbell rang and there was a telegram and he said this is from the government and I was petrified. He said, "Why don't you open it while I'm here?" So I did and that's when I was notified that he was a prisoner of war. At least I knew that he was alive.

Then I didn't hear again, although I had addresses to write to and I wrote every blessed day.... Every August, somehow, I would get a postcard. That was it. On Yom Kippur, 1945, I had just sent Edward to shul, because he was old enough to go to shul by himself, Sandra was home and I had my sister's two infants. The doorbell rang and it was our mailman. I looked down and I screamed. He said, "What's the matter?" I said, "That's my husband's handwriting." It was my husband's letter. He said, "I'm coming home...."

I saw a man walking and knocked on the window and said, "Are you going down to the First Street shul?" and he said, "Yes." I said, "Would you give my father the message that ... Leo's coming home...." He [her father] got up and stopped the service and made the announcement. I understand they made a certain prayer and the first thing I knew my doorbell kept ringing and people kept coming and me with the kids and I'm not dressed.

As the concentration camps were liberated, word began to reach Jews in Portland, as it did elsewhere in America and the world, of the immensity of the Holocaust, the unfathomable extermination of six million Jews and countless others. Of the few who survived, some made their way to Oregon after the war. The experience of the Holocaust can really only be related by those whom it touched directly. Here are the stories of Diana Galante Golden and Chella Velt Meekcoms, who now live in Oregon, as told to Shirley Tanzer and published in the *Scribe* of the Jewish Historical Society in 1978.

Brought together by Harry Glickman during World War II, Jewish servicemen from Oregon and friends gather in San Francisco. Front row from left: Milt Carl, Joe Lakefish and an unidentified person; back row: Sam Benveniste, Sam Menashe, Harold Unkeles, Ruth Schilt, Bob Hasson, Harry Glickman, Irv Potter and Al Lebenzon. Courtesy, JHSO.

Diana Galante Golden

Diana Galante Golden was born on the Isle of Rhodes on February 7, 1922. When Mussolini allied his government with Hitler in the mid-1930s, Jews without Italian citizenship were asked to leave Rhodes, where they had enjoyed amiable relations with the Greek, Italian and Turkish population. Most of the Galante family stayed, however, and soon it was impossible to leave. The Germans occupied the island in the spring of 1944. On July 12, 1944, Jews were ordered to take only what they could carry on their backs and prepare to leave Rhodes.

Diana remembers that they were evacuated by boat after sirens sounded a curfew so that no one would witness their deportation. People were packed into the galleys of two boats where, for the duration of the eight-day voyage to Pireaus, they endured heat, hunger and stench. Some died en route.

The Jews were then taken to an interim camp at Pireaus. Diana's grandmother died there, leaving Diana, a blind aunt whom Diana had cared for in her grandparents' home, her mother and father, her two sisters and a brother.

After three days in the Pireaus camp, up to one hundred people were herded into box-cars . . . for the twenty-eight-day trip to Auschwitz in Poland. The train would sometimes stop for several hours, and these afforded people the opportunity to relieve themselves in the fields and bury their dead. The Galantes left Diana's father in a shallow grave in Yugoslavia after he died in fever and delirium, but Diana remembers that there were no tears for those blessed with a "natural death."

The transport arrived at Auschwitz on August 16, 1944, and the prisoners were un-loaded. Diana was forced by the S.S. guards to let go of her terrified aunt's hand, and she was separated from her aunt, mother and little brother. She never saw them again.

Filthy, hungry and ill, the new arrivals were processed into Auschwitz: they were bru-tally stripped, shaved of body hair, allowed only brief showers and given one piece of in-adequate clothing. Diana and the others were then sent to barracks where they learned that ten people were to share a bunk the size of a double bed. At dawn of the first day, still in shock, they were forced out of the barracks between which ran electric wires that were al-ways charged. There they stood at attention for over an hour. Many died during the first two weeks, a number of them suicides.

Diana recalls that some women from Belgium, France and Italy addressed the issue of survival for the newcomers. . . . "They tried to put it in a few words that we would never be able to see those who were sent to the other side, our elders, small children and moth-ers. . . . 'Now that you are here it's up to you. If you just want to hang yourself on the wires then you just go ahead and do it, that will be quick. But if you want to survive you have to be very strong to survive it. . . . Find someone, even if you don't have anyone who's in your family here, and pledge life for each other.'"

Diana and her sisters did forced labor in Birkenau (Auschwitz) for three months be-fore the proximity of Allied bombing prompt-

Pictured here in 1978, Diana Galante Golden was raised on the Island of Rhodes. In 1944, at the age of twenty-two, she was deported with her family to Auschwitz. Courtesy, Oregon Holocaust Resource Center and Paul Miller.

ed their removal to a munition factory in the south of Germany.

Late in March, this factory closed as the sounds of planes and cannon drew nearer. Diana and the other prisoners were again loaded into boxcars without roofs, so the prisoners were constantly exposed to the snow and cold. People in the boxcars began screaming and crying for food, since they had eaten only a few slices of bread throughout the entire nine days. Finally they were deliv-ered to Therezienstadt, not far from Prague, in Czechoslovakia.

The Jews of Therezienstadt were liberat-ed by the Russians in the early spring of 1945. Over the next several months, Diana and her sisters were taken to Prague, and to Austria and Hungary. The Italian government lacked funds to repatriate its people, and it wasn't until September that, with the help of the

American Jewish Joint Distribution Committee, they arrived in Milano by train from Budapest and "kissed the ground." In a plain room converted to a provisional sanctuary, they celebrated Rosh Hashanah.

Of the many people in Diana's family, only two sisters, two male cousins and two elderly cousins from her mother's side survived the concentration camps.

Sponsored by relatives in Los Angeles, Diana emigrated to the United States. She was reunited with a sister in New York, and three weeks later she was on a train bound for California: "Oh, I was—I was—feeling so wonderful to be able to be in a train, free. To be regarded as a human being and not a slave and not fear and fear and just, you know, I felt I'm free, I'm a human being, I'm myself."

Diana and her husband, Kenneth Golden, settled in Portland in the early 1950s. Reflecting upon the attitude which helped her survive Auschwitz and the rest of her imprisonment, Diana said: "I felt if you have a good feeling towards people, if you want to be friends, it had to begin with you. You cannot expect people to have a feeling of hostility or hate. . . . Instead of being negative I would say, well, this is another hour, this is another minute. I don't know, a type of philosophy."

Rachella "Chella" Velt Meekcoms

After five days of bombing that flattened Rotterdam, the Germans marched into Holland on Chella Velt's twelfth birthday. Chella and her family were forced into hiding where they remained for over two years in Scheveningen near The Hague where Chella had been born in 1928.

Chella had never experienced anti-Semitism and thought of herself as a Dutch child. . . . She remembers how it was to wear the Star of David: "I was only twelve at the time, I remember. So I felt different all of a sudden. It made you feel different." Nevertheless, non-Jewish neighbors stopped Jews on the street to express support and urged them to wear the Star of David proudly.

Then Flora, Chella's older sister who was sixteen, received a letter ordering her to report in a few days with other young people to go to a camp. The family decided that she would not go, and a few days later Flora was in hiding thanks to the Dutch underground. A year later, the entire family was in hiding.

Meanwhile, Chella's father had been forced to go to a labor camp where he broke a leg and both hips in an accident. But he escaped from a hospital and joined his family. He was crippled and walked with great difficulty, and Chella recalls that he returned with a different look in his eyes and a determination that his family should survive.

They almost didn't. Chella remembers a terrifying near-discovery after her stepmother rejoined the family. The Germans were conducting house-to-house searches, and one day they suddenly appeared where the Velts were hiding. The family just barely had time to conceal themselves behind a clothes closet before the men came up the stairs. After they left, everyone was shaking, and Chella herself was rolling on the floor with stomach pains from the tension and terror.

Chella's father told her: "We will never complain about what we have to go through while we are in hiding. We will stick it out, we will never see daylight—that will be fine. But we will never be caught, because that will be the worst thing that can happen to us."

But sadly, his resolve could not spare them. The family had to split up for better security, Flora hiding in Rotterdam and Chella's father and stepmother in the inner city. Chella was hidden elsewhere by a loving family with five children.

Although it was very risky, Chella's family decided to have a reunion to celebrate her father's birthday, so Flora and Chella secretly joined their parents in the inner city and remained for an extended visit. The family slept and read together, and Chella had long conversations with her father. "He was such a wonderful human being. . . . In all our sorrow and worry these were the most marvelous hours I spent with him. . . . I got strength from

Chella and Flora Velt, 1930

Chella Velt Meekcoms, Portland, 1978

Chella Velt Meekcoms and her family had been hidden near The Hague for two years when they were discovered by the S.S. in 1944 and sent to Auschwitz. Courtesy, Chella Velt Meekcoms.

him, strength of character which helped me afterwards through the years in camp."

Then, in February of 1944, the Velts were captured by the S.S. early one morning. Chella remembers that they came one morning when the family was still in bed: "I heard these voices say: 'We've come to get the family Velt, where are they? There are four of them.' And I heard them and I thought I'm dreaming, I'm dreaming. This is not true, I'm dreaming. And father sat up in bed and he said, 'Oh, God, be with us.'"

The Velts were told to dress quickly and were immediately taken to the federal penitentiary, where they remained for six weeks. They were allowed to shower and walk outside once a week. Next they were sent to prison in the province of Westerbrook, where Chella, Flora and their stepmother were together while Mr. Velt was in sick bay. At Westerbrook, Chella and Flora were offered the chance to work in the Phillips factory and re-

main in Holland. Advised by their father to accept the offer, they were then sent to Veught, where Chella had her sixteenth birthday.

But a couple of weeks later, they were put on a transport to Auschwitz. As the transports crossed into Poland, the prisoners threw from the boxcars little scribbled messages addressed to friends. They wrote that they were leaving Holland and didn't know where they were going.

After four days and nights on the transport, they arrived at Auschwitz. As they were unloaded onto the platform, Chella saw the red sky, "like flames going into the sky," and said to those around her, "look at that pretty sky, it's red. I wonder what it is."

The Phillips group was processed into Birkenau (Auschwitz) and eventually put to work. "Work" consisted of carrying bricks from one place to another in sight of those coming in on the transports. Chella quickly lost twenty pounds and was very ill with dys-

entery. Flora took care of her, insisting that she eat and not give up. Working at the gates of Auschwitz near the road to the gas chambers was an experience of overwhelming exhaustion and pain for Chella. The women were physically wasted and mentally depressed, and "just to survive each day was a miracle."

On July 9, 1944, due to Phillips' influence, the group was sent to a Telefunken factory in Reichenbach, Germany. There they were fed hot meals and treated more like workers. As the Russians drew near they were evacuated and forced to walk for four days over the Carpathian Mountains. On the way, they slept in farmhouses or by the roadside; no food was provided and they ate snow to quench their thirst. Flora had been very ill with migraine headaches and a touch of pneumonia at Reichenbach. Knowing that she would not be allowed to live if she remained in the camp "hospital," Chella forced her to leave and physically supported her on the long march through the mountains. Those who fell by the way were shot by the soldiers.

After being transported to Wiesbaden, Germany, where they worked for several weeks in salt mines, the prisoners were again crowded into boxcars and transported from place to place by the Germans, who at that point had no place to deposit them. Finally, on May 4, 1945, Chella and the others realized that they were crossing the German border into Denmark. Danish Red Cross workers boarded the train and informed the prisoners that they were free.

In the station in Copenhagen there were huge barrels of hot cross buns, and everyone received a plate of rolls. Of course, many became ill from this rich food, and the donors learned to be careful how they fed people who had subsisted on so little for so long.

Also in the station at Copenhagen was a man dressed in ordinary clothing who did not identify himself but moved among the ex-prisoners, shaking their hands and congratulating them on their survival and their freedom. They learned later that he was the King of Denmark.

Chella and the other ex-prisoners walked from the train station to the port, where they were to board the boat that would take them to Malmö, Sweden. As she and the others walked to the boat, the people of Copenhagen

Many Oregonians lost family members in the Holocaust. This is the family of Joseph Hertzberg of Portland in Biezun, Poland in 1939. They are his aunts, uncles and grandfather who were deported to the Warsaw Ghetto and then to Auschwitz and Treblinka concentration camps and murdered. Courtesy, Joseph Hertzberg.

lined the streets. The ex-prisoners, who smiled and waved and threw kisses, didn't understand why the Danes were all weeping. But later Chella saw newspaper photos of that march, in which their group looked like "walking dead people."

They arrived at Malmö one week before Chella's seventeeth birthday. Representatives from the Dutch consulate were there to greet the boat, and a group of musicians played the Dutch National Anthem.

In January of 1946, the two women went to England to visit their stepmother who had also survived. With the exception of an aunt (who was in hiding throughout the war) and an older cousin, the rest of her family had been wiped out.

Chella later returned to England, where she married Dan Meekcoms on June 8, 1947. With their new baby, Chella and Dan emigrated to the United States in June of 1952, following Flora, who had married an American of Dutch parentage and was living in Portland, Oregon. The sun was shining in Portland when the Meekcoms arrived on June 7, 1952.

The State of Israel

The Holocaust has become, in the words of historian Henry Feingold, "the touchstone of all Jewish sensibility"—it is with us always. It was surely there when American Jews, with Jews from all parts of the world, fought for the establishment of a Jewish state, Israel, a haven where Jews would, at last, be protected.

After the war, Zionist organizations nationwide dramatically increased their fundraising to assist refugees emigrating to Palestine and to support them once there. In 1948, Hadassah approved a budget of nearly 5 million dollars nationally, and at its convention in Atlantic City the United Jewish Appeal determined to try to raise 250 million dollars, most of it for Palestine. Local Oregon affiliates did their part. Arthur Markewitz described the intense activity:

You put on drives. You had dinners. You honored people and charged fees and you asked people for support. The coming of the State of Israel and the Holocaust made all the difference in the world in the intensity with which Jews would raise funds.

The Council of Jewish Women lobbied President Truman, urging the rescue of Jewish survivors in Europe by opening the doors of Palestine, which had been shut by the British. Oregon Jews poured their energies into helping make Israel a reality. And then came the day. Gussie Reinhardt remembers May 14, 1948:

I broke into tears of joy. I remember vividly the children not understanding why we were crying. We stayed up all night, two nights really, waiting for the decision from the United Nations. The news came through early in the morning. It was as if there was a light from heaven.

Gussie Reinhardt, who was named Oregon's Woman of the Year for 1973 by the Jewish National Fund, went to Israel that year to help plant the first trees in the Oregon Friendship Forest on the hills of Galilee.

After the founding of Israel in 1948, it was essential that funds be raised to help build a nation. In Oregon, Ben Medofsky, long a key supporter of a Jewish state, was asked to be state chairman for the sale of Israel Bonds, a post that he held until his death in the late 1960s. Harry Arnsberg, a young Portland businessman, helped organize the early efforts. In 1967, the Oregon Israel Bond Committee was scheduled to hold its annual dinner at the Benson Hotel on June 7. But that very day the Six Day War began, reservations skyrocketed, and people stood in long lines to buy tickets. Over one million dollars in bonds were sold that night.

The existence of Israel has changed the consciousness of Oregon Jews, as it has for Jews everywhere. Arthur Markewitz, who taught Sunday school for many years, would ask his students whether they were as proud of being Jewish as others were of being Irish, German,

Scandinavian or whatever. Only a few Jewish children would raise their hands. "I asked that question for the thirty years that I was teaching," he said. "Since the formation of the State of Israel, I now get 100 percent raising their hands. That's the difference. It's very important, very important." Harold Schnitzer, raised as an Orthodox Jew in South Portland, believes:

The development of Israel has brought a new kind of glue that holds the Jewish people together. When I was a boy, before 1948, ... we always for centuries prayed for a Jewish homeland and suddenly there is a Jewish homeland. Like a bomb bursting on the world. Our whole religion has ... been affected by the fact that we have a homeland. There is a State of Israel.... Today people around the world speak Hebrew.... There's been a complete revolution here which occurred since 1948 and it has affected the synagogues, our social life. It has affected everything that is Jewish in the world.

Gussie Reinhardt at the ten-thousand-tree Oregon Friendship Forest planted in Israel by the Jewish community of Oregon to honor Gussie and Hershal and Shirley Tanzer. Hershal Tanzer is now the honorary consul in Oregon for the State of Israel. Courtesy, Gussie Reinhardt.

A Unified Community

For Jews, the decade of the 1940s was dominated by international events. The experience of Nazism, the Holocaust and the founding of Israel brought Jewish communities in Oregon and throughout America together as nothing had before. Residential and occupational dispersion which had begun in Oregon in the late 1920s continued, but did not diminish the profound sense of Jews sharing a common destiny brought about by the overwhelming events of the decade.

By 1950, the Jews of Oregon were a mature, well-established community. The older distinctions between German and Eastern European Jews had disappeared. The proud German merchants of the nineteenth century and the dynamic Eastern European immigrants of the early twentieth had blended into one Jewish community: self-aware, resourceful, involved.

Jews continued, as always, to contribute to the broader Oregon community in nearly all areas of endeavor. Lydia Brown, an Orthodox Jew who survived Auschwitz and came to Portland after the war, captured the essence of Jewish commitment when she said—even after all that she had suffered:

I would like, if God would give me strength, to continue to work for the good of the less fortunate than us. For the good of humanity as a whole. I sympathize with anything that is humanistic and needs help. I seem to be able to identify.

Jews can take deep pride in their history in Oregon. It is an illustrious history full of adventure and contributions to the state's development. Through it all, Jews have also retained a deep and abiding sense of being Jewish, a sense of who they are as a people. And it is perhaps this sense of self, of peoplehood, that has allowed Jews to reach out and participate so fully in the building of Oregon.

AFTERWORD

25

A Continuing History

Rabbi Joshua Stampfer leads sabbath services at Ahavai Sholom in 1955. Joshua Stampfer has served as rabbi of Congregation Neveh Shalom and its predecessor, Ahavai Sholom, since 1953. Courtesy, Rabbi Joshua Stampfer.

A great deal has happened in Oregon in the years since 1950. These decades are still too close to us to be judged in historical perspective. However, a brief review of major trends will provide at least an outline of the story of the Jews of Oregon to 1987.

The basic structure of Oregon's Jewish community has remained relatively constant. Its bedrock is—as it has always been—the strong identity that Jews feel through family, synagogue affiliation and participation in the extensive organizational network that exists within the Jewish community.

The three major synagogues in Portland have been unusually fortunate in having rabbis who have each celebrated twenty-five years of service. The first to come to Portland was Joshua Stampfer, who arrived in 1953 to serve as rabbi of Ahavai Sholom. He provided leadership in the merger that created Neveh Shalom (from Ahavai Sholom and Neveh Zedek) and its subsequent move to a new synagogue in suburban Portland. Rabbi Stampfer has also been instrumental in the founding of important Jewish institutions, including the Jewish Historical Society (1974), the Institute for Judaic Studies (1983) and the Oregon Holocaust Resource Center (1983).

Rabbi Yonah Geller came to Portland in 1960. He guided Shaarie Torah through displacement by freeway construction to its new synagogue built in 1965 in Northwest Portland, as well as through significant changes in ritual to develop modern Orthodox practice. He has held various community posts including presi-

Rabbi Emanuel Rose in 1982, at the ceremony of consecration for Beth Israel's Shabbat School. Rabbi Rose has led Beth Israel since his arrival in 1960. Courtesy, BI.

addition, a young, growing congregation, Havurah Shalom, with its recently installed rabbi, Joseph Garon-Wolf, holds services at the Mittleman Jewish Community Center.

Community service has remained a core value for most Jews. In a 1971 study by the Jewish Welfare Federation, over 75 percent of the Jews surveyed volunteered or contributed to Jewish organizations. The major Jewish organizations founded in the past prosper today, albeit in changed, more modern forms. The organizations receiving allocations from the Jewish Federation of Portland (successor to Federated Jewish Societies and the Jewish Welfare Federation) are quite similar to those that received help in 1920, when the Federation was first organized. Beneficiaries for 1986-87 were the Portland Jewish Academy; Jewish Family and

dent of the Jewish Family and Child Service.

Emanuel Rose also came to Portland in 1960 and has served longer than any previous rabbi in Temple Beth Israel's one-hundred-and-thirty-year history. Rabbi Rose has continued the congregation's longtime concern with issues of social justice and has himself taken a leadership role in numerous civic activities, including serving as vice-president of the board of trustees of Lewis and Clark College and chair of the Multnomah County Justice Coordinating Council.

There are also two smaller Orthodox synagogues in Portland. Kesser Israel, located where it has long been at Second Avenue and Meade Street, is associated with Chabad Lubavitch. In 1987, Ahavath Achim, the Sephardic congregation, located on Barbur Boulevard, engaged Shmuel Nechemia, a full-time cantor. In

Rabbi Yonah Geller, who has been the religious leader of Congregation Shaarie Torah for twenty-eight years, prepares for Rosh Hashanah in September, 1962. Courtesy, OHS.

Child Service; Mittleman Jewish Community Center; Portland Jewish Review; and the Robison Jewish Home. The primary changes since 1920 are the large contribution now given to United Jewish Appeal for Israel and the absence of Neighborhood House, now a National Historic Landmark, but no longer utilized by the Jewish community.

Jewish population has remained remarkably consistent over the years. In 1968, it was tabulated at 9,045, approximately the same number recorded in 1918, toward the end of the great influx of Eastern European immigrants. A dip occurred in the years between 1930 and 1950 when many young people sought opportunities outside the state, but Jewish population grew again in the 1960s and '70s. In 1985, the *American Jewish Yearbook* placed Oregon's Jewish population at 11,050 (Portland, 8,950; Eugene, 1,500; Salem, 200; Corvallis, 140). The Jewish Community Center *Yearbook* for 1986-87 estimates the figure is even higher, approximately 15,000, due in part to a large number of unaffiliated Jews who have come to Oregon in the last several decades.

While many trends that began as early as the 1930s have continued to the present date—residential and occupational dispersion, dedication to community service, increased secularism and upward mobility into a stable middle and upper-middle class—a number of significant changes have also occurred. In 1958, Portland voters created the South Auditorium Urban Renewal District, and although there was some opposition, the bulldozers came to the fifty-four block area and demolished all that had been there. While the vibrant Jewish community of South Portland had largely moved away by the Second World War, a number of elderly, more Orthodox Jews stayed. A strong sentimental attachment to the neighborhood remained for many, especially those Eastern European Jews whose parents or grandparents still lived there and who themselves had grown up in its *shtetl* environment.

Some felt that urban renewal improved a deteriorating area. Others, such as Flora Steinberg Rubenstein, who still lives in South Portland, spoke for many Jews for whom freeway construction and urban renewal destroyed the soul of the community that had nurtured them:

It was a lovely neighborhood. We had everything we needed. There were kosher butcher shops. There were bakeries. There were grocery stores. There was everything here and people were friendly. . . .

So what did urban renewal do for the average person who only wanted to exist? Nothing. We now have high-rise buildings. Some people consider that a gorgeous sight, but to me it's an atrocity because no building, no matter how gorgeous or how high it stands, can take the place of people. There are no stores around here. There is absolutely nothing. . . . South Portland community life is . . . done away with; it's dead.

In the period when urban renewal was changing South Portland, many Jews from throughout the city were moving to the suburbs of Southwest Portland and nearby communities. This was a common postwar pattern that was not unique to Jews nor to Portland. As a significant number of Jews concentrated in the southern suburbs, several major Jewish institutions followed: Neveh Shalom in 1964 and the Mittleman Jewish Community Center in 1971, when a large new building was constructed at 6651 SW Capitol Highway.

After 1950, the reemergence of Jewish communities outside of Portland—a process that had begun in the 1930s—gained momentum. There are today Jewish congregations in Eugene, Salem, Corvallis, Medford and Ashland and Jewish activities occur regularly in a number of other smaller Oregon towns.

The social and political upheavals of the 1960s, together with Israel's momentous victory in the 1967 Six Day War, led to an intense new pride in being Jewish. With the 1970s came an infusion of energy and innovation and the creation of new approaches to meet a resurgent interest in Jewish life. New Jewish organizations came to life—both religious and secular—that have given voice to a broad range of Jewish expression. As part of the evolution of Jewish forms, the role of women has been changed profoundly. While Portland has not yet had a female rabbi, it does have two of fifty women cantors in the United States: Judith Schiff at Temple Beth Israel and Linda Shivers at Neveh Shalom.

Another dramatic organizational change occurred with the establishment of the Portland Jewish Academy in 1986. Culminating more than a decade of dialogue, the Portland Jewish Academy was formed from the merger of the Hillel Academy and the Jewish Education Association, creating one community-wide Jewish educational organization. The new Academy is housed in a recently constructed wing adjoining the Mittleman Jewish Community Center.

International events have had a continuing and important effect on Oregon's Jewish community. One of the most momentous was the Second Vatican Council, convened in Rome in 1960 by Pope John XXIII. In 1965, the Council adopted *Nostra Aetate*, which included passages that fundamentally changed the relationship between Roman Catholicism and Judaism:

The church, mindful of the common patrimony with the Jews ... deplores hatred, persecutions, displays of anti-Semitism directed against Jews at any time or by anyone.

Rabbi Rose, who wrote his doctoral dissertation on the Second Vatican Council, states that, "Since *Nostra Aetate*, an exciting new world has opened up in Jewish-Catholic relations." Rabbis of Portland's major congregations have all participated in Jewish-Christian dialogues. Friendship and understanding have grown between these major religions in Oregon as elsewhere. Perhaps related to these closer contacts, two modern trends have increased significantly since the 1960s: intermarriage and conversions to Judaism. Oregon rabbis have approached both issues positively, offering classes and guidance to prepare potential converts and to assist both Jewish and non-Jewish spouses.

The persecution of Soviet Jews has deeply concerned Oregonians. In the years between 1973 and 1978, when Jewish emigration from the Soviet Union increased for a short period, Portland resettled 148 Soviet Jews, a higher number per capita than any other Amerian city. Each year, Oregonians demonstrate to protest the persecution of Soviet Jewry.

While the struggle to help Soviet Jews continues, the survival and flowering of Israel has been paramount for Jews everywhere. The American goverment has responded with military and economic assistance, while Jews in Oregon and throughout the country provide an outpouring of financial support for development and humanitarian assistance. Numerous organizations led by United Jewish Appeal foster our continuing relationship with Israel. Varied activities related to Israel, including the festive Yom Hashmoot, the annual celebration of Israeli Independence, occur in Oregon Jewish communities each year. A direct relationship with Israel was created when the Portland City Council adopted a sister city agreement between Portland and Ashkelon, Israel, in April, 1987. Since its founding in 1948, the pride and sense of well-being of Jews in Oregon and elsewhere has been inextricably entwined with the destiny of Israel.

The contours of Oregon's Jewish community have remained relatively stable. Jews have risen from penniless immigrants to full participants in the economic, political and cultural life of the state. As both American and Jewish culture have become increasingly individualized and private, with less direction from synagogue or family, Jews have nonetheless been able to retain a strong self-awareness as Jews. In fact, in the years since 1950, the presence of Israel together with the creative energies stimulated by postwar social movements have strengthened and broadened Jewish religious and cultural life.

We have always been seekers—from the patriarchs and the prophets of Old, through two thousand years of Talmudic tradition, to the many modern forms of Jewish expression—and it has always been the particular genius of Jews to be able to blend new ways with the ageless truth and ritual of Judaism.

APPENDICES

Glossary

Ashkenazim: Jews who derive from Germany as well as Central and Eastern Europe.

bar mitzvah: the ceremony which recognizes a thirteen-year-old boy as an adult member of his congregation.

bat mitzvah: the ceremony which recognizes a thirteen-year-old girl as an adult member of her congregation.

bris (also *brit* and *b'rith*): the circumcision ceremony performed on the eighth day of a Jewish boy's life.

chazzan: cantor.

daven: to pray.

gefilte fish: fish balls traditionally served on the Sabbath.

gentile: non-Jew.

Goldeneh Medina: the golden land, referring to America.

goyish: gentile-like.

Hanukkah: an eight-day festival of lights held in December to commemorate religious freedom won by the Jewish Maccabees in 167 B.C.E.

havdalah: blessing recited at the end of the Sabbath.

heder: Jewish elementary school.

High Holidays: Rosh Hashanah and Yom Kippur, which occur in early fall at the beginning and the end of ten holy days.

horah: an Israeli folk dance.

kashrut: Jewish dietary code.

kosher: refers to food that is permitted according to Jewish dietary laws.

kibbutz: an Israeli collective community.

Ladino: the language spoken by Sephardic Jews which is composed primarily of Spanish and Hebrew.

luftmensh: literally, air people, those who live without visible means of support.

matzoh: unleavened bread eaten at Passover.

melamed: Hebrew school teacher.

meshuga: crazy.

mikvah: a ritual bath.

minhag: Jewish custom and practice that obtain the force of law.

minyan: the ten adult Jewish males historically required for religious services.

mitzvah (plural *mitzvot*): good deed.

mohel: one who performs circumcision according to ritual.

pe'ot: sidelocks worn by certain Orthodox Jews.

Pesach: Passover, a holiday in spring that commemorates Jewish liberation from Egyptian bondage.

Purim: a joyous holiday commemorating the defeat of Haman and the rescue of Persian Jews as recorded in the Book of Esther.

Rosh Hashanah: the Jewish new year which occurs in September and begins ten days of penitence.

seder: the festive meal usually held on the first night of Passover, at which the exodus from Egypt is dramatically retold.

Sephardim: descendants of Jews who lived in Spain and Portugal before the expulsion of 1492.

Shabbes: the Sabbath, beginning at sundown on Friday and ending at sundown on Saturday.

shadchan: marriage broker, matchmaker.

shammes: caretaker of a synagogue.

shochet: one who slaughters animals in the prescribed kosher manner.

shofar: the ram's horn blown during the High Holidays.

shtetl: village in Eastern Europe inhabited primarily by Jews.

shul: synagogue.

siddur: prayer book.

Simchas Torah: a joyous holiday on which the reading of the Torah in its annual cycle is both completed and begun anew.

Succoth: a holiday during which temporary huts are built to commemorate the Jewish wanderings in the desert after emancipation from Egypt.

tallis: prayer shawl.

Talmud: a massive compendium of commentaries interpreting the Torah.

Torah: the scroll containing the Pentateuch, the first five books of the Old Testament.

tsedakah: charity.

yarmulkah: skullcap worn by Orthodox and Traditional Jews.

Yiddish: the language spoken by Ashkenazic Jews which is composed primarily of German and Hebrew.

yihus: status derived from lineage, learning and wealth.

Yom Kippur: the Day of Atonement, the solemn conclusion of ten days of penitence that begin with Rosh Hashanah.

Sources:

Encyclopaedia Judaica

Feldman, Marianne L., ed., "Glossary" in *Portland Jewish Oral Histories*; unpublished manuscript, 1982, available at the Jewish Historical Society of Oregon, Portland, Oregon.

Howe, Irving and Kenneth Libo, *How We Lived: A Documentary History of Immigrant Jews in America 1880-1930*; New York, Richard Marek Publishers, 1979, p. 345.

Sources

Collections

Jewish Historical Society of Oregon

The principal site for research on the Jews of Oregon is the Jewish Historical Society of Oregon housed at the Mittleman Jewish Community Center. Its collections include:

> original manuscripts, documents and letters;
>
> minute books of various Jewish institutions;
>
> transcripts of 131 oral histories;
>
> standing files by individual, community, congregation and organization;
>
> Jewish newspaper clippings on organizations from 1893 to 1940;
>
> and photographs.

The Oregon Historical Society

The Oregon Historical Society also has valuable collections of manuscripts, scrapbooks, photographs, oral histories, periodicals and books on Jewish history.

Other Archives

The archives of Oregon's synagogues contain numerous significant documents and photographs. Additionally, local historical societies have many useful materials. Jewish and general newspapers are an invaluable resource describing the events of the day as well as providing background and opinion. Other libraries with important holdings and the most important specific works on the subject are listed in the acknowledgments at the front of this book.

Selected Bibliography

Abbott, Carl, *Portland: Planning, Politics, and Growth in a Twentieth-Century City*; Lincoln, University of Nebraska Press, 1983.

Abdill, George, "New Odessa: Douglas County's Russian Communal Colony," Winter, 1965 and Spring, 1966, *Umpqua Trapper*, pp. 10, 16.

American Jewish Historical Society, "The German Jew in America: Businessman, Organizer, Reformer," exhibit brochure, 1984.

American Jewish Historical Society, "Jews in Colonial America," exhibit brochure, 1984.

Angel, Marc D., *The Jews of Rhodes: The History of a Sephardic Community*; New York, Sepher-Hermon Press, Inc. and The Union of Sephardic Congregations, 1980.

Apsler, Alfred, "Jewish Pioneers of Oregon," February 4, 1957 *Congress Weekly*, p. 14.

Apsler, Alfred, *Northwest Pioneer: The Story of Louis Fleischner*; Farrar, Straus and Cudahy and the Jewish Publication Society of America, 1960.

Atwood, Kay, "Minorities of Early Jackson County, Oregon," Jackson County Intermediate Education District, 1976.

Beckham, Stephen Dow, *Land of the Umpqua: A History of Douglas County, Oregon*; Roseburg, Oregon, Douglas County Commissioners, 1986.

Berkowitz, Henry J., "Ben Selling" in *American Jewish Yearbook 5692*, Philadelphia, Jewish Publication Society of America, 1931.

Bernstein, David, book review of "Rabbi Jacob J. Weinstein, 'Advocate of the People,'" ed. Janice J. Feldstein, Fall, 1982 *The Historical Scribe*, Jewish Historical Society of Oregon.

Birmingham, Stephen, *"Our Crowd": The Great Jewish Families of New York*; New York, Harper & Row, 1967.

Birmingham, Stephen, *"The Rest of Us": The Rise of America's Eastern European Jews*; Boston, Little, Brown & Company, 1984.

Blumauer, Blanche, "Council of Jewish Women in Portland: 1905" October, 1976 *Western States Jewish Historical Quarterly*, p. 19, reprinted from *The Jewish Times and Observer*, San Francisco, February 17, 1905.

Blumenthal, Helen E., *New Odessa 1882-1887: United We Stand—Divided We Fall*; unpublished manuscript available at the Jewish Historical Society of Oregon, Portland, Oregon.

Blumenthal, Helen E., "The New Odessa Colony of Oregon, 1882-1886," July, 1982 *Western States Jewish Historical Quarterly*, p. 321.

B'nai B'rith, *The First Hundred Years of the B'nai B'rith Lodge of Portland, Oregon, 1866-1966*; Portland, B'nai B'rith Lodge No. 65, 1966.

Card, Owen J., *A History of the Neighborhood House of Portland, Oregon and the Participation in its Activities by the Failing Elementary School Students*; Masters thesis, University of Portland, 1955.

Clark, Malcolm, Jr., "The Bigot Disclosed: 90 Years of Nativism," 1974 *Oregon Historical Quarterly*, p. 109.

Cline, Robert Scott, *Community Structure on the Urban Frontier: The Jews of Portland, Oregon, 1849-1887*; Masters thesis, Portland State University, 1982.

Cline, Robert Scott, "Creation of an Ethnic Community: Portland Jewry, 1851-1866," April, 1985 *Pacific Northwest Quarterly*, p. 52.

Cline, Robert Scott, "The Jews of Portland, Oregon: A Statistical Dimension, 1860-1880," 1987 *Oregon Historical Quarterly*, p. 5.

Cline, Robert Scott, "Portland's German Jews, 1850-1890," address to the annual meeting of the Jewish Historical Society of Oregon, April, 1982, in Fall, 1982 *The Historical Scribe*, Jewish Historical Society of Oregon.

Cogan, Sara G., *The Jews of San Francisco and the Greater Bay Area 1849-1919: An Annotated Bibliography*; Berkeley, Western Jewish History Center, Judah Magnes Memorial Museum, 1973.

Cogan, Sara G., *Pioneer Jews of the California Mother Lode, 1849-1880: An Annotated Bibliography*; Berkeley, Western Jewish History Center, Judah Magnes Memorial Museum, 1968.

Congregation Ahavai Sholom, *70 Years of Service: 1869-1939*; Portland, Congregation Ahavai Sholom, 1939.

Council of Jewish Women, Portland Chapter, 70th (1966), 75th (1971) and 85th (1981) anniversary publications.

Davidson, Gabriel and Edwin Goodwin, "A Unique Agricultural Colony," May, 1928 *The Reflex*, p. 80.

Dimont, Max, *The Jews in America: The Roots, History and Destiny of American Jews*; New York, Simon & Schuster, 1978.

Dodds, Gordon B., *Oregon, A History*, New York, W. W. Norton & Company and the American Association of State and Local History, 1977.

Durkheimer, Sylvan, "Echos Out of the Past," Bicentennial Biography Project, Oregon Historical Society, March, 1976.

Encyclopaedia Judaica; Jerusalem, The Keter Publishing House, Ltd., 1972.

Engeman, Richard H., *The Jacksonville Story*; Jacksonville, Southern Oregon Historical Society, 1980.

Ettinger, Celia, "A Study of the Portland Hebrew School," seminar paper for Masters degree, Reed College, 1962.

Evans, Elwood, *History of the Pacific Northwest: Oregon and Washington*; Portland, North Pacific History Company, 1889 (2 vols.).

Feingold, Henry L., *Zion in America: The Jewish Experience from Colonial Times to the Present*; New York, Hippocrene Books, Inc., 1974, 1981.

"Feldman Family History," Fall, 1980, *The Historical Scribe*, Jewish Historical Society of Oregon.

Feldman, Marianne L, ed., *Portland Jewish Oral Histories*; unpublished manuscript, 1982, available at the Jewish Historical Society of Oregon, Portland, Oregon.

Fried, Jacob, and Barry D. Lebowitz, *The Portland Jewish Community: 1971*; Portland, Jewish Welfare Federation, 1972.

Friedlander, Alice G., "A Portland Girl on Women's Rights: 1893," January, 1978 *Western States Jewish Historical Quarterly*, p. 146.

Gaston, Joseph, *Portland, Oregon: Its History and Builders*; Portland, S. J. Clarke Publishing Company, 1911 (3 vols.).

Glazer, Michele, "The Durkheimers of Oregon: A Picture Story," April, 1978 *Western States Jewish Historical Quarterly*, p. 202.

Glazer, Michele, *Focus of a Community, Neighborhood House 1897-1929*; unpublished manuscript, 1982, available at the Jewish Historical Society of Oregon, Portland, Oregon.

Goldberg, Deborah B., *Jewish Spirit on the Urban Frontier: Zionism in Portland, Oregon 1901-1941*; B. A. thesis, Reed College, 1982.

Goldsmith, Bernard, papers and dictation; Bancroft Library, University of California, Berkeley, California.

Goodman, Irvin, collected speeches; unpublished, available at the Oregon Historical Society, Portland, Oregon.

Goodman, Irvin, *They Were Called Reds; A Story of Fascist Methods in the Pacific Northwest*; unpublished manuscript, undated, available at the Oregon Historical Society, Portland, Oregon.

Gould, Charles F., "The Jews: A Community Wherever They Gather," October 26, 1975 and January 25, 1976 *Northwest Magazine, The Oregonian*.

Gunns, Albert F., *Civil Liberties in Crisis: The Pacific Northwest 1917-1940*; New York and London, Garland Publishing, Inc., 1983.

Hanzen, Henry Marion, "Joseph-Meier Manuscript," untitled, unpublished manuscript, 1945, available at the Oregon Historical Society Manuscript Collection, MSS. 1019, Portland, Oregon.

Harris, Leon, *Merchant Princes: An Intimate History of Jewish Families who Built Great Department Stores*; New York, Harper & Row, 1977.

Hawthorne, Julian, *The Story of Oregon: A History with Portraits and Biographies*; New York, American Historical Publishing Company, 1892 (2 vols.).

Heilner, Sigmund, *Diary: 1859-1861*; unpublished, available at the Jewish Historical Society of Oregon, Portland, Oregon.

Heilner, Sigmund, letters from his family; Jewish Historical Society of Oregon, Portland, Oregon.

Hertzberg, Steven, *Strangers Within the Gate City: The Jews of Atlanta 1845-1915*; Philadelphia, The Jewish Publication Society of America, 1978.

Hines, Harvey Kimball, *An Illustrated History of the State of Oregon*; Chicago, The Lewis Publishing Company, 1893.

Horwitz, Sheryl, "A Brief Study of Jewish Immigration to Portland Through 1914," unpublished manuscript, 1978.

Howe, Irving, and Kenneth Libo, *How We Lived: A Documentary History of Immigrant Jews in America 1880-1930*; New York, Richard Marek Publishers, 1979.

Howe, Irving, *World of Our Fathers*; New York, Harcourt Brace Jovanovich, 1976.

Jewish Welfare Board, *Population Study*, 1947.

Kramer, William M., "David Solis-Cohen of Portland: Patriot, Pietist, Literateur and Lawyer," January, 1982 *Western States Jewish Historical Quarterly*, p. 139.

Levinson, Robert E., "The Jews of Eugene," Spring, 1968, *Lane County Historian*, p. 3.

Levinson, Robert E., "The Jews of Jacksonville: Genesis to Exodus," Spring, 1962 *The Call Number*, Library, University of Oregon, p. 4.

Levinson, Robert E., *The Pioneer Jewish Community of Jacksonville, Oregon*; Masters thesis, University of Oregon, 1962.

Libo, Kenneth, and Irving Howe, *We Lived There Too: In Their Own Words and Pictures: Pioneer Jews and the Westward Movement of America, 1630-1930*; New York, St. Martin's/Marek, 1984.

Linn, Fletcher, *Memories*, "Morris Mensor," Jacksonville Museum document, Jacksonville, Oregon.

Loewenberg, Ida, *The History of Neighborhood House: 1896-1939*; unpublished manuscript, 1944, available at the Jewish Historical Society of Oregon, Portland, Oregon.

MacColl, E. Kimbark, *The Growth of a City: Power and Politics in Portland, Oregon 1915-1950*; Portland, The Georgian Press, 1979.

MacColl, E. Kimbark, *The Shaping of a City: Business and Politics in Portland, Oregon 1885-1915*; Portland, The Georgian Press, 1976.

MacColl, E. Kimbark, Jr., *The Growth of Citizen Involvement in Urban Renewal: A Selective Case Study of Portland, Oregon, 1945-1972*; senior thesis, Princeton, 1972.

McCann, James, *A Study of the Jewish Community in the Greater Seattle Area*; Seattle, Jewish Federation of Greater Seattle, 1979.

Mackey, William, "A Personal Account of Life in Browntown, Oregon (1934)," in Sigmund Heilner, *Diary: 1859-1961*; available at the Jewish Historical Society of Oregon, Portland, Oregon.

Marcus, Jacob Rader, *Early American Jewry: 1649-1794*; Philadelphia, The Jewish Publication Society of America, 1951.

Meier & Frank Company, "History of the Meier & Frank Company," unpublished, undated, available at the Oregon Historical Society, Portland, Oregon.

Mittleman Jewish Community Center, annual yearbooks.

Mittleman Jewish Community Center, "A Portland Jewish Family Album," 1977.

Mittleman Jewish Community Center, "A Time to Remember," 1976.

Narell, Irene, *Our City: The Jews of San Francisco*; San Diego, Howell-North, 1971.

Neuberger, Richard, *Adventures in Politics: We Go to the Legislature*; New York, Oxford University Press, 1954.

Nodel, Rabbi Julius J., *The Ties Between; A Century of Judaism on America's Last Frontier*; Portland, Temple Beth Israel, 1959.

Nudelman, Eugene R., Sr., *The Family of Joseph Nudelman*; Portland, Eugene R. Nudelman, Sr., 1969.

O'Donnell, Terence, and Thomas Vaughan, *Portland: An Informal History and Guide*; Portland, Oregon Historical Society, 1976, 1984.

"Oregon Pioneer Sigmund A. Heilner," October, 1979, *Western States Jewish Historical Quarterly*, p. 66.

Polier, Justine Wise, and James Waterman Wise, eds., *The Personal Letters of Stephen Wise*; Boston, The Beacon Press, 1956.

Potter, Miles F., *Oregon's Golden Years: Bonanza of the West*; Caldwell, Idaho, The Caxton Printers, Ltd., 1982.

Raphael, Marc L., *Jews and Judaism in a Middlewestern Community: Columbus, Ohio: 1840-1975*; Columbus, Ohio Historical Society, 1979.

Robinson, David, files and papers; Western Jewish History Center, Judah Magnes Memorial Museum, Berkeley, California.

Rochlin, Harriet and Fred, *Pioneer Jews: A New Life in the Far West*; Boston, Houghton Mifflin Company, 1984.

Rosenbaum, Fred, *Architects of Reform: Congregational and Community Leadership, Emanu-El of San Francisco, 1849-1980*; Berkeley, Western Jewish History Center, Judah Magnes Memorial Museum, 1980.

Rosenbaum, Fred, *Free To Choose: The Making of a Jewish Community in the American West, The Jews of Oakland, California from the Gold Rush to the Present Day*; Berkeley, Western Jewish History Center, Judah Magnes Memorial Museum, 1976.

Rothchild, Sylvia, *Voices From the Holocaust*; New York, New American Library, 1981.

Ryan, Kathleen, *The Goldsmith Company: Wholesale Dry Goods Since 1930*; Portland, The Goldsmith Company, 1980.

Scott, Harvey W., *History of Portland, Oregon*; Syracuse, D. Mason and Company, 1890.

The Scribe: A Record of Jewish Life, Special Historical Addendum, "Memory is Survival," May, 1976, Jewish Historical Society of Oregon.

Selling, Ben, papers; Oregon Historical Society, Portland, Oregon.

Simon, Joseph, dictation; Bancroft Library, University of California, Berkeley, California.

Simon, Joseph, scrapbooks; Oregon Historical Society, Portland, Oregon.

Smith, Helen Krebs, ed., *With Her Own Wings: Historical Sketches, Reminiscences, and Anecdotes of Pioneer Women*; Portland, Beattie & Co., 1948.

Solis-Cohen, David, papers; Jewish Historical Society of Oregon, Portland, Oregon.

Solomon, Gus, collected speeches; unpublished.

Solomon, Gus, interview, "Gus J. Solomon on the Beginnings of Legal Aid in Oregon," 1987 *Oregon Historical Quarterly*, p. 52.

Spencer, Omar C., *E. Henry Wemme Endowment Fund*, Portland, Sweeney, Krist & Dimm, undated.

Stampfer, Rabbi Joshua, *The Life and Works of Julius Eckman*, unpublished manuscript, 1975, available at the Jewish Historical Society of Oregon, Portland, Oregon.

Stampfer, Rabbi Joshua, ed., *The Sephardim: A Cultural Journey from Spain to the Pacific Coast*; Portland, The Institute for Judaic Studies, 1987.

Suwol, Samuel M., *Jewish History of Oregon*, Portland, Samuel M. Suwol, 1958.

Teiser, Sidney, *An Autobiographical Memoir*; unpublished manuscript, 1978, available at the Jewish Historical Society of Oregon, Portland, Oregon.

Throckmorton, Arthur L., *Oregon Argonauts: Merchant Adventurers on the Western Frontier*; Portland, Oregon Historical Society, 1961.

Toll, William, "Ethnicity and Stability: The Italians and Jews of South Portland, 1900-1940," May, 1985 *Pacific Historical Review*, p. 161.

Toll, William, "The Female Life Cycle and the Measure of Social Change: Portland, Oregon, 1880-1930," March, 1983 *American Jewish History*, p. 333.

Toll, William, "Fraternalism and Community Structure on the Urban Frontier: The Jews of Portland, Oregon—A Case Study," August, 1978 *Pacific Historical Review*, p. 369.

Toll, William, *The Making of an Ethnic Middle Class: Portland Jewry over Four Generations*; Albany, State University of New York Press, 1982.

Toll, William, "Mobility, Fraternization and Jewish Cultural Change: Portland 1910-1930," in Moses Rischin, ed., *The Jews of the West: The Metropolitan Years*, p. 75; Waltham, Massachusetts, American Jewish Historical Society, 1979.

Toll, William, "The 'New Social History' and Recent Jewish Historical Writing," March, 1980 *American Jewish History*, p. 325.

Toll, William, "Oral History and the Evolution of Portland Jewry, 1850-1970," in Feldman, Marianne L., ed., *Portland Jewish Oral Histories*; unpublished manuscript, 1982, available at the Jewish Historical Society of Oregon, Portland, Oregon.

Toll, William, "They Built a New Home," Spring, 1980 *The Historical Scribe*, Jewish Historical Society of Oregon.

Toll, William, "Volunteerism and Modernization in Portland Jewry: The B'nai B'rith in the 1920s," January, 1979 *Western Historical Quarterly*, p. 21.

Trachtenberg, Gladys G., "Neighborhood House: Its Evolution, Past-Present-Future," Winter, 1978—Spring, 1979, *The Historical Scribe*, Jewish Historical Society of Oregon.

Vorspan, Albert, *Giants of Justice*, New York, Union of American Hebrew Congregations, 1960.

Voss, Carl Herman, ed., *Stephen S. Wise: Servant of the People—Selected Letters*; Philadelphia, The Jewish Publication Society of America, 1961.

Walling, Albert G., *History of Southern Oregon*, Portland, A. G. Walling, 1884.

Webber, Bert and Margie, *Jacksonville, Oregon: The Making of a National Historic Landmark*; Fairfield, Washington, Ye Galleon Press, 1982.

Wise, Stephen S., *Challenging Years: The Autobiography of Stephen Wise*; New York, G. P. Putnam's Sons, 1949.

Wise, Stephen S., papers and letters; American Jewish Historical Society, Brandeis University, Waltham, Massachusetts.

Yarmolinsky, Avraham, *A Russian's American Dream: A Memoir on William Frey, 1839-1888*; Lawrence, Kansas, University of Kansas Press, 1965.

Abbreviations for Photographic Sources

AJHS: American Jewish Historical Society, Brandeis University; Waltham, Massachusetts.

BI: Beth Israel; Portland, Oregon.

DCM: Douglas County Museum; Roseburg, Oregon.

GC: The Goldsmith Company; Portland, Oregon.

HC: The Heilner Collection; Jewish Historical Society of Oregon, Portland, Oregon.

JHSO: Jewish Historical Society of Oregon; Portland, Oregon.

LC: Library of Congress; Washington, D.C.

OHS: Oregon Historical Society; Portland, Oregon.

SOHS: Southern Oregon Historical Society; Jacksonville, Oregon.

UO: University of Oregon Library; Eugene, Oregon.

YIVO: YIVO Institute for Jewish Research; New York City.

Index

This proper name index includes all Jewish names, as well as many non-Jewish names and geographical references.